Data Skills for Media Professionals

Data Skills for Media Professionals

A Basic Guide

Ken Blake
Jason Reineke

This edition first published 2020
© 2020 John Wiley & Sons, Inc.

The right of Ken Blake and Jason Reineke to be identified as the authors of this work has been asserted in accordance with law.

Registered Office
John Wiley & Sons, Inc., 111 River Street, Hoboken, NJ 07030, USA

Editorial Office
111 River Street, Hoboken, NJ 07030, USA

For details of our global editorial offices, customer services, and more information about Wiley products visit us at www.wiley.com.

Wiley also publishes its books in a variety of electronic formats and by print-on-demand. Some content that appears in standard print versions of this book may not be available in other formats.

Library of Congress Cataloging-in-Publication data applied for

Paperback ISBN: 9781119118961

Cover Design: Wiley
Cover Image: © Mordolff/Getty Images

Set in 10/12pt Warnock by SPi Global, Pondicherry, India
Printed and bound in Singapore by Markono Print Media Pte Ltd

10 9 8 7 6 5 4 3 2 1

Contents

Preface

Our students often tell us they don't like doing math. We tell them we don't, either. We've had the conversation often enough to know that students usually are referring to their dislike for the tedium and anxiety of completing such standard-issue math course tasks as solving 20 separate quadratic equations for 20 separate 'x' values, each with no meaning beyond indicating whether one can solve a quadratic equation. Neither of us ever liked doing that kind of thing, or ever will. But computers don't seem to mind it at all. Given valid data and correct instructions, they'll do it without complaint. They'll also do it with much more speed and accuracy than either of us could. So, we let computers do the math. We do the thinking. In this book we focus on getting computers to do the kinds of math behind the kinds of thinking that media professionals must do most often: thinking about what questions to ask, how to ask them, and how to evaluate and communicate the answers.

Perhaps because we have solved, or have tried to solve, far too many abstract mathematical problems ourselves, this book's examples rely exclusively on real, newsworthy data from real sources. Most relate to our home state, Tennessee; our home city, Murfreesboro; or our home institution, Middle Tennessee State University, where we both belong to the faculty of the School of Journalism and Strategic Media. We've provided downloadable data that you can use to follow along with our examples. Just visit this book's companion web site, TheDataReporter.com. But we've also shown you how to download similar real data relevant to anywhere in the United States at whatever time you open this book. Our first three chapters deal with downloading, analyzing, visualizing and mapping October 2018 unemployment rates across Tennessee's 10 metropolitan areas. But you'll find instructions on how to get similar data for the metro areas in any state you happen to be in, and at any time, so that while you are learning, you also can be producing a worthwhile news report.

We also understand that computer tools for working with data can be expensive – perhaps prohibitively so for at least some of those who will use this book. Accordingly, we have focused on using free tools, like Google's spreadsheet and mapping apps, and the open-source QGIS geographic information system software. We also have tried to sidestep computer operating platform differences by emphasizing data and mapping apps that run in a web browser and, thus, work about the same way, regardless of which platform is running the browser. These apps may change between editions of the book. Be sure to check the companion web site for updated tips, "how to" videos, and more.

Like many authors, we made time to write this book by foregoing time with those whom we love. We are grateful to them. Jason would like to thank Heather. Ken would like to thank Amy, Joshua and Justin.

1

Basic Data Analysis

Wrapping up an introduction to data analysis during the first week of a news reporting class recently, one of us asked the two dozen students in attendance whether any of them could name something they had learned from the session. Just when it seemed nobody was going to say anything, a student spoke up. She had learned, she said, that data analysis wasn't terrifying.

We're going to demonstrate some basic spreadsheet skills by showing you how to turn a set of federal unemployment rate estimates for nearly 400 metropolitan areas in the United States into a news story that an audience in the Nashville, Tennessee, area, where we live, would want to read. You'll learn spreadsheet techniques for filtering, computation and sorting. Afterward, you'll be ready to download the latest data and turn it into a news story that an audience in your area would want to read, assuming your area is in the United States and includes at least one sizable city. In short, you'll have everything you need to get started right away on the kind of work we presume you picked up this book in the hope of learning how to do. If we had to choose the one thing we most want you to learn from this first chapter, though, it would be the same thing that student learned: Data analysis isn't terrifying. Nor is it necessarily tedious, confusing or even all that difficult. Instead, it is practical, empowering and, believe it or not, fun.

Some Example Data

Learning data skills requires data, so let's start with the U.S. Bureau of Labor Statistics' October 2018 table of preliminary unemployment rates for each of 387 Metropolitan Statistical Areas in the United States (Bureau of Labor Statistics, 2018a). Figure 1.1 shows what the top of the table looked like at the time we were writing this chapter. The bureau updates the table monthly. After you've worked through the chapter, we encourage you to download the latest data from the bureau's Local Area Unemployment Statistics page, www.bls. gov/lau/, and try writing a story suitable for your area. To find the data, scroll down to the "Tables and Maps Created by BLS" area, and click the

Data Skills for Media Professionals: A Basic Guide, First Edition. Ken Blake and Jason Reineke.
© 2020 John Wiley & Sons, Inc. Published 2020 by John Wiley & Sons, Inc.

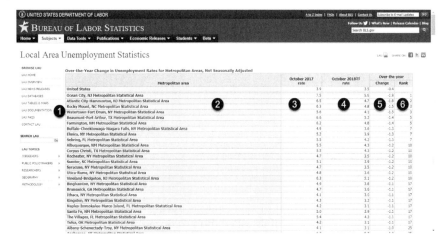

Figure 1.1 Over-the-Year Change in Unemployment Rates for Metropolitan Areas, October 2018. See the link to the data documentation (1). The table shows Metropolitan Statistical Area (2) unemployment data for October 2017 (3), October 2018 (4), and the over-the year change (5) as well as the rank order of the change (6). The data update monthly. *Source:* www.bls.gov/web/metro/laummtch.htm, December 2018.

"Over-the-Year Change in Unemployment Rates for Metropolitan Areas" link. A table like the one in Figure 1.1 will appear and will contain the latest MSA-level unemployment figures.

Always check to make sure you understand how a dataset came to be and what it represents. This one comes from a reasonably reliable source and is accompanied by a link to documentation that clearly explains how and when the data were compiled and what they represent. Specifically, the column labeled "Metropolitan Area" shows the name of each metropolitan area listed. The areas are based on definitions that the Office of Management and Budget updates at least once a decade for federal statistical purposes. Each area name involves at least one city name and one state name that, together, give you an idea of the area's location and scope. MSAs consist of one or more counties. Some areas in the six New England states are based instead on cities and towns. They're called New England City and Town Areas, or NECTAs. Of course, the first entry in the column, "United States," indicates the country as a whole rather than some geographical subdivision.

The column labeled "October 2017 rate" shows the estimated unemployment rate for each area in October of 2017. The "October 2018P rate" column shows the same estimate for October 2018. The "P" indicates that the estimate is still preliminary and may be revised. The bureau bases its estimates on survey data and uses precise definitions to decide who out of the general population qualifies as part of the "labor force," which members of the labor force will be counted as "employed," and which members will be counted as "unemployed." To get the unemployment rate for an area, the bureau divides the number of "unemployed" labor force members by the total labor force, then multiplies the result by 100 to change the figure from a decimal (like .04) to a percentage (like 4 percent, meaning 4 out of every 100).

The "Change" column shows the difference between each October 2017 and October 2018 rate. For example, the Ocean City, NJ MSA's October 2018 unemployment rate of 5.6 percent represents a decline of 1.9 percentage points compared to the area's unemployment rate in October 2017, a year earlier. Finally, the "Rank" column shows where each area ranks when sorted, lowest to highest, by the "Change" column. The Ocean City, NJ, MSA ranked first, because its 1.9 percentage point decline in unemployment compared to October 2017 was the largest decline in the country. Note that areas with identical declines have the same rank. For example, the Rocky Mount, NC, and Watertown-Fort Drum, NY, MSAs both rank third, because both saw an unemployment decline of 1.5 percentage points compared to a year earlier, and that decline was the third-largest decline in the nation. For more about the data, see "How the Government Measures Unemployment" (Bureau of Labor Statistics, 2015).

An Introductory Tool: Google Sheets

If we're going to do much more than look at the data, we're going to need a tool to help us analyze it. Don't bother reaching for your pocket calculator. We'll be way out of its league. We need a spreadsheet, a software program that can import, store, organize, display, filter, sort, analyze and graph data – and more. Probably the most widely used spreadsheet, Microsoft Excel, is a favorite of ours. There are more sophisticated programs designed for general statistical analysis that you may have heard of, like R, SPSS, SAS, and STATA. Many general programming languages can be used for data analysis and visualization, too.

Instead of starting with any of those tools, though, we're going to start with Google Sheets, a Web-based spreadsheet from Google. We picked it as a starting point for several reasons. Because it's Web-based, you never have to install it. You can access it via any web browser on any Internet-connected computer. Also, you can start a project on one computer, log out, log in on a different computer, and pick up right where you left off. That capability comes in especially handy if you're a university student who is constantly switching from your own computer to a classroom computer to a computer in a university lab. Furthermore, because Google Sheets runs in a web browser, it will look and handle the same way regardless of whether you are using a Mac or a PC. It can easily produce and publish online, interactive data visualizations, and it's similar enough to Excel to make switching back and forth between the two fairly easy.

Best of all, it's free. If you have a Gmail account, you already have access to Google Sheets. If you don't have a Gmail account, setting one up is a snap.

Google Sheets has drawbacks, too. For example, it tends to become slow and unstable when handling larger datasets, and some of its features are rudimentary compared to their counterparts in Excel and downright primitive compared to those in the other analytical programs we mentioned. It also would be naïve to assume that data saved on servers maintained by a third party are as confidential and secure as data saved on digital storage media more directly under your control. In short, Google Sheets won't meet all of your data analysis needs. But it's a good place to start, and it's similar enough to some of those other programs to make learning them easier.

Getting the Data into a Google Sheet

Let's open a Google Sheet and get the unemployment data into it. Open the web browser of your choice, and go to http://drive.google.com. If you don't have a Google account, or if you aren't logged in to Google on the computer you're using, your screen will look something like Figure 1.2. If you do not yet have a Google account, click the "Create account" link and follow the directions. You'll be asked to provide your first and last name, make up a unique username as well as a password, and provide a current email address or phone number as well as some demographic information. If you already have a Google account – and if you have a Gmail address, you do – type your full Gmail address into the "Email or phone" box, click "Next," type in your Gmail password, and click "Sign in." There's also a "Forgot email" link, if you need it.

Getting to a screen that looks something like Figure 1.3 means you're in the right place. Depending on your setup, arriving might involve clicking the nine-dot "Google apps" icon in the screen's upper-right corner and choosing the "Drive" icon. The Google Drive shown is brand new, so it's nearly empty. If you're a long-time Google Drive user, your drive's directory may be considerably more cluttered.

Google Sheets is among the applications that come built-in and pre-activated with Google Drive. These apps run in your Google Drive, not on your computer, so there is nothing to download or install. Simply open a blank Google Sheet by clicking the "+ New" button in the upper-left corner, then "Google Sheets," then "Blank spreadsheet." Figure 1.4 illustrates the steps. Google Drive will open a new browser tab and display a blank Google Sheet with the name "Untitled spreadsheet."

The blank grid that will take up most of your screen once the spreadsheet has opened is the spreadsheet's work area. The work area's "columns" run vertically. Each is labeled with one or more letters at its top. The first is "Column A." The work area's "rows" run horizontally and are labeled with numbers. The first is

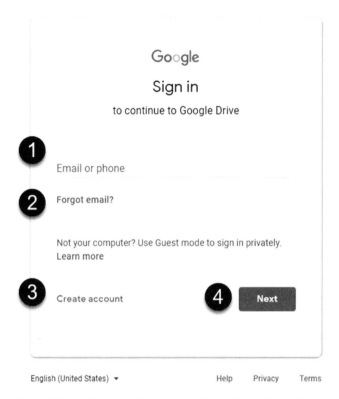

Figure 1.2 Google account login screen. If you already have a Google account, enter your Gmail address or phone number (1) and click "Next" (4). The screen also offers a login/password recovery option (2), and a button for creating a new – or additional – Google account (3). *Source:* http://drive.google.com, December 2018. Google and the Google logo are registered trademarks of Google Inc., used with permission.

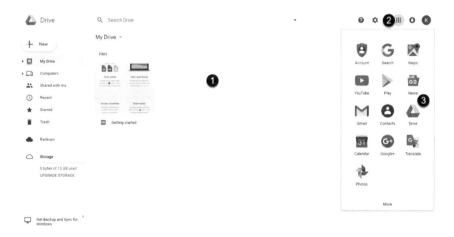

Figure 1.3 Home screen for a newly created Google Drive account. Files you create will appear in the file directory area (1). Click the Google Apps icon (2) to access the pre-installed Google Applications, including Google Drive (3). Google and the Google logo are registered trademarks of Google Inc., used with permission.

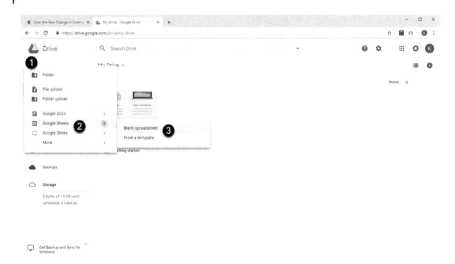

Figure 1.4 Creating a blank Google Sheet. Click the "+ New" icon (1) and choose Google Sheets (2) from the drop-down menu. Then select "Blank spreadsheet" (3). Google and the Google logo are registered trademarks of Google Inc., used with permission.

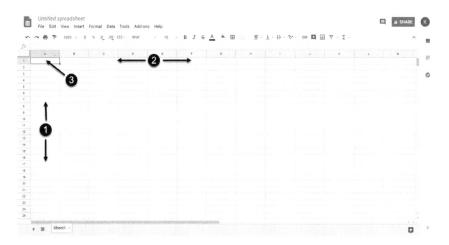

Figure 1.5 Areas of a spreadsheet. "Columns" run vertically and are labeled with letters, like Column A (1). "Rows" run horizontally and are labeled with numbers (2). "Cells," like Cell A1 (3) lie at the intersections of columns and rows. Google and the Google logo are registered trademarks of Google Inc., used with permission.

"Row 1." Each intersection of a row and column forms a "cell." Each cell has a unique "address" consisting of the cell's column letter or letters followed by its row number. In Figure 1.5, the box in the upper-left corner of the work area is Cell A1, because it lies at the intersection of Column A and Row 1. The cell to its immediate right is Cell B1, and the cell directly below it is Cell A2.

If this sounds confusing to you, just think back to a skill you probably mastered in grade school: plotting points on a grid. The teacher would give you a paper grid and a pair of "X-Y coordinates," and you had to pencil in a dot on the grid at the position the coordinates indicated. The "X" coordinate gave you a starting point on the horizontal axis, the "Y" coordinate gave you a starting point on the vertical axis, and you penciled in a dot at the one spot where lines passing through those starting points perpendicular to their axes intersected. You've probably used that skill many times since – for example, to find the seat that corresponds to the ticket you bought to a sporting event, or to play a certain board game involving pegs, grids and fleets of plastic warships. Well, here is yet another useful application. The column letters in your spreadsheet are like the "X" coordinates from your grade school days, and the column numbers are like the "Y" coordinates. Together, column letters and rows define cells, just like "X" and "Y" coordinates, together, defined the location of each dot on the grid.

Knowing how to specify cells in a spreadsheet is fundamentally important. As you'll soon see, a lot of spreadsheet work involves putting instructions in one cell that tell the spreadsheet to go to one or more different cells, retrieve information stored there, do something with the information, then display the results.

There are a couple of ways to get the MSA unemployment data out of the table on the Web page and into your Google Sheet. The most direct might be to use your computer's mouse to highlight and copy the column headings and data from the Web page table, then switch to your Google Sheet, click on Cell A1, and paste the data into the Google Sheet by holding down the "Ctrl" key (or the "Cmd" key on a Mac) while pressing the "v" key. But that approach can produce a variety of outcomes, depending on which combination of browser and computer operating system you're using. Give it a try, if you like. If it works, you'll have a nice shortcut.

A more reliable approach involves clicking on Cell A1, then carefully typing this set of instructions, making sure to include every quote, comma and parenthesis:

=importhtml("https://www.bls.gov/web/metro/laummtch.htm","table",2)

Once you have typed what's above and double checked your work, press the "Enter" key. If you typed everything correctly, a "Loading ..." message will appear for a moment in Cell A1. Then, the column headings and data from the MSA unemployment table will fill the spreadsheet.

You've just used one of the more than 400 "functions" that the developers of Google Sheets built into the program to help you do particular things more easily. You can find a list of these functions, and instructions for using each one, in the online manual for Google Sheets (Adielsson et al., 2005). The =IMPORTHTML function imports data from a table or a list on a Web page. The first part of the code you typed into Cell A1 consists of a "=" symbol, which tells Google Sheets that a function is being used, followed by the name of the function:

=importhtml

The next part provides three pieces of information the function needs in order to work correctly. The first of the three pieces of information is the URL of the page you want Google Sheets to go to in order to find the data. We're using the URL for the MSA unemployment data, but any URL would work. Note that the URL has to appear within double quote marks. You also have the type a left parenthesis in front of it to mark the start of the information the function needs:

=importhtml("https://www.bls.gov/web/metro/laummtch.htm"

Next comes a comma, which signals the end of the first piece of additional information. After the comma comes the second piece of information, which can be either "table" or "list," depending on which you want Google Sheets to import data from. Note that "table" or "list" must be surrounded by double quote marks, just like the URL had to be:

=importhtml("https://www.bls.gov/web/metro/laummtch.htm","table"

The final piece of information comes after another comma and tells Google Sheets which table or list on the page to import data from. A "1" specifies the first table to appear in the page's .HTML code, a "2" specifies the second table to appear in the page's .HTML code, and so on. The same is true for lists. You can examine the .HTML code to figure out which number indicates the table or list you're interested in, or you can figure it out by trial and error. Note that the table number should not be surrounded by double quote marks. Furthermore, it has to be followed by a right parenthesis, which marks the end of the function's code:

=importhtml("https://www.bls.gov/web/metro/laummtch.htm","table",2)

On the page we got the MSA unemployment data from, the unemployment data table happened to be the second table in the code. That's why the function used a 2 at the end. The first table on the page contains the navigation links on the left side of the page and the "Last Modified Date" information toward the bottom of the page. If you use a 1 in the function rather than a 2, Google Sheets will import the information from that table instead of from the table of unemployment rates. Use "list" and 1 in the code instead of "table" and 2, and Google Sheets will import the information from the list that shows up as the dropdown menu on the page's "Home" tab. Perhaps you can see how flexible and useful this function can be.

Getting a Fixed Copy of the Data

This might seem odd, but the unemployment data you're looking at on your screen aren't actually there. Not in the sense of being permanent or fixed, at least. Each time you do anything to this Google Sheet, it will execute the =IMPORTHTML function over again, reimporting the data from the specified Web page and table. If you put anything in the way of the data the function tries to retrieve, the function will halt the import and give you an error message. For example, if you click on Cell A3, replace "United States" with "U.S.," and press "Enter," your newly imported data will vanish. You'll see nothing in the spreadsheet besides "U.S." in Cell A3 and "#REF!" in Cell A1. Hover your mouse curser over "#REF!," and a pop-up error message will read, "Array result was not expanded because it would overwrite data in A3." The error message means that Google Sheets tried to run the =IMPORTHTML function but stopped when it tried to put "United States" in Cell A3 and found Cell A3 was already occupied with "U.S."

It would be impossible to analyze a dataset that either disappeared or reverted to its original form every time you tried to do something to it. Fortunately, there's an easy solution to this problem. All you have to do is select and copy the data, then paste it to a new spreadsheet as "values only." Pasting the data as "values only" removes any functions, like =IMPORTHTML, and leaves just the text and numbers the functions produced. Any formatting that might have been used, like bold-facing or formatting to display 0.25 as 25%, will also be removed. Figure 1.6 highlights key areas involved in the process. Here's what to do, step by step:

- Delete "U.S." from Cell A3. Also delete any spaces or other characters you might have entered into Cell A3, whether accidentally or on purpose.
- Press "Enter." The unemployment data should reappear.
- Select the entire dataset by using your mouse to click once in the blank rectangle directly below the "fx" icon in the upper-left corner of the spreadsheet's work area. The rectangle is to the right of the A label for Column A and above the 1 label for Row 1. Clicking in the blank rectangle will select (that is, shade) the entire spreadsheet – cells that contain the unemployment data as well as cells that are blank.
- Hold down the "Ctrl" key (or the "Cmd" key on a Mac), and press the "c" key to copy the data you've highlighted.
- Click the small + symbol in the lower-left corner of the spreadsheet's work area. This step will open a second spreadsheet in a "tab" labeled "Sheet2." The tab will appear right next to the "Sheet1" tab in the lower-left corner of your screen. Sheet1 is the tab you've been working in all along.
- Click on Cell A1 in Sheet 2. Doing so tells Google Sheets that this is where you want to paste the data you're copying.
- Press and hold the "Ctrl" and "Shift" keys, then press the "v" key to paste the data you've copied. Including the "Shift" key tells Google Sheets to paste only

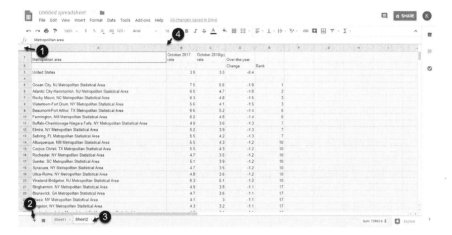

Figure 1.6 Pasting a "values only" copy of the spreadsheet data to a new spreadsheet tab. Start by clicking the blank rectangle in the sheet's upper-left corner (1) to select the entire spreadsheet. Hold down the "Ctrl" key (the "Cmd" key if you're using a Mac) and press the "c" key to copy the data. Click the + symbol (2) to open a new tab named Sheet2 (3) containing a blank spreadsheet. Paste the data's values into Sheet2 by clicking on the new sheet's Cell A1 and holding down the "Ctrl" or "Cmd" key, also holding down the "Shift" key and pressing the "v" key. Once the data are pasted, you can widen the columns by double-clicking on the boundary line between the Column A and Column B headings (4). Google and the Google logo are registered trademarks of Google Inc., used with permission.

the numbers and text in the data you've copied, omitting any formatting or functions.

- Notice how Column A of the pasted data isn't quite wide enough to show the full name of each MSA? You can tell Google Sheets to automatically widen each column to whatever width each column needs in order to display its widest content. Just float your mouse cursor over the boundary between the "A" and "B" column headings, or between any other adjacent pair of column headings. When the cursor changes to a double-ended arrow, pause, and double-click. Each column you have selected will widen automatically.

A few notes about what just happened: By pasting only the unemployment data values, you stripped out the =IMPORTHTML function that was in Cell A1 and kept only what the function had produced: the text and values imported from the Web page's table. Because the text and values are now fixed, rather than temporary, you can edit and analyze them without having your work overwritten or interrupted by a re-execution of the =IMPORTHTML function.

However, the =IMPORTHTML function is still plugging away back on Sheet1. You could delete Sheet1 now, if you like, by clicking the little down-pointing triangle to the right of the "Sheet1" label and choosing "Delete" from the pop-up menu. But you might be better off leaving it in place. Because guess what's going to happen next month, when the next round of MSA unemployment data get posted on the Web page? If you reopen the spreadsheet then and click on "Sheet1," the =IMPORTHTML function will run automatically, and you'll have the latest data waiting to be copied to a new sheet and analyzed for a whole new story.

In fact, you can rename Sheet1 and Sheet2 so you can better keep track of what each one contains. Click that down-pointing triangle beside the "Sheet1" label, but instead of choosing "Delete," choose "Rename." The "Sheet1" label turns blue and becomes editable, allowing you to name it something like "Latest data." Do the same with Sheet2, and you can rename it "October 2018p," or something like that.

There's at least one other thing to notice about what just happened. Google Sheets generally prefers that you copy and paste things using keyboard commands, like "Ctrl/c" or "Cmd/c" and "Ctrl/v" or "Cmd/v." Try to use a mouse to copy or paste data in Google Sheets, and you might get an error reading something like, "These actions are unavailable via the Edit menu, but you can still use Ctrl+C for copy, Ctrl+X for cut, Ctrl+V for paste." Your particular result will depend on your browser type and settings. In our experience, for example, mouse-based copying and pasting works fine in the Chrome browser for PC but not in the FireFox browser for PC.

Formatting the Data

Spreadsheets work best when the cell at the top of each column contains a short, descriptive label identifying the column's data, and there are no gaps or blank cells in the data columns beneath these column headings, at least until after the last row of data. The unemployment data on your screen don't quite meet either criteria yet. Instead, the data appear in the spreadsheet pretty much the same way they appeared in the table on the Web page. For example, columns D and E contain the over-the-year change in the unemployment rate and the rank order of the change. But Column D's heading is split across two cells. Cell D1 contains "Over-the-year," and Cell D2 contains, "Change." Next door, Cell E1, where the column heading ought to be, is blank. The heading appears instead in Cell E2, "Rank." Finally, there are blanks in cells A2 through C2, as well as in cells A4 through E4. To remedy these problems:

- Insert a single blank row above the "United States" row. You can do it by right clicking on the "3" to the left of "United States" and choosing "Insert 1 above" from the drop-down menu.
- Click the first cell in the blank row you just inserted. That cell is now Cell A3. The "United States" text has shifted down one row, to Cell A4.
- Type "Area" and press "Enter."

Figure 1.7 The formatted spreadsheet, shown with October 2018 data. Google and the Google logo are registered trademarks of Google Inc., used with permission.

- Click Cell B3 and type or copy what's in Cell B1. For the data we're using here, that would be "October 2017 rate." If you're using more current data, you obviously would want to use a label that accurately describes the more current data.
- Similarly, type "October 2018(p) rate" (or the month and year of the data you're working with) in Cell C3, "Change" in cell D3, and "Rank" in Cell E3.
- Type "N/A" (for "Not applicable," or some similar notation) into Cell E4, to remind yourself that the United States can't really be ranked the way the MSA rates can.
- Delete rows 1, 2 and 5 in their entirety. You can do so by right clicking on the shaded number to the left of each row you want to delete, then choosing "Delete row." Google Sheets will delete the row, then automatically shift the rows below up by one.
- Finally, scroll all the way to the bottom of the dataset (or get there fast by clicking on Cell A1 and pressing Ctrl/down arrow or Cmd/down arrow). You'll probably see a couple of footnotes from the Web page table. Delete those rows, too.

Once you're done, Sheet2, now renamed to match the current month, should look something like the one in Figure 1.7.

Cleaning the Data

"Cleaning the data" means checking it for errors, omissions and similar data quality problems. Failing to clean your data inevitably will bring you grief, so please make it a habit. For example, look through the unemployment figures for any that seem unrealistically large or small. In the October 2018 data, the unemployment rate for the El Centro, California, MSA was listed as 19.4 percent. Really? That's quite a bit more than the typical unemployment figures in the dataset. Could nearly one in five people in the El Centro area truly be out of work? Or did someone at the Bureau of Labor Statistics accidentally type 19.4 when the actual figure was 9.4? Such mistakes are more common in datasets than one might think, even in datasets from usually reliable sources. It's also possible to accidentally introduce mistakes when transferring data from a source to a spreadsheet for analysis. In this case, though, the figure was probably correct. We found the same number on the Bureau of Labor Statistics' "Economy at a Glance" page (Bureau of Labor Statistics, 2018b), under the section for the El Centro, California, MSA. Also, a Google search using the terms "El Centro unemployment" turned up a number of news articles from reliable sources indicating that the area has a history of high unemployment rates, due largely to its agriculture-based economy. We used the same method to check other seemingly high unemployment figures in the list as well as several that seemed pretty low. Finally, we checked to see that the first record in the imported data (United States) and the last one (Texarkana, TX-AR Metropolitan Statistical Area) matched the first and last records on the Web page's table, and that the number of MSAs listed in both places was the same (389). All in all, these data look pretty accurate, and the import seems to have worked well. But data cleaning tactics vary from one dataset to another, and data cleaning involves being alert for odd results throughout your analysis, not just at the beginning.

Planning your Analysis

It's also important to come up with at least a general plan for your analysis. The plan should consider both what analyses are possible, given the nature and limitations of your data, and what audience you plan to try to interest in the analysis results. Suppose, for example, you are a local news reporter for WPLN, the all-news National Public Radio affiliate based in Nashville, Tennessee, our home turf. The station's over-the-air listening area corre-sponds roughly to the boundaries of the Nashville-area MSA. Your audience members probably would be most interested in how the Nashville area's October 2018 unemployment rate compares to the October 2018 unemploy-ment rates in Tennessee's other metro areas and, perhaps secondarily, to the rate for the nation as a whole. They would feel reassured if the Nashville area's unemployment rate fell in the relatively moderate or low range and concerned if it fell in the relatively high range. The comparison you have in mind would require filtering out all of the records except those for Tennessee MSAs and the overall U.S. rate. Some rearranging of the data would be needed, too. The

Bureau of Labor Statistics has sorted the data by unemployment rate change since October 2017, with the largest unemployment rate decline at the top of the list and the largest unemployment rate increase at the bottom. You would need to sort the data to put the smallest October 2018 unemployment rate at the top and the largest October 2018 unemployment rate at the bottom. Some calculations might prove helpful, too, like determining the average rate across the Tennessee MSAs and maybe each MSA's difference from the average. Your Google Sheet can do all of those things and more. Let's get started.

Filtering

You can specify a filter in Google Sheets that displays only the data you want and hides everything else. We're going to use a filter to display only the MSAs in Tennessee, and then copy those MSAs to a new Google Sheet tab so we can work with them without involving all the other MSA records. Clicking through the Bureau of Labor Statistics' "Economy at a Glance" page (Bureau of Labor Statistics, 2018b) to the page for Tennessee reveals that there are 10 Tennessee MSAs:

- Chattanooga, TN-GA
- Clarksville, TN-KY
- Cleveland, TN
- Jackson, TN
- Johnson City, TN
- Kingsport-Bristol-Bristol, TN-VA
- Knoxville, TN
- Memphis, TN-MS-AR
- Morristown, TN
- Nashville-Davidson–Murfreesboro–Franklin, TN

You could find and copy them individually. But who has time for that, especially on deadline? Setting up a filter would be much faster (see Figure 1.8). To set one up in your Google Sheet:

- Click "Data," then "Create a Filter." Google Sheets will highlight the entire dataset and place, at the top right of each column, three lines in the shape of a tiny, down-pointing arrow.
- Click the down-pointing arrow at the top of the "Area" column (Column A). The filter menu will open.
- Under "Filter by values," choose "Clear" to uncheck all of the records in the spreadsheet.
- Click in the search box (the box with the magnifying glass icon) and type something that will uniquely, or at least nearly uniquely, identify the records you want to find. We've learned, for example, that typing "TN," without the

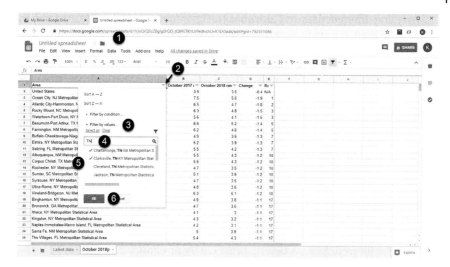

Figure 1.8 Setting up a filter in Google Sheets. Click Data (1), then "Create a Filter," then the down-pointing arrow at the top of the "Area" column (2). Under "Filter by values," click "Clear" (3), then type a suitable search term in the search box (4). Click each of the resulting MSAs you want the filter to display (5). When you have clicked on each MSA you want, click "OK" (6). Google and the Google logo are registered trademarks of Google Inc., used with permission.

quotes or the comma, will bring up all 10 Tennessee MSAs but none of the remaining MSAs.

- Scroll through the resulting list of MSA names and click on those that name a Tennessee MSA. Google Sheets will put a check mark beside each one you click on. If you're searching for the MSAs in some other state, use that state's abbreviation instead of "TN," and be aware that MSA names not in your state might show up. Just leave them unchecked.
- When you have checked all of the appropriate MSA names (make sure you didn't miss any, and make sure you didn't accidentally include any that you don't want), click "OK."

Once you click "OK," Google Sheets will display only the rows for only the MSAs your filter selected. The rows for the other MSAs haven't been deleted. They're just hidden from view. Google Sheets gives you two hints that the data have been filtered. First, the down-pointing arrow at the top of the "Area" column has changed to a funnel, indicating that a filter has been applied to the data in the "Area" column. Also, notice the gaps in the row numbers. When filtered for the Tennessee MSAs, for example, the row numbers start with Row 1 but then skip to Row 307, which is where the Kingsport-Bristol, TN-VA MSA data are, then jump to Row 320, the location for the Chattanooga, TN-GA MSA.

Analyzing filtered data has drawbacks. The analyses you perform tend to include the hidden rows in ways you might not always be aware of. Also, any time you ask Google Sheets to do something with the data, it has to spend time and processing power taking the hidden data into account. As a result, the best thing to do is to open a third spreadsheet tab and copy the filtered data there. To do so:

- Use your mouse to highlight the filtered data. Specifically, click on Cell A1, hold down the left mouse button, drag the mouse pointer down to the lower right corner of the filtered data, and release the mouse button. Alternatively, you can simply click the blank rectangle in the sheet's upper-left corner, which highlights all displayed cells in the sheet.
- Copy the highlighted data (as before, press Ctrl/c or Cmd/c on your keyboard).
- Click the small plus sign in the lower-left corner of the sheet to add "Sheet3."
- Click Cell A1 in Sheet3.
- Paste the filtered data (as before, press Ctrl/v or Cmd/v on your keyboard).
- Adjust the column widths, as you did before, by selecting all the data and double-clicking on the boundary between the "A" and "B" column labels, or the boundary between any other adjacent pair of column labels.

Recall that one aspect of the analysis we have in mind involves comparing each MSA's unemployment figures to the national unemployment data. The national data are still back on the sheet containing the filtered data. They're just hidden, because of the filter. To copy them to this new sheet:

- Click on the Sheet2 tab, which you might have renamed "October 2018p" or something similar by now.
- Remove the filter by clicking "Data / Turn off filter." Removing the filter should make all of the rows visible again, including Row 2, which contains figures for the "United States."
- Highlight and copy everything from "United States" under the "Area" heading to the "N/A" under "Rank."
- Click on the Sheet3 tab.
- Click on the first blank cell in Column A, the "Area" column. This click will tell Google Sheets where to paste the data you've copied.
- Use "Ctrl/v" or "Cmd/v" to paste the United States data.
- Click somewhere else – perhaps the next cell in Column A – to clear the highlighting from the United States data you just pasted.
- You might want to rename this new tab to something descriptive. We used, "Oct. 2018 data for TN." Renaming new tabs as you create them is a good idea. The more tabs you create, the easier it becomes to forget what you put where. Analysis mistakes can result.

Notice, too, that we're generally avoiding deleting data. That's a good habit to get into. Deleted data is difficult to retrieve if you discover at some later point in your analysis that you need it more than you thought you would. In some

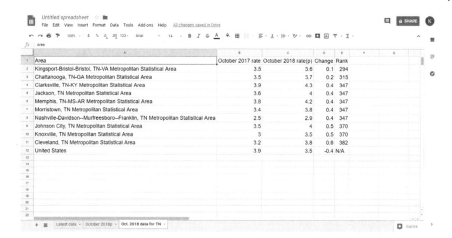

Figure 1.9 The filtered data, pasted into a new tab. Google and the Google logo are registered trademarks of Google Inc., used with permission.

cases, it might be impossible to retrieve. Assuming you have enough memory and storage space available, it's best to keep successively pared versions of your data in separate tabs, or, if necessary, in separate Google Sheets.

If you did everything correctly, your screen should look something like Figure 1.9.

Calculating

So far, we've merely filtered and rearranged the original data. Let's get a number that the Bureau of Labor Statistics didn't give us. Specifically, let's calculate the difference between the Kingsport-Bristol MSA's October 2018 unemployment rate and the October 2018 unemployment rate for the whole country. Calculating the difference will require subtracting the U.S. rate from the Kingsport-Bristol MSA rate. If you were using a pocket calculator, you'd punch in Kingsport-Bristol's 3.6 rate, press the "minus" key, punch in the U.S. rate, 3.5, and press the "Equals" key. The calculator would show you the difference, which is 0.1, meaning that Kingsport-Bristol's unemployment rate is one-tenth of a percentage point higher than the U.S. rate. To do the same math in your spreadsheet, you click on an empty cell in the spreadsheet and type in a set of instructions called a "formula." The formula tells the spreadsheet where to find the two unemployment rates and what kind of computation to do with them. Figure 1.10 gives an overview of the steps. Here are detailed instructions:

- Click on an empty cell. You could choose any cell you like, but the result will end up looking neater and more organized if we use Cell F2.

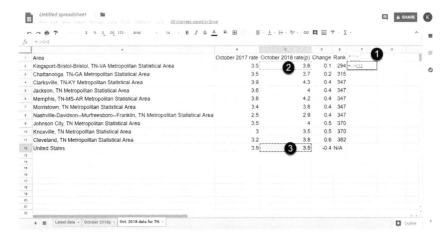

Figure 1.10 Writing a formula to compute the difference between the Kingsport-Bristol area's rate and the United States rate. Click Cell F2, then type a "=" symbol (1). Click Cell C2, then type a "-" symbol (2). Click Cell C12 (3). Press "Enter" to execute the formula and display the results in Cell F2. Google and the Google logo are registered trademarks of Google Inc., used with permission.

- On your keyboard, press the "=" key. That's how you tell a spreadsheet that you're about to type instructions rather than data.
- Using your mouse, click once on Cell C2, the cell containing the Kingsport-Bristol area's October 2018 unemployment rate of 3.6 percent. Notice that Google Sheets sticks the "C2" cell address right next to the equal sign you typed.
- Type a minus sign ("-") to signal that you want to subtract something from the number in Cell C2.
- Click on Cell C12, the cell with the 3.5 percent unemployment rate for the entire country.
- Press "Enter," and Google Sheets will display in Cell F2 the results of the computational instructions you just gave it: 0.1.

If you want to review what the computational instructions were, just click on Cell F2, then look in the upper-left corner of the spreadsheet, right above the "A" column heading. This area is called the "formula bar." You should see the instructions: =C2-C12. If you click on the instructions, Google Sheets will go back to something like Figure 1.10, which is what the screen looked like right before you pressed "Enter" to save the instructions in Cell F2.

By itself, what we've just shown you probably isn't all that impressive compared to what a calculator can do. So let's go somewhere else in the spreadsheet for a moment and demonstrate a few things that might change your mind. It would be informative to calculate the average October 2018 unemployment

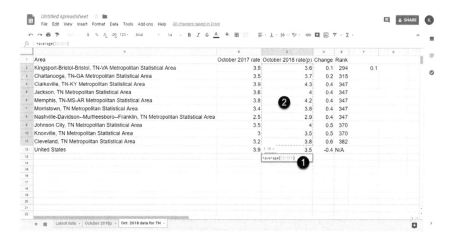

Figure 1.11 Averaging the MSA unemployment rates. Click Cell C13 and type =average(into the cell (1). Use your mouse to highlight cells C2 through C11 (2), then press "Enter." Be sure to exclude Cell C12 from the cells to be averaged, because Cell C12 contains the U.S. rate, not a rate for one of the MSAs. Google and the Google logo are registered trademarks of Google Inc., used with permission.

rate among the 10 MSAs listed. The average would give you an idea of how high or low any one MSA's rate is compared to the typical MSA unemployment rate statewide. To compute this average on a calculator, you'd have to punch in each unemployment figure, press the calculator's "plus" key between each figure, then press the calculator's "equal" key, press the "division" key, punch in the number of MSAs (10), then, finally, the "equal" key. By our count, that's close to 50 individual button pushes, each of which is an opportunity to make a mistake. To compute the same average in Google Sheets:

- Click Cell C13.
- Type: =average(
- Use your mouse to highlight the unemployment figures you want to average. Remember to exclude the U.S. figure, which is in Cell D12. Your screen should look like Figure 1.11.
- Press Enter.

The average, 3.78, should now be displaying in Cell C13. That's four steps compared to nearly 50.

Impressed yet? If not, try this:

- Click Cell C13, the one containing the average you just calculated.
- Copy the cell's instructions by pressing "Ctrl/c" or "Cmd/c" on your PC or Mac keyboard, respectively.

- Click Cell B13, the first blank cell in the column of unemployment rates from a year earlier, October 2017.
- Paste the instructions by pressing "Ctrl/v" or "Cmd/v".

You've just calculated the average of the October 2017 Tennessee MSA figures. Click Cell B13 so you can look at the instructions in the formula bar, in the upper-left corner of the spreadsheet. You'll see that Google Sheets was smart enough to understand that you wanted it to borrow the instructions for averaging the October 2018 figures, alter the cell addresses to those for the October 2017 figures, and show the result (3.39) in Cell B13. You can use the same process to get the average of the figures in the "Change" column (0.39). Clearly, someone using a spreadsheet can run circles around someone using a calculator – and be much more likely to make deadline with error-free results.

The "=AVERAGE" part of what you just did is another of Google Sheets' built-in functions, like the =IMPORTHTML function you've already learned how to use. If you're feeling adventurous, try using the =MEDIAN, =MIN and =MAX functions in the same way you used the =AVERAGE function.

Now that you've seen how a spreadsheet can copy instructions from one place to another, automatically updating them as needed, let's return to the instructions in Cell F2, the ones computing the 0.1 difference between the Kingsport-Bristol area's 3.6 percent October 2018 unemployment rate and the whole country's 3.5 percent October 2018 unemployment rate. As you might suspect, Google Sheets can replicate those instructions to produce the difference for each of the other October 2018 unemployment rates. First, though, we have to tell Google Sheets to keep the same cell address for the 3.5 percent national figure (Cell C12) when updating the instructions to refer to the cell address for each MSA's figure. Otherwise, Google Sheets will end up looking in the wrong places for the national figure. To better understand what we mean, try this:

- Click Cell F2, the cell with the formula computing the 0.1 difference between the Kingsport-Bristol area's 3.6 percent October 2018 unemployment rate and the whole country's 3.5 percent October 2018 unemployment rate.
- Click the "=C2-C12" instructions in the "formula bar" in the upper-left corner of the screen. Clicking the instructions allows you to edit them.
- Type a dollar sign, $, in front of both the "C" and the "12" in the "C12" cell address, so that the instructions look like this: =C2-C12.
- Press "Enter."
- Now, copy Cell F2's instructions to cells F3 through F11 by clicking Cell F2, pressing "Ctrl/c" or "Cmd/c," highlighting cells F3 through F11, then pressing "Enter."

Google Sheets will respond by keeping the cell address for the national unemployment rate the same while updating the MSA cell address to the one appropriate for each row. Omit the dollar signs, and Google Sheets will increment both cell addresses. The results would be incorrect, because, starting

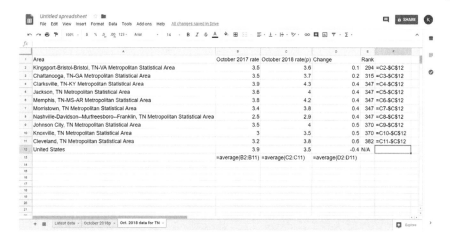

Figure 1.12 The spreadsheet, with the formulas we've added made visible by pressing and holding the "Ctrl" key, followed by the "~" key. On a Mac, use the "Cmd" key instead of the "Ctrl" key. Google and the Google logo are registered trademarks of Google Inc., used with permission.

with the instructions for the Chattanooga area in Cell F3, Google Sheets would be looking somewhere other than Cell C12 for the national figure to subtract from the MSA's figure.

So, the bottom line, here, is that you can save a bunch of time by copying calculation instructions from one place to another in your spreadsheet. And, when necessary, you can control how the spreadsheet updates the cell addresses in those instructions. Figure 1.12 shows all the formulas we have added to the spreadsheet so far. You can toggle between this view of your spreadsheet and the regular view by pressing Ctrl/~ or Cmd/~.

Labeling and Tidying Up

This is a good place to pause and add some labeling and formatting to avoid confusing ourselves about what's what in the spreadsheet. Clicking on Cell A13 and typing "MSA Average" will help you to remember that the figures in cells B13 through D13 are averages of the October 2017, October 2018, and "Change" figures for each MSA. Highlighting cells A12 through F13, then clicking the large, dark "B" on the tool bar will bold-face the contents of those cells, indicating that they are distinct from the rows above, which deal with individual MSAs. Clicking on Cell F1, then typing "Diff. from U.S. Rate" will give the column a label. You can expand the column by double-clicking the border between the "F" and "G" column labels. Bold-facing the column labels in cells A1 through F1 would look nice, too. Some columns may need resizing.

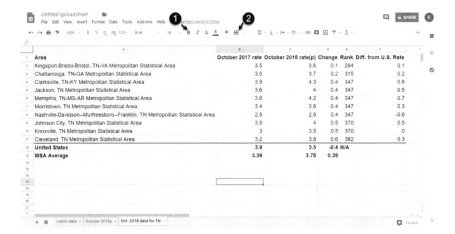

Figure 1.13 The spruced-up spreadsheet, with the locations of the bold-facing (1) and cell border (2) tools highlighted. Google and the Google logo are registered trademarks of Google Inc., used with permission.

Remember: Just highlight the column or columns, point at a column boundary until the cursor changes to a double-ended arrow, and double-click. The column width will adjust automatically. Finally, highlighting cells A11 through F11, clicking the toolbar's "Borders" icon (the icon looks like a square divided into four smaller squares) and choosing the "Bottom border" option will put a nice dividing line between the MSA rows and the "United States" and "MSA Average" rows. Figure 1.13 shows the spruced-up version of the spreadsheet.

Sorting

Looking at the list, it's fairly easy to see that the Nashville area has the smallest October 2018 unemployment rate (2.9 percent) out of the 10 MSAs, while the Clarksville area has the largest (4.3 percent). It wouldn't be so easy, though, if the list were longer. Besides, we think the smallest rate should be at the top of the list, not the bottom. The top of the list is for better things, like small unemployment rates, not worse things, like large unemployment rates. Like other spreadsheet programs, Google Sheets lets you quickly and easily sort data from high to low or low to high. Let's use the sort tool to put the MSAs in ascending order by their October 2018 unemployment rates. Figure 1.14 illustrates the steps. Here are detailed directions:

- Highlight rows 1 through 11 – the column labels and the data for all 10 MSAs. Leave rows 12 (the row for the United States) and 13 (the row with the MSA average figures) unhighlighted. Doing so will omit them from the sort. You can highlight the data by clicking on Cell A1 and dragging down to Cell F11.

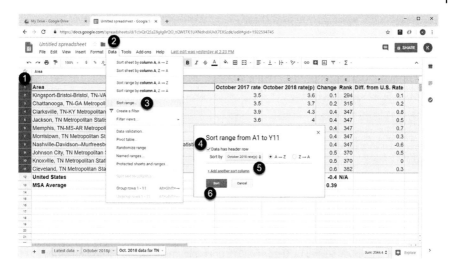

Figure 1.14 Sorting in ascending order by the October 2018 unemployment rates. Highlight the rows 1 through 11 (1), click "Data" (2), then "Sort" (3). When the sort dialog box appears, check the "Data has header row" box (4), choose the "October 2018 rate(p)" column from the "Sort by" list (5), and click the "Sort" button (6). Google and the Google logo are registered trademarks of Google Inc., used with permission.

Alternatively, you can click on the "1" to the left of Row 1 and drag down to the 11 to the left of Row 11.

- Click "Data," then click "Sort range ..."
- A window will pop up. In the window, click the box beside "Data has header row." This step will keep the column labels, like "Area," "October 2017 rate," etc., from being included in the sort.
- Click the down arrow next to the "Sort by" box. A list of the column headings will appear. If you see only column letters, like Column A, Column B, etc., it's because you didn't check the "Data has header row" box on the previous step. Choose the "October 2018 rate(p)" column.
- Make sure the radio button next to "A -> Z" is selected, indicating that you want Google Sheets to sort the data by putting small numbers higher than larger ones.
- The "+ Add another sort column" option is there in case you want to add one or more "nested" sorts. For example, adding "Area" as a second sort column would sort the data first by unemployment rate, then, for areas that have the same unemployment rate, alphabetically by area name. We're going to keep things simple for now and skip that step, but you're welcome to try it out.
- Click "Sort."

Google Sheets will rearrange the data so that the MSA with the smallest unemployment rate, Nashville, is at the top of the list, and the MSA with the largest unemployment rate, Clarksville, is at the bottom of the list, as shown in Figure 1.15.

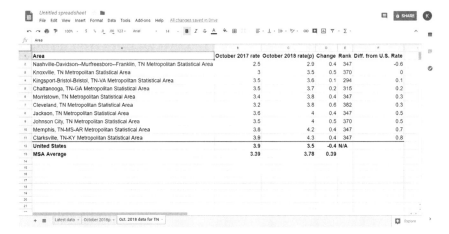

Figure 1.15 The data, sorted by October 2018 unemployment rate in ascending order. Google and the Google logo are registered trademarks of Google Inc., used with permission.

Where's the "Save" Button?

Did you notice, by the way, that we haven't "saved" the data. In fact, if you click the "File" button in Google Sheets and look for a "Save" or "Save as …" option, you won't find one. That's because Google Sheets automatically saves your work as you go. Even better, it keeps a copy of each earlier version. Look for, and click on, the "All changes saved in Drive" link next to the "Help" button in the navigation menu, and you'll see links to your earlier versions in a list running down the right side of the screen. The closest thing to a "Save" or "Save as …" button on Google Sheets' "File" menu is a "Download as …" option, which will let you download a copy of your spreadsheet in a variety of file formats.

One thing you might want to do, though, is change your spreadsheet's name from "Untitled spreadsheet" to something more descriptive, like "MSA unemployment rates." Simply click once on the "Untitled spreadsheet" name. It will become editable. Type the new name, and press "Enter."

Writing About the Analysis Results

While more could be done with these data, the techniques demonstrated so far would enable you to write the beginnings of a news piece for a Nashville-area audience:

> *Just under 3 percent of the Nashville region's workforce lacked a job in October, the lowest unemployment rate among the state's 10*

metropolitan areas but a slight increase compared to a year earlier, federal figures released on Thursday show.

Nashville's preliminary October 2018 unemployment rate stood at 2.9 percent, up from 2.5 percent in October 2017 and below the national figure of 3.5 percent unemployment for the month.

The Knoxville, Tennessee, area posted a 3.5 percent unemployment rate, the next-lowest in the state. The Clarksville, Tennessee, area's 4.3 percent unemployment ranked highest, just ahead of the 4.2 percent unemployment rate in the Memphis, Tennessee, area. Unemployment edged upward across all 10 of the state's metro areas compared to October of last year, with the largest increase appearing in the Cleveland, Tennessee, area, where unemployment rose from 3.2 percent in October of last year to 3.8 percent this October.

Nationwide, Nashville's unemployment rate was identical to that of a dozen other metro areas, some of them geographically nearby, such as Gainesville, Georgia, and Raleigh, North Carolina. The lowest unemployment rate for the month among all U.S. metro areas was Ames, Iowa's 1.1 percent rate. The highest was 19.2 percent in El Centro, California.

The Nashville metropolitan area consists of Metro Nashville / Davidson County as well as 13 surrounding counties, including Rutherford and Williamson. The U.S. Bureau of Labor Statistics released the data Thursday and will release similar estimates on Jan. 3 for November 2018.

The above story needs additional sourcing to provide verification, reaction and context. But writing something like it could give you a head start on gathering such material. The lead suggests a need to contact private, governmental and academic sources with insights into the Nashville-area and statewide employment situations. The third paragraph suggests contacting similar sources in the Clarksville area. The fourth paragraph might lead to a more in-depth comparison of the Nashville area and the areas with unemployment rates similar to Nashville's, especially if the similarities persist over time. And as you might infer, we used filtering and sorting on the full dataset to identify the dozen metro areas with unemployment rates identical to Nashville's and to single out the areas with the lowest and highest unemployment rates in the nation.

Note, too, the implied promise in the final paragraph. New, more recent data will be available in January, so your audience can expect an update then. The Bureau of Labor Statistics publishes a calendar showing which reports it will release when, so you can plan accordingly (Bureau of Labor Statistics. 2018c). The possibility leads us to this chapter's final point about spreadsheets. Just for fun, go to your Google Sheet and change the U.S. unemployment rate from 3.5 percent to, say 6 percent. Just click Cell C12, type "6," and press "Enter." Did you notice what happened over in column F? All of the calculations in Column F are tied to the national unemployment rate in Cell C12. So, when you changed the number in Cell C12, all of the calculations in Column F updated automatically. That means that when next month's data come out, you could copy this month's sheet to a new tab, paste in the new numbers, and get up-to-date calculations without having to reprogram any of them. Just redo the sorting, and you'll be ready to write.

Don't forget, by the way, to change the national unemployment rate back to the accurate figure.

Recap

This chapter has introduced you to Google Sheets, a free, Web-based spreadsheet you can use from any Internet-connected computer, PC or Mac. You've seen how to import data into Google Sheets from any table or list on the Web, specify a filter to display data that meet particular criteria, create and manage tabs within a Google Sheet, perform calculations using basic mathematical instructions as well as the "=average" function, sort data, and update data. You've also learned the importance of questioning data, checking data for obvious errors, and planning an analysis with a particular audience in mind. You've also seen an example of how to begin writing about the results of a data analysis. Finally, if you've downloaded and analyzed current data for your own area, well, quit wasting time. You've got a story to finish writing.

References

Adielsson, Magnus, Richard Barnes, Peter Kupfer, Iain Roberts, and Jean Hollis Weber. 2005. "Google Sheets Function List." Accessed Dec. 8, 2018. https://support.google.com/docs/table/25273?hl=en&ref_topic=9054531.

Bureau of Labor Statistics. 2015. "How the Government Measures Unemployment." Accessed Dec. 7, 2018. www.bls.gov/cps/cps_htgm.htm.

Bureau of Labor Statistics. 2018a. "Over-the-Year Change in Unemployment Rates for Metropolitan Areas." Accessed Dec. 5, 2018. www.bls.gov/web/metro/laummtch.htm. For the latest data, visit the Local Area Unemployment Statistics page, www.bls.gov/lau/, scroll down to "Tables and Maps Created by BLS," and click the "Over-the-Year Change in Unemployment Rates for Metropolitan Areas" link under the "Metropolitan Area Data" heading.

Bureau of Labor Statistics. 2018b. "Economy at a Glance." Accessed Dec. 13, 2018. www.bls.gov/eag/.

Bureau of Labor Statistics. 2018c. "Release Calendar." Accessed Dec. 15, 2018. www.bls.gov/schedule/2019/01_sched.htm.

2

Data Visualization

Tables of data like the one at the end of the last chapter (Figure 1.15) may be informative. They're typically not much to look at, though. More importantly, they can obscure important patterns and trends in the data they hold. For example, it's not immediately apparent that all 10 Metropolitan Statistical Areas saw an increase in their unemployment rates in October 2018 compared to October of the previous year. You have to study the table long enough to understand that the "Change" column compares the current figures with the figures from a year ago, that all of the "Change" column's figures are positive, and that their being positive means that all of the current figures are greater than the year-old figures.

Figure 2.1 presents the same data in an easier-to-understand fashion. Once you've grasped that the light-shaded bars represent last year's figures and the dark-shaded bars this year's figures, you can easily determine that this year's figures are all higher than last year's for each of the 10 MSAs. You also can easily see that the Nashville MSA had the lowest unemployment rate, that the Clarksville MSA had the highest, and that only the Nashville MSA had an unemployment rate lower than the national rate. Finally, if you were using a tablet, smartphone or computer to view the chart online, you would find that tapping on, or hovering your mouse pointer over, any set of bars in the chart would cause a small box to appear telling you the MSA's name and the precise unemployment rate each of its two bars represents. Figure 2.1 shows such a box for the Nashville MSA. This chapter will show you how to make a chart like Figure 2.1 using the Tennessee MSA unemployment data from Chapter 1 and publish the chart on the Web. You'll also learn about making two other types of charts, a line chart and a pie chart, and a little bit about how to tell when to use which type of chart.

Data Skills for Media Professionals: A Basic Guide, First Edition. Ken Blake and Jason Reineke.
© 2020 John Wiley & Sons, Inc. Published 2020 by John Wiley & Sons, Inc.

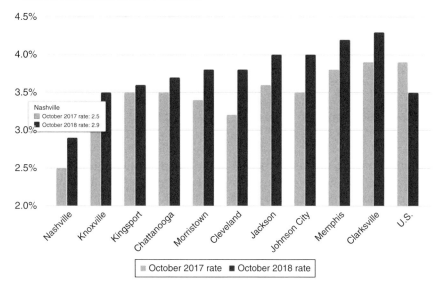

Metro area unemployment in Tennessee

Source: U.S. Bureau of Labor Statistics

Figure 2.1 The unemployment data from Chapter 1, presented in a Google Sheets column chart. Note the pop-up box for the Nashville MSA. When the chart is published online, a similar box will pop up for each metro area in the chart when users tap on, or mouse over, the area's bars. Google and the Google logo are registered trademarks of Google Inc., used with permission.

Preparing Your Data

Begin by opening the "MSA Unemployment rates" Google Sheet that you cre-ated in Chapter 1 and going to the "Oct. 2018 data for TN" tab, or whatever tab you used to store your year-to-year unemployment rate comparison. Now, copy your data to a new tab so that you can make the chart without disturbing your work from Chapter 1. You could do so by creating a new tab, then highlighting, copying and pasting your data into the new tab. But there's a handy shortcut:

- Click on the small, downward-pointing arrow on your data's tab. It's just to the right of the tab's label.
- Click "Duplicate" on the pop-up menu.

You should now be looking at an exact copy of your original data, but in a new tab labeled "Copy of Oct. 2018 data for TN" (or "Copy of," followed by the name of the tab you copied). Now the data and analysis on the original tab can stay the way they were at the end of Chapter 1. Meanwhile, you can change the data on this new tab in any way necessary to make the chart. And only one

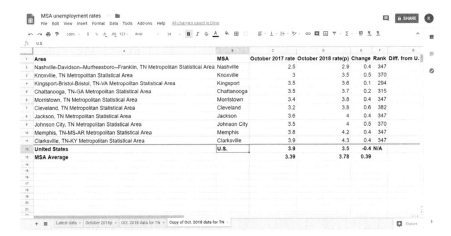

Figure 2.2 The unemployment data, after inserting a blank Column B and filling it with shortened versions of the area names in Column A. Google and the Google logo are registered trademarks of Google Inc., used with permission.

change is needed. The names in the "Area" column (Column A) are too long and complex to display in the chart. Let's insert a blank column between columns A and B, then type a shorter, simpler name for each MSA. To insert a blank column between columns A and B:

- Hover your mouse over the "B" at the top of Column B until a small, down-pointing arrow appears.
- Click the arrow.
- Choose "Insert 1 left" from the pop-up menu.

Google Sheets will insert a blank Column B and shift the "October 2017 rate" and each column after it exactly one column to the right. Give the new, blank Column B a label by typing "MSA" into Cell B1. Then, in the rows beneath it, type a short version of each MSA name from Column A. We used the first city name in each longer MSA name. For example, "Nashville-Davidson–Murfreesboro–Franklin, TN Metropolitan Statistical Area" in Column A became just "Nashville" in Column B, and we used "U.S." for "United States." We also resized the column. Figure 2.2 shows the results.

Making a Column Chart

Making a column chart involves using your mouse to select the column headings and data you want to include in the chart, telling Google Sheets to produce its best guess about the kind of chart you want, then customizing the chart Google Sheets produces. Figures 2.3 and 2.4 illustrate the steps. Here's the process in detail:

- Use your mouse to highlight everything between Cell B1 (the "MSA" column label) and Cell D12 (the October 2018 unemployment rate for the U.S.). To do so, click on Cell B1, hold down the mouse's left button, drag down to include Cell D12, highlighting everything in between, and release your mouse button. Google Sheets will shade the cells you have selected and will frame them with a thin rectangular outline that has a small square on the lower-right corner.
- Click "Insert," then click "Chart" on the drop-down menu. Google Sheets will insert a chart and automatically open the "Chart Editor" on the right side of the screen.
- Google Sheets can produce three kinds of column charts: a basic "Column chart," a "Stacked column chart," and a "100% stacked column chart." It will guess which type of column chart you want. Chances are, it will guess incorrectly. For example, Google Sheets usually gives us a "Stacked column chart." Such a chart would be useful if columns C and D in the data represented parts of some whole, like if Column C contained the number of unemployed workers who had no college degree, Column D contained the number of unemployed workers who had earned a college degree, and both, when combined, represented all unemployed workers. But that's not the case. columns C and D represent unemployment rates for two different months, October 2017 and October 2018. Accordingly, we need a plain "Column chart" showing one column for each October 2017 unemployment rate, grouped with a column representing the corresponding October 2018 unemployment rate.
- To switch from a stacked to a plain column chart, click the down arrow next to "Stacked bar chart," scroll down to the "Column" area on the drop-down menu, and choose the "Column chart" style. The style's icon shows a chart with red and blue columns next to each other instead of stacked on top of each other, and a "Column chart" label will pop up when you hover your mouse pointer over the icon.
- When you click on the "Column chart" style icon, the chart Google Sheets made from the unemployment will switch to a plain column chart style.

Even if Google Sheets gives you the right type of chart by default, you'll probably want to customize things about the chart, like its title, axis labels, scale, colors, and so on. The "Customize" tab on the Chart editor offers drop-down menus that let you edit these and several other characteristics of the chart. Here, organized by drop-down menu, are the customization options we selected to make the chart in Figure 2.4 look like it does in Figure 2.1:

- On the "Chart style" menu:
  - We checked the "Compare mode" box. Doing so makes the pop-up box for each metro area display the data for both of the metro area's bars at the same time. Leave the box unchecked, and the information for each bar will display separately.

Figure 2.3 Inserting a column chart. Highlight the data you want included in the chart (1), click "Insert" (2), then "Chart" (3). Google Sheets will insert a chart (4) and open the Chart Editor (5). Google and the Google logo are registered trademarks of Google Inc., used with permission.

Figure 2.4 Switching the column chart's style. Click the down arrow in the Chart Editor's "Chart type" area (1), scroll down to the "Column" area, and click the "Column chart" icon (2). Google Sheets will switch the chart to a plain column chart style (3). Google and the Google logo are registered trademarks of Google Inc., used with permission.

- We left the "3D" box unchecked, but you might try it out to see whether you like the look it produces.
- On the "Chart & axis titles" menu:
  - We deleted the default chart title, "October 2017 rate and October 2018 rate(p)," and replaced it with "Metro area unemployment in Tennessee."
  - We changed the "Title font size" from "Auto" to 30.
  - We changed the "Title text color" from "Auto" to black by selecting the black square from the color options. Note that if you click the "Custom …" link, you have a wider range of color choices and also can enter custom color codes.
  - We clicked the down arrow next to "Chart title" in the "Type" area and selected "Chart subtitle." On the "Title text" line, we typed, "Source: U.S. Bureau of Labor Statistics." We also changed the "Title font size" to 18 and the "Title text color" to black.
  - Using the down arrow in the "Type" area, we switched to the "Horizontal axis title" and deleted "MSA" from the "Title text" line. It's obvious that the items on the horizontal line are areas, so we saw no need to label them as such.
- On the "Series" menu:
  - We clicked the down arrow next to "Apply to" and selected "October 2017 rate." There, we changed the color to "dark gray 1."
  - Changing the "Apply to" selection to "October 2018 rate(p)," we changed the color to "dark cornflower blue 3."
- On the "Legend" menu:
  - We selected "Bottom" under "Position."
  - We changed the text color to black.
- On the "Horizontal axis" menu:
  - We changed the text color to black.
- On the "Vertical axis" menu:
  - We changed the text color to black.
  - We changed "Number format" to "Custom," then added a "%" symbol to the "Suffix" line.
  - We changed the minimum axis value to two by putting a "2" next to "Min."
- We changed nothing on the "Gridlines" menu.
- Finally, we used the mouse to grab the small, blue square at the top of the blue outline around the chart and, keeping the mouse button held down, stretch the chart vertically until it became more of a square than a landscape-oriented rectangle. The stretch made the chart look a little less crowded and allowed more room for the metro area names.

You can style your chart however you like, of course. At least one of the choices we made in styling ours requires some careful thought, though. The "Min" and "Max" settings on the "Vertical axis" menu define the minimum and maximum values the chart will display on its vertical axis. Setting the minimum value to 2 decreases the vertical axis scale's range and, as a result, emphasizes the differences between the unemployment rates in the chart. Emphasizing the differences in this way helps readers make comparisons more easily, but it also might subtly mislead them about the size of the differences involved.

To see what we mean, pick two bars whose values are pretty close to each other, like the October 2018 rates for Clarksville (4.3 percent) and Memphis (4.2 percent). If you set the "Min" value to zero, the two bars look almost identical. And they probably should look almost identical. Remember, they differ by only one-tenth of one percentage point. If you set the "Min" value to "2," the difference between the two bars looks bigger, even though it's still just a tenth of a percentage point. Is that misleading? Maybe. But it would be at least equally misleading to suggest that zero percent unemployment is a realistic value. Even in the best of times – and October 2018 was a time of historically low unemployment rates across the nation – there are always at least some people looking for a job. In short, there probably is no perfect choice, here. Our point is that you should make the choice mindfully.

Once you have finished editing your chart, you can close the chart editor by clicking any spot in the spreadsheet that isn't occupied by the chart or the editor. To reopen the chart editor, click the chart, click the three vertical dots in the chart's upper-right corner, and choose "Edit chart ..." Another way to reopen the chart editor is to double click on whatever chart element you want to edit. For example, double click the chart's title, and the chart editor will open to the "Chart & axis titles" menu. Clicking once on the chart also will let you try out the chart's pop-up boxes. Just drag your mouse over the chart and watch the box appear for each pair of columns. Clicking the chart also lets you select it so that you can use your mouse to drag it to any location in the Google Sheets tab. For example, if the chart is covering up your data table, you might want to move it elsewhere so you can see both the data and the chart.

Publishing the Chart to the Web

You can publish the finished chart on the Web so anyone with a Web browser can view it as a stand-alone Web page or as an element embedded in a Web page along with other content. Figures 2.5 and 2.6 illustrate the steps. Specifically:

- Click the chart once to select it.
- Click the three vertical dots the chart's upper-right corner.
- Click "Publish chart ..."
- On the "Publish to the web" window, click "Publish."
- Click "OK" when Google Docs asks, "Are you sure you want to publish this selection?"

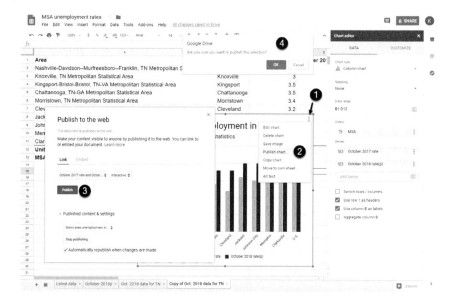

Figure 2.5 Publishing your chart. Click the chart once, then click the three vertical dots in the chart's upper-right corner (1). Choose "Publish chart" (2), then "Publish" (3). If the chart has never been published before, click "OK" to confirm that you are ready to publish it (4). Google and the Google logo are registered trademarks of Google Inc., used with permission.

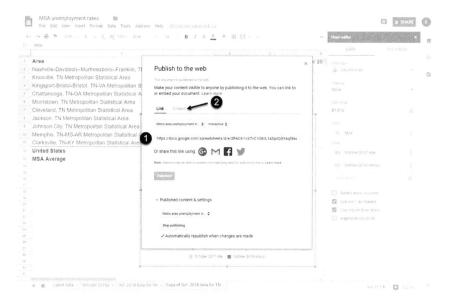

Figure 2.6 The URL for your published chart (1) and the "Embed" tab (2), which will give you code for embedding your chart on a Web page. Google and the Google logo are registered trademarks of Google Inc., used with permission.

The "Publish to the web" screen will then show you a URL under a "Link" tab. Copy that URL and paste it into a Web browser, and the browser will display your chart. The same URL can be emailed or shared via social media. Meanwhile, click the "Embed" tab, and you will see embed code that you can use to embed your chart in a Web page, including a WordPress.com or WordPress.org page or post.

Choosing the Right Type of Chart

A column chart, while versatile, isn't the best choice for every data visualization purpose. Consider, for example, these data, which show the Nashville MSA seasonally adjusted unemployment rates for the 12 months leading up to October 2018 and also for the previous 12-month period. We extracted the data from the Bureau of Labor Statistics' table of seasonally adjusted unemployment rates for all U.S. Metropolitan Statistical Areas (Bureau of Labor Statistics, 2018a).

At first glance, the data look structurally the same as the data in columns B, C and D in Figure 2.2 that you just finished illustrating with a column chart. The "Month" column contains the names of months, all of which are text information, as were the MSA names in Column B of the table in Figure 2.2. The last two columns both contain numeric data, as did columns C and D in Figure 2.2. In fact, you could represent Table 2.1's data as a column chart made by following the steps in Figures 2.3 and 2.4.

But there's one important difference between the two datasets: The months represent a time sequence. January comes before February, which comes before March, which comes before April, and so forth. There is no such time sequence in the MSA names from the table in Figure 2.2. Furthermore, the time sequence in the Table 2.1 data is kind of a big deal. The month-to-month changes are a big part of what make the data newsworthy. So, a chart that emphasizes the sequential nature of the data might be better than a column chart. In such situations, a line chart like the one in Figure 2.7 would be better.

The figure shows the pop-up window that appears when a user hovers a mouse over the chart's March data points. You can make the same line chart by punching the numbers into a Google Sheet, highlighting the three columns, then choosing "Insert," then "Chart," and selecting "Line chart" under "Chart type." After inserting the chart, click chart editor's "Customize" tab. Then, if you want to make your chart look like Figure 2.7:

- On the "Chart style" menu, check the "Compare mode" box
- On the "Chart & axis titles" menu:
  - Choose "Chart title" next to "Type," then:
    - Key in a chart title like, "Monthly unemployment in the Nashville metro area."
    - Choose black under "Title text color."

Table 2.1 Monthly Nashville MSA Unemployment Rates.

Month	Jan.–Dec., 2017	Jan.–Oct., 2018
January	3.6	2.6
February	3.4	2.7
March	3.2	2.7
April	3	2.6
May	2.8	2.5
June	2.8	2.8
July	2.8	2.8
August	2.7	2.8
September	2.6	2.9
October	2.6	3
November	2.7	
December	2.6	

Monthly unemployment in the Nashville metro area
Source: U.S. Bureau of Labor Statistics

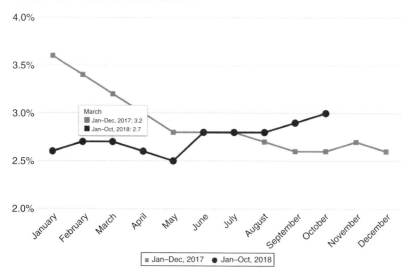

Figure 2.7 A Google Sheets line chart showing monthly unemployment rates in the Nashville metro area for 2017 and for 2018 through October. Note the interactive pop-up window showing detailed data for March. Google and the Google logo are registered trademarks of Google Inc., used with permission.

- – Choose "Chart subtitle" next to "Type," then:
  - ○ Key in something like, "Source: U.S. Bureau of Labor Statistics."
  - ○ Again, choose black under "Title text color."
- – Choose "Horizontal axis title," then:
  - ○ Delete "Month" under "Title text," and leave the line blank.
- On the "Series" menu:
  - – Choose "Jan–Dec, 2017" next to "Apply to," then:
    - ○ Change the color to "dark gray 2."
    - ○ Change "Point size" to "7 px." This setting controls the size of the markers on the series line. Note that your markers have to be larger than the thickness of your line. Otherwise, the markers won't show up well.
    - ○ We left the "Point shape" for this series on the default, "Circle." Also, we left the "Data labels" and "Trendline" boxes unchecked; we think the elements they introduce would make this particular chart too crowded. But you might try clicking on them, if only to see what they do.
  - – Choose "Jan–Oct, 2018" next to "Apply to," then:
    - ○ Change the color to "dark cornflower blue 3," or whatever color you like. The point is to pick a color that sufficiently contrasts with the color you chose for the Jan–Dec. 2017 line.
    - ○ Change the "Point size" to 7px.
    - ○ Change the "Point shape" to something other than a circle, like a square.
- On the "Legend" menu:
  - – Choose "Bottom" under "Position."
  - – Choose black under "Text color."
- On the "Horizontal axis" menu:
  - – Change "Text color" to black.
- On the "Vertical axis" menu:
  - – Change the text color to black.
  - – Change "Min" to 2. Recall, here, our earlier discussion about the pros and cons of showing a limited scale range in a chart.
  - – Change "Number format" to "Custom," then place a "%" symbol under "Suffix." This step adds the percent sign after each value on the vertical scale.
- Leave the "Gridlines" menu on its default settings.

Finally, stretch the chart up a little, until the chart's overall shape is a square, or approximately so. Once you are done, you can share and/or embed this chart using the same steps shown in Figures 2.5 and 2.6.

Next, look at the data in Table 2.2, which represent the number of jobs per major economic sector in the Nashville MSA during the month of October 2018 (Bureau of Labor Statistics, 2018b).

This time, there's something special about the column of numeric "Jobs" data. Each value in the column represents a unique portion of the total number

Table 2.2 Jobs in the Nashville, Tennessee MSA, by Sector, October 2018.

Sector	Jobs
Trade, Trans., Utilities	194,100
Professional, Business Svcs.	171,400
Education, Health	154,100
Government	120,100
Leisure, Hospitality	115,200
Manufacturing	82,100
All other	175,800

Jobs in the Nashville area, by sector
Source: U.S. Bureau of Labor Statistics

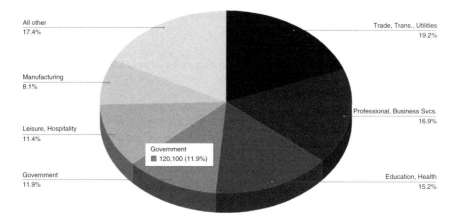

Figure 2.8 A Google Sheets pie chart showing Nashville-area job totals by employment sector. The interactive pop-up window shows the detailed information for the "Government" sector. Google and the Google logo are registered trademarks of Google Inc., used with permission.

of non-farm jobs in the Nashville MSA for that month. What's most newsworthy, here, is how those portions compare to one another. For example, which portion contains the most jobs, how much bigger is it than the portion with the next-largest number of jobs, and so forth. In situations like this one (and if there aren't more than about seven portions to represent), a pie chart like the one in Figure 2.8 can work nicely.

The figure shows the pop-up window that appears when a user hovers a mouse over the chart's "Leisure, Hospitality" slice. You can make Figure 2.8 by keying the data into Google Sheets, selecting both columns, then clicking "Insert," then "Chart," and choosing the "3D pie chart" icon from the "Pie" tab area under "Chart type." After inserting the chart, click the chart editor's "Customize" tab, then:

- On the "Chart & axis title" menu:
  - Choose "Chart title" next to "Type."
    - Change the "Title text" to something like, "Jobs in the Nashville area, by sector."
    - Change the title text color to black.
  - Choose "Chart subtitle" next to "Type."
    - Change the "Title text" to something like, "Source: U.S. Bureau of Labor Statistics."
    - Change the title text color to black.
- On the "Series" menu:
  - Select the first slice, "Trade, Trans., Utilities," from the drop-down menu next to "Apply to."
  - Choose a color for the slice. We went with black.
  - Repeat the procedure for each remaining slice, choosing a different color each time. We used gradually lighter shades of gray.
- On the "Legend" menu:
  - Change the text color to black.

Of course, you can share or embed a pie chart online as easily as you can a column or line chart, and by using the same procedure. See Figures 2.5 and 2.6. Describing the best situations for every type of chart available in Google Sheets would be beyond the scope of this book. The main point to see here is that you should choose the type of chart thoughtfully, and with an eye toward emphasizing what is newsworthy about the data. Column charts (or their cousins, bar charts) are good for comparing how one thing (like an unemployment rate) differs across different things (like metro areas). Line charts excel at showing how one thing (like an unemployment rate) for one thing (like a metro area) has changed over time. Pie charts are best for showing how a complete set of things (like jobs in the Nashville metro area) is divided into component categories (like employment sectors).

Google Sheets will help you by trying to guess which type of chart is best suited for your data. Don't trust it uncritically, though. It often guesses incorrectly. Also, Google Sheet's "Chart" function works best when the data you want to visualize are all in contiguous columns. If organizing the data that way isn't possible or convenient, you can highlight non-contiguous columns by holding down the "Ctrl" or "Cmd" key on your keyboard as you highlight the data columns you want to include. Google Sheets might have a difficult time recommending correct chart types to you, though.

Figure 2.9 A pair of Google Sheets table charts, one showing its data sorted by October 2018 unemployment rate (1) and another showing its data sorted by over-the-year unemployment rate change (2). To the right is the "Customize" menu for table charts. Google and the Google logo are registered trademarks of Google Inc., used with permission.

We encourage you to play around with each of the other chart types. You can learn about each one by visiting Google's "Types of charts & graphics in Google Sheets" page (Google, 2018). We especially recommend taking a look at the "Table chart" type. It lets you display your raw data in a dynamically sortable table. When the table is posted online, users can sort the table's data from lowest or highest, or highest to lowest, by clicking on the arrow at the top of any table in the column. We started out in Chapter 1 with a spreadsheet of unemployment rates for each of the United States' 388 Metropolitan Statistical Areas. That's way too much data to put into a column chart. But put it in an dynamically sortable table, with columns for the metro area's name, current unemployment rate, rate from a year ago, and over-the-year change, and users will have multiple ways of looking at how the areas compare. Figure 2.9 shows the data file plus two table charts, one sorted to show the metro area with the highest unemployment rate, and the other sorted to show the metro area with the biggest unemployment rate decline.

You should know that Google Sheets is not the only, or even the best, tool for making online, interactive graphics. A growing number of sites offer free or low-cost data visualization tools. At the time of this writing, such sites include Datawrapper (www.datawrapper.de) and Flourish (https://flourish.studio/). By the time you pick up this book, still others may have become available.

Recap

You've learned in this chapter how to use Google Sheets to turn a table of data into an interactive column chart and share that chart via the Web. You've also learned how to customize the layout and look of the chart. Finally, you've seen how to choose and customize other types of charts that might be more suitable for visualizing the data you are working with.

References

Bureau of Labor Statistics. 2018a. "Table 1. Civilian Labor Force and Unemployment by Metropolitan Area, Seasonally Adjusted." Accessed Dec. 17, 2018. www.bls.gov/lau/metrossa.htm.

Bureau of Labor Statistics. 2018b. "Economy at a Glance: Nashville-Davidson–Murfreesboro–Franklin, TN." Accessed Dec. 19, 2018. www.bls.gov/eag/eag. tn_nashville_msa.htm.

Google. 2018. "Types of charts and graphs in Google Sheets." Accessed Dec. 19, 2018. https://support.google.com/docs/answer/190718?hl=en.

3

Making Online Maps

There's one critical type of information that the charts you learned how to make in the last chapter can't convey: None of them can show you where the Metropolitan Statistical Areas they allude to are located. Most Tennessee natives probably would know that Memphis is in the western part of the state, Nashville is in the middle, and Knoxville is in the east. They'd probably have a tougher time placing the likes of Jackson, Cleveland and Morristown. People new to Tennessee, or people who live elsewhere, probably would have even less familiarity with the state's geography. Also, MSAs sometimes cross state lines. The Memphis metropolitan statistical area (MSA), for example, includes parts of Mississippi and Arkansas.

If you're analyzing data about places, you're eventually going to need to display them on a map and maybe also customize their appearance based on something you want to convey about them. That's what this chapter will show you how to do. For example, Figure 3.1 shows an online map of the 10 Tennessee metropolitan area's we've been looking at. The map's legend categorizes the areas as "lowest," "midrange" or "highest" based on their October 2018 unemployment rates. On the map itself, each area is shaded to indicate which category it falls within. Those in the "lowest" category are shaded blue, those in the "midrange" category, gray, and those in the "highest" category, red. The map is interactive, too. If you click on an area's name in the legend or shape on the map, a detail window slides into view telling you the area's October 2017 and October 2018 unemployment rates as well as the difference between the two rates.

Google Sheets' chart editor, which you learned to use in Chapter 2, offers "Geo chart" and "Geo chart with markers" options that can make maps similar to the one in Figure 3.1. But as of this writing, both tools can map only countries, continents or regions. If you want to map data about Metropolitan Statistical Areas – or states, counties, political district, U.S. Census Bureau divisions, cities, zip codes or pretty much anything else that has geographic borders – you're going to need more flexibility. In the next few pages, we'll walk you through the best approach we've found, which involves three general steps

Data Skills for Media Professionals: A Basic Guide, First Edition. Ken Blake and Jason Reineke.
© 2020 John Wiley & Sons, Inc. Published 2020 by John Wiley & Sons, Inc.

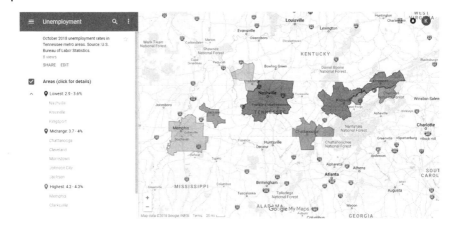

Figure 3.1 An online, interactive, choropleth-style Google My Map showing Tennessee's 10 Metropolitan Statistical Areas sorted and shaded according to their October 2018 unemployment rates. Google and the Google logo are registered trademarks of Google Inc., used with permission.

and a couple of new tools we'll introduce you to along the way. Specifically, you'll learn how to:

- Download a premade geographic shapefile that includes the borders of whatever areas you want to map.
- Use a separate mapping application to open the shapefile, combine it with data for the areas you want to map, filter out any unneeded areas, and export the results as a map file compatible with Google Drive.
- Use your Google Drive's "My Maps" app to import and further customize the map file, then publish it as an online, interactive map.

Downloading a Shapefile

A shapefile is a compressed set of component files containing information about the location, borders and characteristics of geographic features. Shapefiles are available from a range of online sources, but the collection of "Cartographic Boundary Shapefiles" offered by the U.S. Census Bureau at https://www.census. gov/geographies/mapping-files/time-series/geo/carto-boundary-file.html is a pretty good place to start. Clicking on the page's "Metropolitan and Micropolitan Statistical Area and Related Statistical Area" link will take you to the page shown in Figure 3.2. For this example, we're downloading the file cb_2017_us_cbsa_500k. zip, which contains borders for every metropolitan statistical area in the United States as of the year 2017. The Census Bureau offers two other versions of the same file, each with higher resolutions. But the lower-resolution file will do just fine for our purposes. By the time you pick up this book, there might be shapefiles

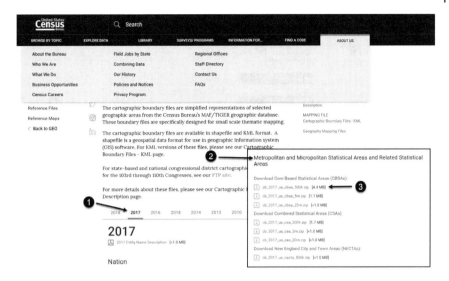

Figure 3.2 Downloading the U.S. Census Bureau shapefile that contains borders for all Metropolitan Statistical Areas in the United States. Visit the page, https://www.census.gov/geographies/mapping-files/time-series/geo/carto-boundary-file.html, click the tab for the most recent year (1), then download the 500 k file under "Download Core-Based Statistical Areas (CBSAs).

available for years more recent than 2017. Metro area boundaries can change, so it's a good idea to use the most recent shapefile available.

We're not going to need – or want – the boundaries for every metro area in the nation, of course. We're looking for only the ones in Tennessee. But don't worry about that for now. When the time comes, we'll delete any unneeded metro areas. Finally, notice that each shapefile has a ".zip" extension, meaning that it is a compressed file and that you will have to decompress or extract the files inside the .zip file before you can use them. The process for downloading and decompressing the file will vary, depending on your computer's combination of operating system, Web browser, and Web browser settings. Generally, though, the process will involve clicking on the .zip file's link, choosing a place to save the .zip file on your computer's hard drive, navigating to the .zip file once it has finished downloading, double-clicking on the .zip file, and telling your computer where to store the files it extracts from the .zip file. Make a note of where you stored the extracted files. You'll need that information shortly.

Importing the Shapefile into QGIS

Now that you have the shapefile downloaded and its contents extracted to a directory on your computer, you need software that will enable you to work with it. There are many options, including ArcGIS. Their prices range from free

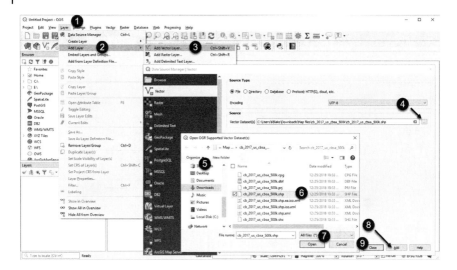

Figure 3.3 Opening the metro area shapefile with QGIS. Open QGIS. The "untitled project" window will appear. Click "Layer" (1), "Add Layer" (2), and "Add Vector Layer" (3). On the "Data Source Manager | Vector" window, click the navigation icon (4), and navigate to the directory on your computer that contains the Census Bureau shapefile contents that you extracted (5). Find, and click once on, the file with the ".shp" extension (6), and click "Open" (7). Finish by clicking "Add," (8) then "Close" (9).

to definitely not free. We assume you're on a budget that you exhausted when you bought this book. Accordingly, we recommend QGIS, a free, open-source geographic information systems application available for Windows, Mac OS, Linux, BSD, and Android operating systems. You can download it from https://qgis.org. Our demo, below, uses QGIS 3.4.3 "Madeira," released Dec. 21, 2018, running on a 64-bit Windows 10 PC. We installed it by downloading and running the md5 QGIS Standalone Installer Version 3.4 (64 bit). You'll of course want to download whatever version is both current and suitable for your computer system. While the software is free, the installation process will give you the option of making a donation in support of QGIS's continued development.

We'll be using only a fraction of QGIS's capabilities. Describing the full range of what QGIS can do would be well beyond the scope of this book. But be aware that QGIS users from all around the world have produced an extensive body of "how to" materials and plugins that you can access online at no cost. If you want to get something done in QGIS but don't know how, a few minutes of Googling likely will turn up some helpful guidance.

For now, download and install QGIS. Open the program to an "untitled project" window, then follow these steps, which Figure 3.3 illustrates:

- Click "Layer / Add Layer / Add Vector Layer." In GIS terms, "vector" data consists of individual points on a map, map points connected to make a line, and/or a line that eventually connects to its origin to form a shape called a polygon. The map in Figure 3.1 uses polygons to represent the metro areas. Meanwhile, the term "layer" refers to features and information contributed to a map by a particular geographic dataset. You can have multiple layers on a map, with each layer coming from a different dataset.

- The "Data Source Manager | Vector" window will open. Click the file navigation icon to the right of the "Vector Dataset(s)" box, and then navigate to the directory where you stored the files you extracted from the Census Bureau shapefile.
- Find, and click once on, the file that has a ".shp" extension. The file's full name should be "cb_20xx_us_cbsa_500k.shp," with the last two digits of the file's year replacing the "xx."
- Click "Open."
- After the navigation window closes, click the "Data Source Manager | Vector" window's "Add" and "Close" buttons.

A map of every metro area in the U.S., including those in Hawaii, Alaska and Puerto Rico, will appear in the QGIS work area, and the name of the shapefile you opened will be visible in the "Layers" area in the lower-left portion of the screen.

Examining the Shapefile and Joining it with the Unemployment Data

You can't do much more with the shapefile until you've had a look at its contents. Right click on the shapefile name in the "Layers" area, then select "Open Attribute Table" from the menu. Figure 3.4 illustrates the steps. QGIS will show you a spreadsheet-like grid of the data contained in the shapefile. You may have to click the small "Switch to table view" icon in the window's lower right corner. As in a spreadsheet, the grid will contain a row of data for each metropolitan statistical area, and field names in the first row (CSAFP, DBSAFP, AFFGEOID, etc.) will identify the data in each column. Some of the columns aren't especially helpful for our purposes. For example, the "AWATER" column indicates how much of each metro area's surface is covered by water.

But one column, the "NAME" column, will prove indispensable. This column shows the name of each metropolitan statistical area. By clicking on the "NAME" heading, you can sort the metro areas alphabetically by name, then easily scroll to any particular one you want to look at. In Figure 3.4, we've scrolled to the row for the Nashville metro area. Notice that its name in the shapefile, "Nashville-Davidson–Murfreesboro–Franklin, TN," nearly perfectly matches the full name of the Nashville metro area in the unemployment data you obtained from the Bureau of Labor Statistics. The only difference is that the Bureau of Labor Statistics data added a space plus the words "Metropolitan Statistical Area" to the name. Compare the names of Tennessee's other metro

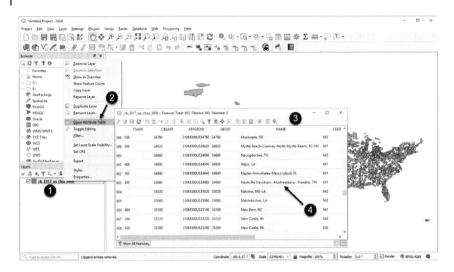

Figure 3.4 Viewing the shapefile's contents with QGIS. Right click on the shapefile's name (1) and choose "Open Attribute Table" (2). QGIS will show you the shapefile's data in the form of a grid. You may need to click the "Switch to table view" icon in the window's lower-right corner. Here, we clicked the "NAME" column heading (3) to sort the shapefile's data alphabetically by metro area name, then scrolled to the row for the Nashville metro area (4).

areas in the shapefile and unemployment data file, and you'll see the same pattern. In each case, the addition of "Metropolitan Statistical Area" – with a single space in front of "Metropolitan" – is the only difference.

This commonality between the shapefile and the unemployment dataset means that you can combine your unemployment data with the shapefile. All you have to do is make the metro area names in both files match exactly, then tell QGIS to import the unemployment figures into the shapefile and use the metro area name to pair everything up correctly.

Editing the metro area names in the spreadsheet to match those in the shapefile will be much easier and faster than editing the metro area names in the shapefile to match those in the spreadsheet. Accordingly, go to your Google Sheet containing the unemployment data, and copy the "Area," "MSA," "October 2017," "October 2018(p)," and "Change" data for each metro area to your computer's clipboard. Again, do so by highlighting the data with your mouse, then pressing "Ctrl/c" or "Cmd/c." Next, open a new, blank Google Sheet (from Google Drive, click "New / Google Sheets / Blank spreadsheet"), and paste the data into Cell A1 of the new sheet. You might also want to expand the new sheet's columns so that all of the pasted data becomes visible. Also, go ahead and give this new Google Sheet a descriptive name, such as, "October 2018 unemployment data for map." Finally, edit the names in the "Area" column to match the format of the names in the shapefile by deleting "Metropolitan Statistical Area" from each name, taking care to delete the space in front of

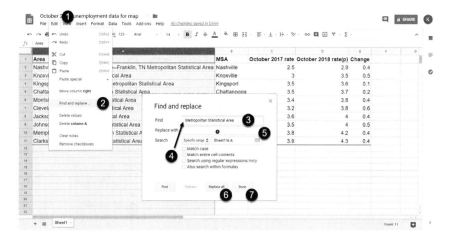

Figure 3.5 Using "Find and replace" to edit the metro area names in the unemployment Google Sheet so that they match the metro area names in the shapefile. Click "Edit" (1), then "Find and replace …" (2). On the dialog box, type " Metropolitan Statistical Area" in the "Find" box (3), taking care to include the single, blank space in front of "Metropolitan" (4). Leave the "Replace with" box completely blank (5), and click "Replace all" (6), then "Done" (7). Google and the Google logo are registered trademarks of Google Inc., used with permission.

"Metropolitan." You could edit the names one at a time, or you could click the "A" in Column A to highlight the entire column, then use "Edit / Find and replace …," as shown in Figure 3.5.

Now, download the Google Sheet you've just edited to a folder on your computer so that you can import it into QGIS. Specifically, download the sheet as a comma-separated value file, which is a data file format compatible with QGIS. In Google Sheets, you do it by clicking "File / Download as / Comma-separated values (.csv, current sheet)." Figure 3.6 shows the steps. Be sure to note where on your computer you stored the file, because you'll have to navigate to it in just a moment. We prefer to store the data file in the same folder as the contents of the decompressed shapefile.

By the way, a comma-separated value file is simply a text files containing data with a comma marking the boundary between each piece of data. In other words, when you save a spreadsheet file as a comma-separated value file, you're simply replacing each column boundary in the spreadsheet with a comma – and, in some cases, putting the column contents in quote marks to ensure that any commas within the content of a column don't get mistaken for column boundaries. Many data applications can read data from, or save data as, a comma-separated value file.

The next step is to import the edited unemployment data into QGIS and join it with the shapefile, matching the unemployment data's "Area" column to the shapefile's "NAME" field. You can import the unemployment data file into

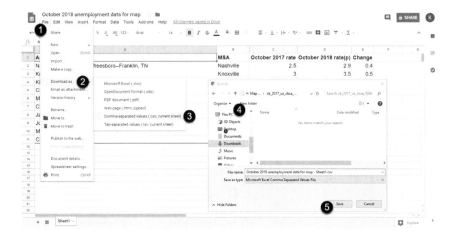

Figure 3.6 Downloading the edited Google Sheet as a comma-separated value file. Click "File" (1), "Download as" (2), and "Comma-separated values (.csv, current sheet)" (3). On the "Save as" dialog box, navigate to wherever you want to store the downloaded file (4), then click "Save" (5). Google and the Google logo are registered trademarks of Google Inc., used with permission.

QGIS using the same procedure, depicted in Figure 3.3., that you used to import the Census Bureau shapefile. In QGIS:

- Click "Layer / Add Layer / Add Vector Layer."
- Click the navigation icon to the right of the "Vector Dataset(s)" box.
- Navigate to the directory on your computer where you stored the comma-separated value file containing the edited unemployment data.
- Click once on the filename to select the file.
- Click "Open."
- Click "Add."
- Click "Close."

The unemployment data file should appear above the "cb_2017_us_cbsa_500k" shapefile in the "Layers" area in the lower-left portion of the QGIS screen. To combine the unemployment data and the shapefile:

- Right click on the "cb_2017_us_cbsa_500k" shapefile, then choose "Properties ..." to open the "Layer Properties" window. Note that the "Layer Properties" window is not the same as the "Attribute Table" you used to examine the shapefile data earlier. Double-clicking on the shapefile name offers a short-cut to the "Layer Properties" window, if you prefer to use it.
- Click on the "Joins" icon in the tool area that runs vertically along the left side of the "Layer Properties" window.

- Click the "+" icon in the lower-left corner of the "Layer Properties" window to open the "Add Vector Join" window.
- Use the dropdown menu next to the "Join layer" box to select the unemployment data file.
- On the "Join field" dropdown menu, select the unemployment data file's "Area" column.
- On the "Target field" dropdown menu, select the shapefile's "NAME" field.
- Check the box beside "Custom Field Name Prefix." A box will appear beneath and display the name of the field plus the name of the unemployment data file. Delete this text, so that the box is completely blank. If you skip this step, the column label in the resulting file will end up reading "October 2018 unemployment data for map – Sheet1_October 2018 rate(p)." That label will be too long for our purposes later. Following this step will omit the name of the source file and produce a more manageable column label: "October 2018 rate(p)."
- Click "OK."
- Click "OK" again.

Figure 3.7 summarizes the steps. To translate what you've done: You've told QGIS to open the unemployment data file, take the first record, look at the metro area name in the record's "Area" field, search through the shapefile until

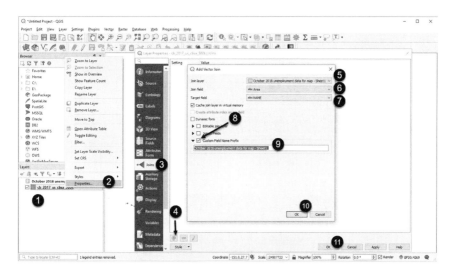

Figure 3.7 Joining the unemployment data and the shapefile. Right click on the shapefile (1), then choose "Properties …" (2) to open the "Layer Properties" window. Click on the "Joins" icon (3), then the "+" icon (4) to open the "Add Vector Join" window. Select the unemployment file on the "Joins Layer" menu (5), the unemployment file's "Area" field on the "Join field" menu (6), and the shapefile's "NAME" field on the "Target field" menu (7). Check the "Custom Field Name Prefix" box (8) and delete all text in the box (9) so that the box is blank. Finish by clicking "OK" (10), and "OK" again (11).

finding a record with a matching metro area name in the shapefile's "NAME" field, and associate the unemployment data with that record.

If you reopen the Attribute Table (right click on the shapefile and choose "Open Attribute Table") and scroll down to the row for the Nashville metro area, you'll see that QGIS has made some changes. First, it has added columns for the October 2017 rate, the October 2018(p) rate, and the change. Second, the Nashville area's record has values for these columns (2.5, 2.9, and 0.4). Scroll to Tennessee's other metro areas, and you'll see that each of them also has data in the new columns. But all of the non-Tennessee metro areas have no data in the new columns. For these areas, the new columns are instead marked as "NULL."

Do you remember learning about Google Sheets' filtering capabilities back in Chapter 1? You used them to filter out all metro areas except those in Tennessee. QGIS has filtering capabilities, too. You can use them to identify and delete each metro area that has a NULL value in the October 2018 unemployment rate column, leaving a map consisting only of the Tennessee metro areas. Look at Figure 3.8 to see the steps. Here are details:

- Open the shapefile's Attribute Table (Right click on the shapefile name, then choose "Open Attribute Table.").

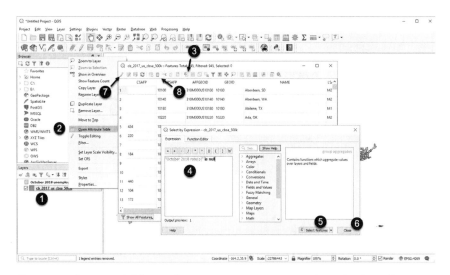

Figure 3.8 Filtering and deleting all non-Tennessee metro areas. Open the shapefile's Attribute Table by right clicking on the shapefile name (1) and choosing "Open Attribute Table." Click the "Select features using an expression" icon (3) to open the "Select by Expression" window. In the window's editing area (4) type, in double quotes, the name of the shapefile field you want to filter the data based on (in this example, "October 2018 rate(p)") then type "is null" (without the quote marks). Click "Select features" (5), then "Close" (6). Back on the Attribute Table, click the pencil-shaped "Toggle editing mode" icon (7) until the trash can icon (8) turns red, then click the trash can icon to delete the selected records.

- Click the "Select features using an expression" icon. It's a tiny "E" in front of a yellow square. The label "Select features using an expression" will pop up when you mouse over it.
- Type an expression telling QGIS which records to select. Here, the goal is to select all records for which the "October 2018 rate(p)" field is null – that is, has no data. One expression that will work is:

"October 2018 rate(p)" is null

… being careful to include the double quote marks around the "October 2018 rate(p)" field name.
- Click "Select features," then "Close." Most of the records in the Attribute Table will turn blue, indicating that the filtering expression you just wrote found and selected them.
- Click the small, pencil-shaped "Toggle editing mode" icon in the Attribute Table's upper-left corner.
- The trash can-shaped "Deleted selected features" icon will turn red. Click it to delete the selected records – the ones with no data in the "October 2018 rate(p)" field.

If all went well, you'll be left with records for only the 10 metro areas in Tennessee. Close the Attribute Table, and you'll see that the map in the QGIS work area now shows only the selected metro areas.

In case you haven't realized it yet, QGIS just saved you an appreciable amount of time and bother. Without QGIS's "Join" capabilities, you would have had to find each Tennessee metro area, one at a time, and manually add its unemployment information. Without QGIS's filtering capabilities, you then would have had to manually find, select and delete each non-Tennessee metro area's record. That's not too terrible of a task for 10 metropolitan areas, each with three data points. But imagine yourself mapping data for each of Tennessee's 95 counties, or for each of its 1,497 Census tracts, and you can begin to see the power of QGIS's shapefile joining and filtering capabilities.

The final thing we need to do with QGIS is use it to export the edited, filtered shapefile as a map file that Google Drive can recognize. Figure 3.9 gives an overview of the steps. Here are details:

- Right click on the shapefile name.
- Choose "Export" from the pop-up menu.
- Choose "Save Features As …" to open the "Save Vector Layer as …" window.
- Click the down arrow in the right corner of the "Format" box. You'll see a dropdown menu showing a range of different map file formats. Your Google Drive prefers the "Keyhole Markup Language [KML]" map file format, so select that format from the menu. Keyhole Markup Language map files have a ".kml" extension.

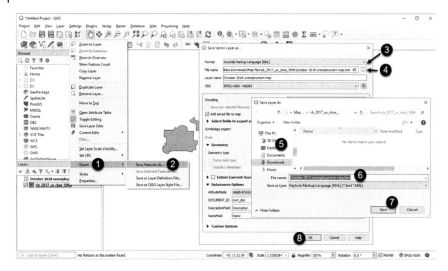

Figure 3.9 Exporting the map file from QGIS. Right click on the shapefile name (1), then choose "Save Features As …" (2). On the "Save Vector Layer as …" window, change "Format" to "Keyhole Markup Language [KML]" (3), and click the navigation icon beside "File name" (4). Navigate to wherever on your computer you want to store the exported map file (5), compose a suitable file name (6), then click "Save" (7) and "OK" (8).

- Click the three-dot navigation icon in the right corner of the "File name" box to open the "Save Layer As" window, navigate to wherever you want to store your exported mapfile, type a suitable file name, like "October 2018 unemployment map," and click "Save."
- The "Save Layer As" window will close, leaving you on the "Save Vector Layer as …" Window. Click the window's "OK" button.

You're finished for now with QGIS. If you like, you can save your work by clicking "Project / Save As …," navigating to wherever you want to store the file, composing a suitable file name, and clicking, "Save." Or, you can just close QGIS without saving anything.

Customizing and Publishing the Map File with Google My Maps

You probably already know how to use Google Maps to find a place you want to go and generate turn-by-turn directions for getting there. If so, Google My Maps will look and feel familiar to you. Open your Google Drive by typing drive.google.com into a Web browser and, if you're not already logged in, provide your login credentials. Then click "New / More / Google My Maps." Or

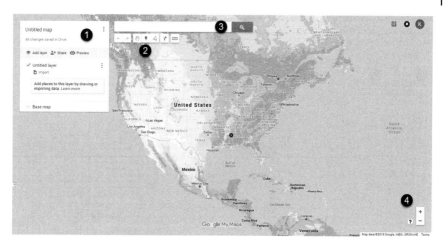

Figure 3.10 A blank Google My Map. Note the map title and layer editing area (1), the tool box (2), the search bar (3), and the zoom controls (4). Google and the Google logo are registered trademarks of Google Inc., used with permission.

you can type mymaps.google.com directly into your browser's address bar. Log in, if necessary, using your Google credentials, and choose "+ Create a new map." Either route should open a blank Google My Map like the one in Figure 3.10.

As with the Google Maps you're accustomed to using, this one is interactive. You can drag the map view to different regions of the world, and you can zoom in and out. Zooming in on an area reveals increasingly detailed map information and features like city names, road names and, eventually, names of local restaurants and businesses. The map also provides a search box; some tools for adding markers, lines or routes and measuring distances; and an area in the upper-left corner for labeling the map and adding and editing layers of map features.

To bring the .kml map file you made with QGIS into Google My Maps (also see Figure 3.11):

- Click "Import" under "Untitled layer" in the screen's upper-left area to open the "Choose a file to import" window.
- Make sure the "Upload" tab is selected, because you will be uploading the .kml file from your computer. Note, though, that it is possible to bring files in from your Google Drive or even from your Google photo albums.
- Click "Select a file from your computer."
- Navigate to wherever you stored the .kml file that you made with QGIS.
- Click on the .kml file.
- Choose "Open."

Figure 3.11 Importing the .kml file made with QGIS into a Google My Map. Click "Import" (1), and make sure the "Upload" tab is selected (2). Choose "Select a file from your computer" (3), navigate to the .kml file's location (4), select the .kml file (5), and click "Open" (6). Google and the Google logo are registered trademarks of Google Inc., used with permission.

My Maps will import the .kml map file and use it to add the outlines of the metro areas to your map. Click one of the outlines, and a pop-up window will display the data embedded in the .kml, including the unemployment data you added using QGIS. You can still reposition the map view and zoom the map in and out, but be careful if you do. It is possible to accidentally "pick up" a metro area and move it to somewhere on the map other than where it is supposed to be. If it happens, you can use the "Undo" button on the tool bar to put the metro area back in its correct location. But if you need to reposition the map, the safest way to do so is to zoom out until you can "grab" a portion of the map that is not inside any of the metro areas, then reposition the map.

The metro areas are probably pretty difficult to see, because, by default, Google My Maps doesn't shade them. It shows only their borders. Back at the start of the chapter, Figure 3.1 showed each metro area not only filled in, but filled with shading that indicated whether its October 2018 unemployment rate fell into the "Lowest," "Midrange" or "Highest" category. Before you can get Google My Maps to do that, you have to make a copy of the October 2018 unemployment figures but convert them from text – the default format QGIS imported them as – to numbers, the format My Maps needs them to be in before it can use them to categorize each metro area and shade it accordingly. There is a procedure for overriding QGIS's defaults and getting QGIS to store the unemployment rates as numbers, rather than as text, when making the map file. It involves manually creating a specially-named text file containing headings that indicate which type of data each column in the data file holds.

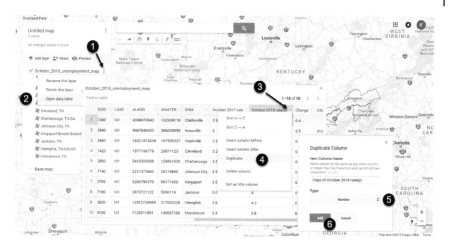

Figure 3.12 Making a numeric copy of the "October 2018 rate(p)" data for My Maps to use when shading the metro areas by their unemployment rates. Click the layer editing icon (1), and choose "Open data table" (2). Scroll to the right in the data table until you see the "October 2018 rate(p)" data column, and click the down arrow on the right side of the column's heading (3). Choose "Duplicate" (4), and change "Type" to "Number" (5), then click "Add" (6). Google and the Google logo are registered trademarks of Google Inc., used with permission.

But dealing with the problem here, within My Maps, ends up being a lot less complicated. Figure 3.12 shows the process. Here are detailed steps:

- Click the editing icon for the map layer that contains the metro area outlines and data. The icon looks like three dots arranged vertically, and it appears to the right of the layer's name.
- Choose the "Open data table" option from the menu. Doing so is similar to clicking "Open Attribute Table" for a layer in QGIS. The move allows you to see the data embedded in the map file.
- Scroll to the right in the data table until the "October 2018 rate(p)" column slides into view. Then, click the down arrow to the right of the column's name.
- Choose "Duplicate" from the menu.
- On the "Duplicate Column" window, change the "Type" to "Number."
- Click "Add."

My Maps will make a copy of the "October 2018 rate(p)" column and place it to the right under a label that reads, predictably, "Copy of October 2018 rate(p)." Aside from the difference in their headings, the two columns will appear identical. They're not, though. The original contains the unemployment figures as text, while the copy contains them as numbers. Because the figures in the copied column are numbers, rather than text, My Maps can do numeric things with them, like figure out which ones are low, moderate, and high, and shade the metro areas accordingly. Once you have finished duplicating the unemployment figures as numeric data, close the data table by clicking on the "x" in the table's upper-right corner.

You're finally ready to start styling the map – that is, to start choosing the details about how the map will look and function. If the process seems to have gotten a little dull, this is the point at which it might start getting fun again, because this is the point at which you can start doing things your own way. For example, one thing you might want to do next is determine how to shade the metro areas according to their unemployment rates. We ended up grouping the metro areas into three categories: a "Lowest" group, shaded blue; a "Midrange" group, shaded gray; and a "Highest" group, shaded red. Those choices made sense to us, given the number of metro areas we were working with, the range of the unemployment rates involved, and the colors we preferred to use. If you're working with different metro areas with different rates, you might want to pick a different number of categories, different colors, and so on. That's perfectly fine.

If you want to replicate what we did:

- Click "Individual styles" next to the paint-roller-shaped icon in the metro areas layer.
- Under "Group places by," click on "Individual styles," then click on the name of the numeric unemployment rates. In our case, the name is "Copy of October 2018 rate(p)." By default, My Maps will treat each metro area rate as a unique category and will fill each metro area on the map a unique color.
- To set your own colors for the metro areas, click the radio button next to "Ranges," and specify the number of ranges you want. The default is "4." We changed it to "3."
- Close the "paint roller menu" by clicking on the "x" in the menu's upper-right corner.

The map will show each metro area filled with one of three shades of the same color. In our case, the color was blue. The map legend will show the unemployment rate ranges corresponding to each shade. In our case, the lightest shade of blue indicated each of the three metro areas with rates between 2.9 and 3.6 percent, while the middle shade marked the five metro areas with rates between 3.7 and 4 percent, and the darkest shade of blue stood for the two metro areas with rates between 4.2 and 4.3 percent. My Maps determines the range of each category automatically and attempts to pick ranges that it thinks best represent the range of values being depicted.

We decided to choose colors with more contrast, though. It was a little difficult to distinguish one shade of blue from another. We also wanted to make the range labels more descriptive. For example, the first range label, "2.9 – 3.6 (3)," is supposed to convey that the range includes three metro areas, each with an unemployment rate of between 2.9 and 3.6 percent. We thought a label like, "Lowest: 2.9 – 3.6%" would be clearer. Again, if you want to do what we did:

- Hover your mouse pointer over the first range in the legend, the one that reads, "2.9 – 3.6 (3)."

- An icon shaped like a paint bucket will appear. Click the icon.
- Change the range label to "Lowest: 2.9 – 3.6%" by typing the new label into the box beneath the original label.
- Uncheck the "Use range color" box under "Color," then pick the color you want to use for the range instead. We picked "RGB (1, 87, 155)," a medium blue.
- Click the "x" in the editing window's upper-right corner.
- Repeat the process for each of the other two ranges. We used "Midrange: 3.7 – 4%" and "RGB (117, 117, 117)," a medium gray, for the second range, and "Highest: 4.2 – 4.3%" and "RGB (165, 39, 20)," a red, for the third range.

Next, we customized the map title, added a subtitle and customized the title for the metro area layer. To edit a title, simply click once on the title, then type the new title in the editing window that will appear. We changed the main title (which, unfortunately, has to be pretty short in order to fit) to read simply "Unemployment." The subtitle allows for a bit more information, so we typed, "October 2018 unemployment rates in Tennessee metro areas. Source: U.S. Bureau of Labor Statistics." We also changed the metro area layer's title to "Areas," and added "(click for details)" in the hope of signaling to users that the map is interactive. Figures 3.13 through 3.16 illustrate key steps in the process.

If you click on one of the map's metro areas and look at the information window that appears, you'll probably notice something else that needs to be customized. For example, if you click on the Nashville metro area, the pop-up window will show the awkwardly lengthy "Nashville-Davidson–Murfreesboro–Franklin, TN,"

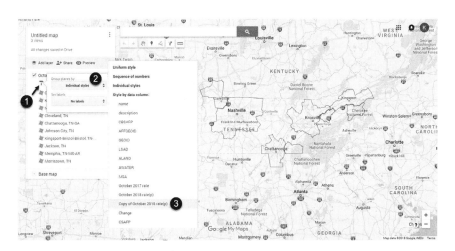

Figure 3.13 Telling My Maps to shade the metro areas according to the numeric version of the October 2018 unemployment rates. Click the metro area layer's paint-roller-shaped icon (1), then change the "Group by" setting from "Individual styles" to the data table field that contains the numeric copy of the latest unemployment rates (3). Google and the Google logo are registered trademarks of Google Inc., used with permission.

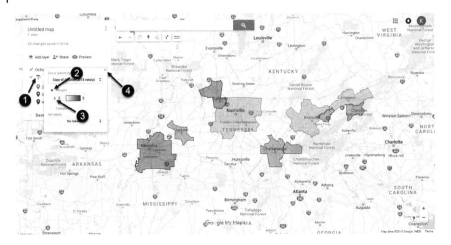

Figure 3.14 Dividing the unemployment rates into three ranges. Click the metro area layer's paint-roller-shaped icon (1), select the "Ranges" radio button (2), and change the number of ranges to 3 (3). Click the "x" in the window's upper-right corner to close the window (4). Google and the Google logo are registered trademarks of Google Inc., used with permission.

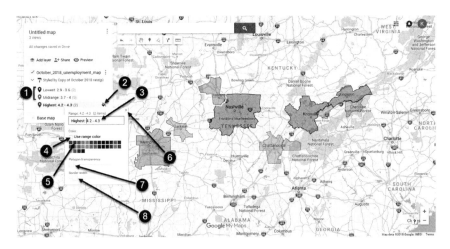

Figure 3.15 Customizing the legend labels and colors. Here, the "Lowest" and "Midrange" categories have been edited already (1). Hover your mouse over the last category until the paint-bucket-shaped icon appears (2). Click the icon, then type a custom name for the category, if desired (3). Uncheck the "Use range color" box (4), and check the color you want (5). Finish by clicking the "x" in the window's upper-right corner (6). Note, too, the sliders for adjusting the transparency of the metro area colors (7) and the width of the metro area borders (8). Google and the Google logo are registered trademarks of Google Inc., used with permission.

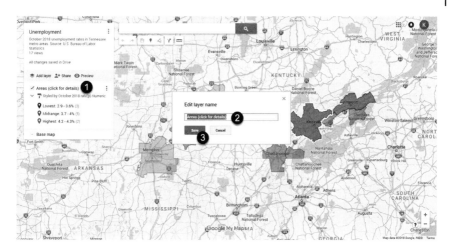

Figure 3.16 Editing a layer title. Click on the title you want to edit (1), type the new title (2), and click "Save" (3). Google and the Google logo are registered trademarks of Google Inc., used with permission.

as the area's name. Furthermore, it will show every one of the shapefile's embedded data fields, most of which a user wouldn't be able to make sense of. Fortunately, My Maps gives you an easy way to select which data fields will appear in the window. Just click the pencil-shaped icon in the lower-right corner of the window. First, click the down arrow beside the box at the top of the window and choose which field you want to use as the pop-up window's headline. Selecting the "MSA" field will display the shortened metro area names instead of the official, much more complex ones. Second, uncheck the box beside each remaining field that you would like to hide from view. We unchecked all except the "October 2017 rate," "October 2018 rate(p)," and "Change" fields. When you are finished, click "Save." Changes you make in one window will be automatically applied to every other metro area's pop-up window. Figure 3.17 illustrates the key steps.

Note that a more complicated, but equally effective, way to simplify the pop-up window would be to reopen the layer's data table and delete each field you no longer need. If the .kml map file you are using has a large number of data fields and/or a large number of records, this approach can reduce the time the map will take to load in a user's Web browser. In most cases, though, simply hiding unneeded fields from view will suffice.

A final step before publishing your map on the Web involves fixing the map's center point and zoom level. See Figure 3.18 for an overview. Here are the steps to follow:

- Click somewhere on the map that is not inside a metro area border (recall, here, our earlier warning about the possibility of accidentally picking up and relocating one of the metro areas).

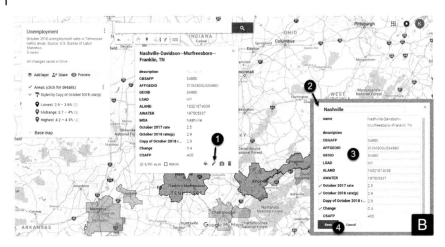

Figure 3.17 Simplifying the map's pop-up information window. Click on any metro area to open its information window, then click the window's editing icon (1). The window will switch to editing mode (see Inset B). Select "MSA" as the window's title field (2), then uncheck any fields you would like to hide from view when the window opens (3). Finish by clicking "Save" (4). Google and the Google logo are registered trademarks of Google Inc., used with permission.

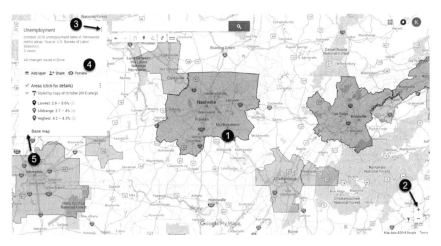

Figure 3.18 Setting the map's default position and zoom level. Center the map on your screen (1), then zoom in one level by clicking the "+" icon (2). Click the editing icon next to the map's title (3) and choose "Set default view" from the menu that will pop up. To check the results, click "Preview" (4). Note that you can change the base map if you don't like the default one (5). Google and the Google logo are registered trademarks of Google Inc., used with permission.

- Drag the map so that it is at least roughly centered on your screen. The city of Murfreesboro happens to be the geographic center of Tennessee, and we happen to know that, mainly because there is a big, stone marker in town announcing as much. Accordingly, we try to drag the map around until Murfreesboro is at about the screen's center point.
- Now, zoom in until the map looks about one zoom level too large for the screen. If you use the "+" icon in the screen's lower-right corner, you can zoom without affecting your positioning of the map.
- Click the three vertical dots next to the map's title in the upper-left corner. If you're using our title suggestions, that would be the word "Unemployment."
- On the pop-up menu, click "Set default view." My Maps will flash a brief message indicating that "Your current view has been saved as default for this map." Now, regardless of how much you zoom and drag the map, this default view is the one My Maps will use when displaying the map on the Web.
- To see what the map will look like to map users, click the eye-shaped "Preview" icon. My Maps will open the map in a separate browser tab and show you the map as it will appear to visitors on the Web. The preview is fully functional; you can click on the metro areas to see their information windows, drag and zoom the map, and even toggle between satellite and street map views.
- If something isn't quite right about the centering or zoom level, just repeat the above steps until you get it right. Some trial and error is almost inevitable.

Once you are ready to publish your map on the Web:

- Click the "Share" button in the upper-left area of the map screen.
- By default, the sharing will be set to "Private," meaning that the map can be seen only by you, or at least by someone who has logged into your Google Drive account using your user name and password. Click the radio button next to "On – Public on the web."
- Click "Save."
- The link displayed in the box under "Link to share" will display your map if pasted into a Web browser's address bar. The link is always quite lengthy, so if you are going to share the link via email or social media, using a URL shortener might be a good idea.
- Click "Done" to close the sharing settings.

Note that if you paste the "Link to share" into a browser's address bar while you are logged into your Google Drive on that same browser, you will see the map's editing mode, not the user mode shown in the preview. If you want to embed the map on a Web page, click the three vertical dots next to the map's title and choose "Embed on my site" from the pop-up menu. My Maps will show you the embed code – but only if you have first shared the map as

Figure 3.19 Publishing the map on the Web. Click the "Share" button (1), then Change …
(2), and select "On – Public on the web" (3), followed by "Save" (4), and "Done" (5). The map
will be accessible via the "Link to share" link (6) or the embed code available by clicking the
three dots beside the map's title (7) and choosing "Embed on my site" from the menu.
Google and the Google logo are registered trademarks of Google Inc., used with permission.

described above. Try to get the embed code before sharing the map, and My
Maps will ask you to share the map first. Handily, both WordPress.com and
WordPress.org pages offer native support for embedding Google My Maps.
Figure 3.19 shows the steps involved in sharing your map.

The process for making this map might have seemed long and complex. But
the more you use it, the faster you'll get at completing it, especially if you are
reusing a shapefile you already know your way around in. All the same, here's a
tip that might come in handy: It is possible to update the map's data from the
"Data table" window, click the first unemployment figure, type a new figure,
and move on to the next one. If you make a copy of the map first (click the three
vertical dots to the right of the map's title, then choose "Copy map"), you can
preserve the original map and use it as a template for the new one. If you decide
to use this approach to keeping your maps updated, it might be a good to use
field names like "Current month unemployment" and "Unemployment 12
months ago" instead of "October 2018 rate(p)" and "October 2017 rate."

Mapping Specific Points with Latitude and Longitude Coordinates

Inevitably, you will need to map things that have to be represented as a specific
location. For example, Figure 3.20 maps sites in Tennessee at which facilities
released 1,000 pounds or more of lead compounds during the year 2017. Data
for the map came from the United States Environmental Protection Agency's

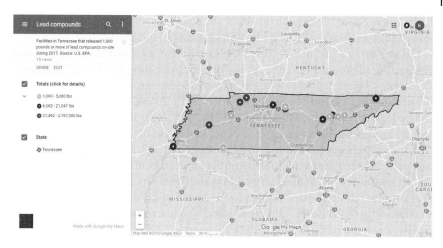

Figure 3.20 Map of facilities in Tennessee that released 1,000 pounds or more of lead compounds on-site during 2017. Google and the Google logo are registered trademarks of Google Inc., used with permission.

Toxics Release Inventory Program. The program provides publicly available data reflecting annual amounts of toxic chemicals released or otherwise handled by facilities across the United States. Download a given year's dataset from the program's Web site, and you'll find that you have one row of data for each toxic chemical handled by a given facility. Fields provide details about how the chemical was handled, the facility that handled it, and – most importantly for our purposes – latitude and longitude coordinates specifying the site at which the material was handled. This section will show you how to make the map in Figure 3.20, or, if you prefer, a similar map for an area of interest to you. After you've learned how to make a map using latitude and longitude coordinates, we'll show you how to make a map using street addresses and even how to make a map by simply finding things on the map and marking their locations.

Let's start by looking at the available data and downloading what we need. As with any dataset, you should learn about this one's scope and limitations. The program's Web site, www.epa.gov/toxics-release-inventory-tri-program, explains what you need to know in order to report accurately about the data. For example, the amount of a toxic chemical released at a facility doesn't necessarily indicate the level of exposure or health risk faced by people living near the facility. A lot depends on additional factors, including the toxicity of the chemical released, how quickly the chemical degrades in the environment, whether the chemical tends to accumulate over time in components of the food chain, the method by which the chemical was released, and more. But properly contextualized information about how much of a chemical was released, and where, can be an important starting point in assessing such risks (U.S. Environmental Protection Agency, EPA, 2015). In short, no matter how impressive your map looks once you're done with it, don't start writing your Pulitzer acceptance speech just yet. You'll still have a lot of investigation and reporting to do.

We'll be using a file of 2017 Toxics Release Inventory data for Tennessee. You can get the file (or a different one, if you like) by visiting the EPA's "TRI Basic Data Files" page at www.epa.gov/toxics-release-inventory-tri-program/tri-basic-data-files-calendar-years-1987-2017 (EPA, 2018a). Find the year 2017 in the table, change the location from "US" to "TN," and click "Go." Your browser will download the data as a comma-separated value file. You might remember that Google Sheets gave you a comma-separated value file when you downloaded the metro area unemployment data so you could import it into QGIS. This is the same type of file. Each value in the file is separated by a comma, and the commas tell data applications how to organize the data into columns. Also download the "TRI Basic Data Files Guide" from www.epa.gov/toxics-release-inventory-tri-program/tri-basic-data-files-guide (EPA, 2018b). The file describes what each column in the data file means and explains other things you need to know in order to understand and use the data.

Once you have both files downloaded, create a blank Google Sheet. Figure 3.21 summarizes the import process steps. Here are some details:

- In your Google Drive, click "New," then "Google Sheets," then "Blank spreadsheet."

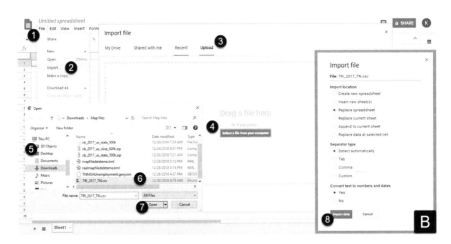

Figure 3.21 Importing the Toxics Release Inventory comma-separated value file into Google Sheets. From a blank Google Sheet, click File (1) and Import (2) to open the "Import file" window. Click the window's "Upload" tab (3), navigate to wherever you stored the data file (5), click on the file (6), and click "Open" (7). Google Sheets will display a second "Import file" window (Inset B) asking for details about the file you are importing. Choose the settings shown, then click "Import data" (8). Google and the Google logo are registered trademarks of Google Inc., used with permission.

- When the new sheet opens, click "File," then "Import."
- Google Sheets will open the "Import file" window. Click the "Upload" tab, the "Select a file from your computer" button, and then navigate to wherever you stored the comma-separated file you just finished downloading from the Toxics Release Inventory Web page. Click on the file, then click "Open." Alternatively, you can drag the file into the "Import file" window.
- Google Sheets will open a second "Import file" window. This one will ask you for details about the file you are importing. Make sure "Replace spreadsheet" is selected under "Import location." This setting tells Google Sheets to replace your blank Google Sheet with the data you are importing. The "Detect automatically" setting under "Separator type" should work fine. Google Sheets will figure out that the separator is a comma. But note that you can specify the separator as a comma, a tab, or even some custom character. Some files, for example, use a vertical bar (|) as a separator. Also, let Google Sheets convert numbers and dates stored as text in the file you are importing.
- Click "Import data."

The import could take a few moments. How many moments depends on the speed of your Internet connection and the size of the file you are importing. Tennessee's 2017 file should load in under 30 seconds with a typical high-speed Internet connection, despite containing 2,212 rows and 109 columns of data per row. Once the file has imported, go ahead and replace the generic "Untitled spreadsheet" name with something more descriptive, like "TN Toxics Release Data 2017."

You'll realize pretty quickly that the file contains far more data than you need for a basic map of lead compound releases in Tennessee amounting to 1,000 pounds or more. Fortunately, you learned about Google Sheets' filtering capabilities while working with the metro area unemployment data back in Chapter 1. You'll simply use the same tool here. Opening the "TRI Basic Data Files Guide" you downloaded will help you figure out what you need to keep, and where to find it in the file. A "Basic file contents" table begins on about page 5 of the documentation. The table contains four columns that identify each data column's number, field name, type, and description, respectively. For example, the very first column in the data has the field name "YEAR" and contains, "The calendar year in which the reported activities occurred." Pretty straightforward. We don't really need to keep the year column, though. We already know we're working with 2017 data, and the data file does not contain data from other years. So, scroll down until you find something that you'll need to make your map.

The first candidate appears in Column 4, the "FACILITY NAME" field, which contains the "Name of the reporting facility." On the map, that would make a nice title for the detail window that slides into view when a user clicks on one of the map's markers. A quick look at the dataset shows that the "FACILITY NAME" field for the first record is "WACKER POLYSILICON NA." Let's plan on keeping that one. Columns five through nine contain components of the street address of the reporting facility. It would be possible to combine these components into street addresses that Google My Maps could map. But there would be a problem. It turns out that the street address doesn't always reflect where the toxic material was handled. For example, a facility might report the street address of its corporate headquarters but handle toxic materials at a remote mining or processing site that might not even have a street address. We're interested in the location of the toxic materials, which is why we're after latitude and longitude coordinates rather than street addresses. The latitude and longitude coordinates finally show up in columns 12 and 13, so we'll keep those, too.

The next interesting column is probably "INDUSTRY SECTOR," in Column 16, which can help indicate whether the facility is involved in mining, power generation, manufacturing, or some other type of activity. From there, skip to the "CHEMICAL" field, in column 30. It gives the name of the toxic chemical released. You can pick any chemical you like, of course. We decided to focus on "Lead compounds," which refers to a number of toxic substances that consist of lead combined with other things. Releases of pure lead are reported separately, which is why you'll find "Lead" in the "Chemicals" field along with "Lead compounds." We focused on lead compounds because, at least in Tennessee, they are released in larger quantities than pure lead is. An interesting aside: Many of the larger releases of pure lead in Tennessee occur at shooting ranges operated by the U.S. military. That's right: Firing bullets into backstops counts as releasing lead, and the military releases a fair amount of it that way.

You're probably getting the idea by now. After scanning through the rest of the file documentation, we decided to keep two additional fields. The first is the "ON-SITE RELEASE TOTAL" field, which indicates the "total quantity of the toxic chemical released to air, water and land on-site at the facility." That might sound pretty scary, but remember that even this type of release doesn't necessarily indicate risky levels of exposure for humans. Clearly, though, it's good to know where such releases are happening, and in what amounts. Also, on-site release totals don't account for other types of releases, including material sent for recycling or disposal off site. Other fields in the dataset give more details about how much material goes where. The final field we decided to keep, "PARENT CO NAME," indicates the name of the entity that controls the facility.

We also considered how to filter the data. We already know that all of the releases occurred in Tennessee, because we downloaded the Tennessee file instead of the (much larger) U.S. file, which contains all releases for all facilities across the country during 2017. We also have decided, as noted above, to focus on releases of lead compounds. That means we'll want to filter the "CHEMICAL" field for "Lead compounds." Finally, we decided to look only at facilities that released 1,000 pounds or more of lead compounds on-site. There's nothing significant about 1,000 pounds compared to, say, 900 pounds or 1,100 pounds. More than anything else, we picked 1,000 pounds as a cutoff point in order to keep the dataset and map manageable for purposes of the exercise at hand. Obviously, releasing 100 pounds of lead components into a community's drinking water source would be more dangerous than releasing 1,000 pounds of lead components into an isolated, carefully monitored landfill. Again, feel free to adapt our choices to your own needs and preferences.

To summarize, then, here are the fields we've decided to keep and the filters we've decided to use:

FACILITY NAME
LATITUDE
LONGITUDE
INDUSTRY SECTOR
CHEMICAL (filtered for "Lead compounds")
ON-SITE RELEASE TOTAL (filtered for amounts of 1,000 pounds or more)
PARENT CO NAME

You could do this next part in a couple of different ways, but we recommend applying the filters to the full dataset, selecting and copying the filtered data into a new Google Sheet, then deleting any unneeded columns from the new Google Sheet. You'll end up keeping all of the original data intact, in case you need it for some additional analysis, while having a small, easily managed dataset to work with when producing your map.

You should already know how to filter the "CHEMICAL" field for "Lead components." The process is similar to the process you used for filtering the metro areas for those in Tennessee. See Figure 1.8, in Chapter 1. Here, you would click "Data / Create a filter," find the "CHEMICAL" column, click the down arrow at the top of the column, to the right of the column's label, click "Clear," scroll through the list (or use "Search") to find "Lead compounds," and click "OK." Google Sheets will hide all rows except those that list "Lead compounds" in the "CHEMICAL" column.

Filtering the "ON-SITE RELEASE TOTAL" field for amounts of 1,000 pounds or more will be a bit different, because you'll be filtering based on a numeric expression rather than a simple text match. Figure 3.22 summarizes the process. Specifically:

- With the "CHEMICAL" filter already in place for "Lead compounds," click the down arrow to the right of the "ON-SITE RELEASE TOTAL" field's name.
- Click "Filter by condition" from the menu.

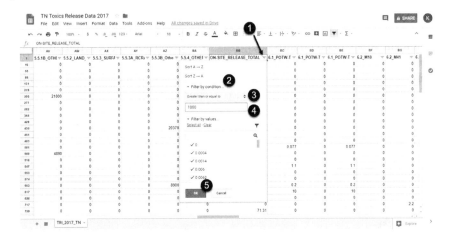

Figure 3.22 Filtering the Toxics Release Inventory data's "ON-SITE RELEASE TOTAL" column for amounts of 1,000 pounds or more. With the "CHEMICAL" filter already in place, click the down arrow beside the column's label (1), click "Filter by condition" (2), select "Greater than or equal to" as the condition (3), and type "1000" as the value (4). Finish by clicking "OK." Google and the Google logo are registered trademarks of Google Inc., used with permission.

- Change "None" to "Greater than or equal to."
- Type "1000" in the "Value or formula" box.
- Click "OK."

Now, use your mouse to select the filtered data. Remember, the shortcut, here, is to click once on the blank rectangle in the spreadsheet's upper-left corner – the one directly beneath the "fx" symbol. Press Ctrl/c or Cmd/c to copy the highlighted data, then create a new spreadsheet to paste the data into. You could go back to your Google Drive and click "New / Google Sheets / Blank spreadsheet," but a perhaps handier route is to choose "File / New / Spreadsheet" from the menu bar of the Google Sheet you're already in. Either way, click on Cell A1 of the new spreadsheet and paste the data by pressing Ctrl/v or Cmd/v. If you're working with exactly the same data we are, pasting the data into the new spreadsheet should leave you with 18 rows of data, including the column labels in the first row. Now, delete the columns you don't need. Highlighting multiple data columns with a mouse can be a little clumsy. An alternative approach is to click on the top of the first column you want to delete, like the "YEAR" column, then hold down your computer's "Shift" key while tapping the right arrow key. Google Sheets will highlight the next column each time you tap the arrow key. When you reach the Column D, the "FACILITY_NAME" column, which you want to keep, stop highlighting, use your mouse to right click on one of the highlighted columns, and choose "Delete Columns A-C." Google Sheets will comply, shifting the remaining columns left, so that the "FACILITY_NAME" column becomes Column A. Continue in this way until you have deleted all columns except the seven we have decided to keep.

Having reduced the data to just what you need for your map, you can do a couple of things that will make your map turn out nicer. First, compose more natural-sounding names for the columns you're going to include in the information window that will slide into view when a user clicks on a map icon. Specifically, "FACILITY_NAME" isn't going to look all that great in the information window. So, change it to "Facility name:" or something similar. We changed:

"INDUSTRY_SECTOR" to "Industry sector:"
"ON-SITE_RELEASE_TOTAL" to "On-site release (in pounds):"
"PARENT_CO_NAME" to "Parent company:"

Also, notice that some facilities have reported their releases to one or more decimal places, while others have probably rounded their totals off to the nearest whole number. Fractions of a pound don't amount to much when you're looking at releases of a thousand pounds or more, so rounding everyone's totals off would add consistency. You can round all of the figures at once by selecting the "On-site release (in pounds:)" column, then clicking the "Decrease decimal places" icon on the Google Sheets' tool bar. The icon looks like ".0" above a small arrow that is pointing left. Click the icon until all of the release totals appear as whole numbers. Incidentally, the icon to its right, which looks like ".00" above a right-pointing arrow, will let you add decimal places, and the "123" icon next to the down-pointing arrow will let you choose from a range of other number formats, including ones you can customize. Just for fun, we also sorted the data by the "On-site release (in pounds):" column, from largest to smallest. Finally, replace the dataset's "Untitled spreadsheet" name with a descriptive one, like, "Lead compounds release data."

Considering what you went through to make the metro area unemployment map, you're going to love how easy this next part is. See Figure 3.23 for the steps involved. More specifically:

- Go to your Google Drive and click "New / More / My Maps" to create a blank Google My Map.
- Click "Import" in the "Untitled layer."
- The "Choose a file to import" window will open. Click the "Google Drive" tab, because the file you are wanting to import, the "Lead compounds release data" Google Sheet, is sitting in your Google Drive.
- The window will change its appearance once you click the "Google Drive" tab, and you'll see a listing of the files in your Google Drive, with your most recent ones at the top of the list. Click on the "Lead compounds release data" sheet to tell My Maps that's the file you want to import.

Figure 3.23 Importing the release data into a My Maps layer. Open a blank My Map and click "Import" (1). Click the "Google Drive" tab (2), and choose the release data's spreadsheet (3). Make sure the LATITUDE and LONGITUDE fields are checked (4), then click "Continue" (5). Pick "Facility name" as the detail window's title (6), and click "Finish" (7). Google and the Google logo are registered trademarks of Google Inc., used with permission.

- My Maps will inspect the file and ask you which column, or columns, you want it to use when determining where to place things on your map. It will guess that you want to use the "LATITUDE" and "LONGITUDE" columns, and that guess is, of course, correct. If My Maps guesses incorrectly for some reason, manually select the two columns. When you are ready to proceed, click "Continue."
- On the next screen, My Maps will ask you which column you want to use as the label for each map marker's detail window. We suggest using the "Facility name:" column. You can use whichever one you prefer, though.
- Click "Finish."

My Maps will draw your map and use the latitude and longitude coordinates to place a marker at each release site. Obviously, using My Maps to map things that can be represented with points is much easier and faster than using My Maps to map things that have to be represented by borders.

You can now style the map using the same techniques you used to style the metro area unemployment map. For example, click "Uniform style" and group the places by the "On-site release (in pounds):" field to group and shade the map markers according to the sizes of the releases they represent, just like you grouped and shaded the metro areas according to the sizes of their unemployment rates. Similarly, you can customize the label for each group of markers and the color of the group's markers. While customizing the marker colors, you'll also notice that you can change the marker shapes. My Maps offers 14 "Popular Icons" and more – as well as a custom icon option – via a "More icons" button. Don't forget to customize your detail windows by unchecking the "Latitude" and "Longitude" fields and any others that you don't want showing up when users click on a map icon. You might also experiment with different base maps. Our example map, in Figure 3.20, used the "Simple Atlas" base map and "Square (Small)" icons for map markers. Of course, you can share and embed this map just like you did the metro area unemployment map. See Figure 3.19 to review the steps.

You might be wondering how we got the outline of Tennessee to show up on the example map. It's simply a .kml file imported into a second map layer. We made the .kml by downloading the Census Bureau's shapefile of all U.S. states. See the shapefile archive at https://www.census.gov/geographies/mapping-files/time-series/geo/carto-boundary-file.html. After downloading and extracting the file's contents, we imported the state borders into QGIS using the same procedure shown earlier for importing the metro area borders (see Figure 3.3). We then used a variation of the filtering process shown in Figure 3.8 to delete all borders from the file except those for Tennessee. The only difference involved using the expression:

"Name" is not 'Tennessee'

… instead of the expression:

"October 2018 rate(p)" is null

… as in Figure 3.8. In the state borders file, the "Name" field contains the full name of the state, so the expression selects all states with a name that is not "Tennessee." Note that, in the expression, there are double quotes around the field name ("Name") and single quotes around the specified field content ('Tennessee'). Having selected all states besides Tennessee, we deleted them by clicking the pencil-shaped icon, then the trash can icon (Steps 7 and 8 in Figure 3.8). Next, we exported the file in .kml format, following the process showing in Figure 3.9. Finally, we clicked "Add Layer" in the "Lead compounds" My Map and imported the Tennessee border .kml file into the new layer, as illustrated in Figure 3.11. It's not a bad idea, in fact, to make a set of .kml files showing the borders of places you will be mapping frequently – your state, your metro area, your county, etc., – and keep them on hand for when you need them.

Mapping Specific Points with Addresses

Using street addresses to map things in My Maps is just about as easy as using latitude and longitude coordinates. And addresses are often easier to come by. There is one complication you should know about, though. We'll demonstrate how to deal with it by showing you how to make the map of Murfreesboro, Tennessee, alternative fuel stations shown in Figure 3.24.

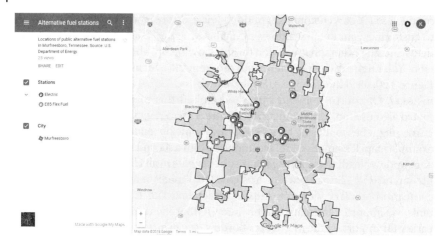

Figure 3.24 A Google My Map of alternative fuel stations in Murfreesboro, Tennessee. Google and the Google logo are registered trademarks of Google Inc., used with permission.

The data for the map come from the U.S. Department of Energy's online directory of alternative fuel stations, at https://afdc.energy.gov/stations/#/analyze. Choosing your state from the page's "State / Province / Territory" menu will get you in the general neighborhood. If you want to get more specific, you can search within specified miles of a particular address or zip code. By default, the page searches for all alternative fuel types and for active stations that are open to the public. There is, you might point out, a "Map Results" button that automatically generates a nice-looking interactive map. And if you generate the map, you might also notice the "</> Embed Tool" link below the map that will hand you code for embedding the map on a Web page. So why, you might reasonably ask, would you need to know how make your own map? Mainly, to learn about mapping address-based data that doesn't hand itself to you on a silver platter. But for the record, the embed code the site offers doesn't work on WordPress.com pages. My Maps embed code does. So, that's another reason.

In any case, using the page to filter for Tennessee stations selects 497 records as of this writing. A "Download results" link in the lower-right corner of the page lets you pull down a comma-separated value file that you can save on your computer. You can then import the data into Google Sheets using the same technique you used to import the comma-separated value file containing the Toxics Release Inventory data. See Figure 3.21 for a refresher. Filtering the "City" column for "Murfreesboro" (see Chapter 1, especially Figure 1.8) yielded 20 rows of data, including the column header row at the top of the file.

Figure 3.25 illustrates both the problem with the imported data and the start of a solution. The problem is that the data file has separated the address components into different columns. The street address is in one column, Column C, while the city name is in another, Column D. The state name is in still another

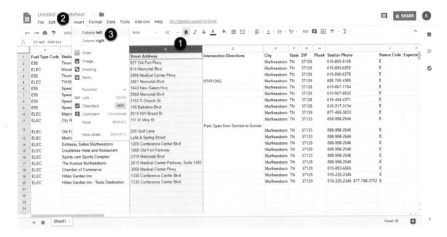

Figure 3.25 Inserting a blank column. Click on the top of Column C (1), Click "Insert" from the menu bar (2), then choose "Column left" (3). Google and the Google logo are registered trademarks of Google Inc., used with permission.

column, F, and the zip code is in a fourth column, G. To map an address accurately, My Maps needs all address components placed in a single column, preferably with the components separated by commas. For example, we need a new column that shows the first address as "927 Old Fort Pkwy, Murfreesboro, TN, 37129" with commas (rather than columns) separating the street, city, state and zip information. Fortunately, Google Sheets offers an easy fix for this problem. First, you'll need a blank column somewhere near the address information. As shown in Figure 3.25, insert a blank column in front of the "Street Address" column by clicking on the top of the "Street Address" column to highlight the entire column, then choosing "Insert / Column left" from the menu bar. Type a new column heading, like "Full Address," at the top of this new column. Next, use the "concatenate" function to retrieve the disparate parts of the address from their columns and place them all in the blank column you've inserted:

- Click Cell C2, which is now the first blank cell in the new column.
- Click on Cell D2, which contains the street portion of the first address.
- Carefully type: =concatenate(D2," ",F2," ",G2," ",H2,").
- Press "Enter" after you've typed the closing parenthesis.

If all went well, Google Sheets will display "927 Old Fort Pkwy, Murfreesboro, TN, 37129" in Cell C2. Note that, in the function, there is a comma and a space, not just a comma, between each pair of quote marks. The pattern in the function's cell addresses, commas and quote marks may not be readily apparent, so here's an explanation: Google Sheets understands the "D2" cell address as something like, "Go get what's in Cell D2 and display it here." The comma right after "D2" tells Google Sheets something like, "OK, here's what to do next." And

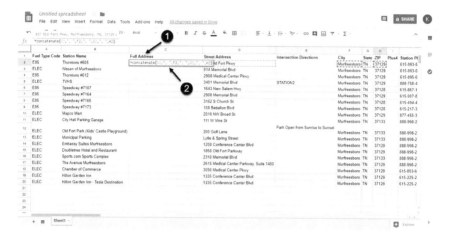

Figure 3.26 Using the = concatenate function. Type a label for the newly inserted column (1), carefully type = concatenate(D2,", ",F2,", ",G2,", ",H2) into Cell C2 (2), then press "Enter." Copy the function to the other cells in Column C to replicate the concatenation for each of the remaining records. Google and the Google logo are registered trademarks of Google Inc., used with permission.

the next thing to do is "Display a comma, then a space, which I've put between quote marks so you know to display it as text instead of trying to read it as a command." The next comma is another, "OK, here's what to do next" signal, and the pattern repeats. Figure 3.26 shows the function just before we pressed "Enter." After you press "Enter," you can copy the function to the other cells in Column C to repeat the concatenation for each of the remaining fuel stations. Recall that you can copy the function by clicking Cell C2, using your mouse the highlight the remain cells in the column (C3 through C20), then pressing Ctrl/v or Cmd/v. To get it done even faster, click on Cell C2, then point your mouse at the small, blue square in the highlighted cell's lower-right corner until the mouse pointer changes to a plus sign, and double click.

Once you have each station's full address displaying in Column C and have given the Google Sheet a suitable name, like "Alternative fuel stations," you can import the data into a Google My Map layer using pretty much the same process you used to import the Toxics Release Inventory data. The only difference involves unchecking the "Latitude" and "Longitude" columns (yes, there are latitude / longitude columns in the dataset) and instead specifying Column C, the "Full Address" column, as the column for My Maps to use when placing the stations on the map:

- Return to your Google Drive, and click "New / More / Google My Maps" to create a fresh map.
- Click "Import" under "Untitled layer."

- On the "Choose a file to import" window, click the "Google Drive" tab; click on the name of the Google Sheet containing the fuel station data, and click "Select."
- On the "Choose columns to position your placemarks" window, check the "Full address" field, which is where the concatenated address information is stored in the Google Sheet. Also, scroll down until you see the "Latitude" and "Longitude" fields, and uncheck those. We could have used them, but we're choosing to use the address information instead.
- Click the window's "Continue" button.
- On the "Choose a column to title your markers" window, select "Station Name," so that the station's name will become the title for each station's detail window.
- Click the "Finish" button.

My Maps will mark each station's location with the default map marker, currently a blue one shaped like an upside-down teardrop. Especially when mapping with address information, it's a good idea to zoom as far out as possible to make sure My Maps didn't misinterpret an address (or correctly interpret incorrect address information) and stick a marker in some obviously wrong location. On our first attempt at mapping the Murfreesboro fuel stations, for example, one marker ended up on Memorial Boulevard in Nashville rather than Memorial Boulevard in Murfreesboro. Fixing an error in the concatenation function solved the problem.

Now you can style the map according to your preferences, using the techniques you've already learned. Figure 3.24 shows that we grouped the stations by "Fuel type code," chose different colors for each fuel type (green for E85 Flex Fuel and blue for electric charging stations), went into the "Other icons" menu and found a gas pump icon to use as markers, and added a second layer displaying a .kml of Murfreesboro's city limits. The .kml came from the Census Bureau's repository of shapefiles for "Places," at https://www.census.gov/geographies/mapping-files/time-series/geo/carto-boundary-file.html. We used QGIS, and specifically a "NAME" is not 'Murfreesboro' expression, to select and delete all place borders except those for Murfreesboro. You could to the same for your city by using your city's name instead of 'Murfreesboro.' Again, note that the field name must be in double quotes ("NAME") and the city name in single quotes ('Murfreesboro') in order for the expression to work properly.

Making a Map When You Have no Geolocation Data to Import

A strong-arm robbery occurred on Thursday, March 3, 2016, near Smith Hall on our campus, Middle Tennessee State University in Murfreesboro, Tennessee. The victim, a female student, told university police she had been near Smith

Hall on the university's campus when an attacker had approached her from behind and had pushed her, causing her to drop her belongings. The attacker had then run away with some of the items she had dropped. The incident, reported at 5:41 p.m., was the last of five reported to university police that day, according to the university police department's media log (Middle Tennessee State University Police Department, 2016). Earlier in the day:

- A victim reported a stolen car at 9:48 a.m. on the Jackson Parking Lot.
- Someone reported at 1:04 p.m. that a door in the Student Union Building had been vandalized.
- A driver reported 4:12 p.m. that his vehicle had been struck while it was parked on the Softball Parking Lot.
- A driver reporter at 4:57 p.m. that her vehicle had been struck while it was parked on the Honors Parking Lot.

A map showing the location of each incident could have considerably enhanced a news report about the incidents. However, the police log gave no latitude or longitude coordinates for the incident locations. Also, many buildings and locations on campus don't have specific addresses. Smith Hall is just "Smith Hall," and the Jackson Parking Lot is just the Jackson Parking Lot. But you can still use My Maps to make a map of these incidents. In fact, it's so easy, you could do it not only on a computer but also on an Internet-connected tablet or smartphone. Figure 3.27 shows a map we made indicating the location of each incident and providing details about what happened.

To make the map, we began by using My Map's "Draw a line" tool to manually draw MTSU's campus borders onto a fresh My Map we had opened and zoomed

Figure 3.27 A My Map of incidents reported to MTSU Police on March 3, 2016. Google and the Google logo are registered trademarks of Google Inc., used with permission.

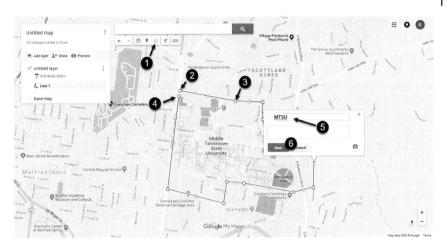

Figure 3.28 Drawing boundaries on a My Map. Click the "Draw a line" tool (1), then click once on the point at which you want to begin drawing the line (2). Click once each time you reach a point at which you need to change direction (3). Double click to set the line once you reach the point where you want to stop (4). After the line is set, you can move the end of the line on top of the starting point to make a complete shape. Type a name for the line in the detail box that appears (5), then click "Save" (6). Google and the Google logo are registered trademarks of Google Inc., used with permission.

in to show MTSU's campus. Figure 3.28 illustrates the process. The tool's icon looks like three dots arranged in a triangle and connected with a line. It lies between the "Add marker" tool and the "Add directions" tool under the map's search box. To use it, click on it with your mouse, position the mouse pointer at the spot on the map where you want to begin drawing (we picked the intersection of Middle Tennessee Boulevard and Greenland Drive, on the northwest corner of campus) and click once. You can then stretch a straight line from that point to any other point on the map by moving the mouse pointer. Click the mouse once, and My Maps will anchor the line there and let you continue in a different direction. With a little practice, you can easily draw a line that navigates around corners and bends. If you need to move to a spot that isn't on screen, use the arrow keys to pan the screen in the direction you need to go.

If you click your way back to where you began, the end of the line will "snap to" the beginning. Click once, and My Maps will form a polygon like those used to show the metro area borders on the map you made in Chapter 2. For small-scale maps like this one, though, it might be a good idea to double click a bit short of the beginning of the line. Doing so leaves what you've drawn as a line rather than turning it into a polygon. After you've double-clicked, you can click on the end of the line and drag it onto the line's starting point. The advantage of doing so is that you can now draw other shapes inside the campus borders, whether lines or polygons. In My Maps, nesting one polygon inside another can cause problems. Specifically, if map users click on the bigger polygon, they can't then click on the smaller, nested polygon unless they go back to the main navigation menu and select it. Confusion can result.

Using the "Draw a line" tool to draw complex borders, like those for a city, county or state, would be pretty tedious and probably produce inaccurate results. For such bigger jobs, finding a shapefile is a far better approach. But there simply isn't a premade shapefile available for MTSU's campus borders. Also, the borders aren't all that intricate. Mostly, they're straight lines that parallel roads. In such situations, the "Draw a line" tool will do just fine. You'll probably discover, too, that you can adjust the line. Each time the line changes direction, My Maps adds a point halfway between the sections' beginning and end points. Grab that point with the mouse, and you can move it around. When you drop it, My Maps will add a halfway point to each of the two sections you created. You can then move those points around, too.

Next, we added a map layer to contain a marker for each incident. We also edited the layer's data table in a way that would enable each marker to show its incident's description, time and location name in a detail window that would appear when a user clicked the marker. Figure 3.29 illustrates the process. Here are step-by-step directions:

- Click the "Add layer" button in the map editing area. My Maps will add a layer and label it "Untitled layer."

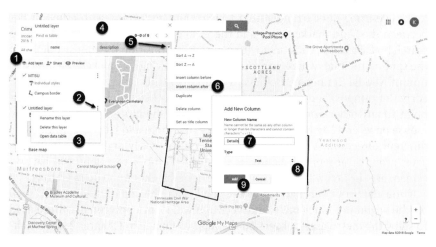

Figure 3.29 Adding a field to a My Maps layer data table. Click the "Add layer" button (1) to add a new layer. Click the new layer's three-dot icon (2), and choose "Open data table" (3). When the layer's data table opens (4), click the "description" field's arrow (5) and select "Insert column after" (6). On the "Add New Column" window, type a name for the new field (7), choose the field type as "Text" (8), and click "Add" (9). Google and the Google logo are registered trademarks of Google Inc., used with permission.

- Click the new layer's three-dot icon, and choose "Open data table." You've done this before. Recall that you opened the metro area unemployment map's data table earlier in this chapter so you could make a numeric copy of the map's "October 2018 rate(p)" field. This time, though, you'll be adding, rather than duplicating, fields.
- Opening the data table reveals that My Maps has created two fields by default: a "name" field, and a "description" field. Ignore these two fields, though. You can't change the first field's lowercase "name" label, and the label isn't going to look very good in a detail window. The same is true for the second field's "description" label. Instead, click the down arrow to the right of the "description" label and choose "Insert column after." The "Add New Column" window will open, allowing you to create a new field with a label that is more suitable for display. We chose "Details" as a label, because this field will contain the type of incident reported, like "Strong-arm robbery," or "Stolen car."
- Make sure "Text" is selected as the field type.
- Click "Add." My Maps will add a data table field labeled "Details."
- Use the same click sequence to add two more data table fields, one labeled "Time," and one labeled "Place." We kept both fields as "Text" fields. There is a "Date & Time" field type available under the "Type" dropdown menu, but that field type requires you to enter the date and time in a particular format. We chose to keep it as a text field, so that times could be entered in a simple format, like "5:41 p.m." Note that you can add more, or different, fields, if you like, depending on the information you have available and what you want your map users to know. You might want to add a field for the police incident report number, for example, or maybe the incident's current status, like "Under investigation" or "Closed" or "Arrest made."

Next, we added a marker for the Smith Hall robbery and formatted the marker's detail window, as illustrated in Figure 3.30. To follow along:

- Zoom on Smith Hall. My Maps currently doesn't label it by default, but it sits at the corner of Alumni Drive and Old Main Circle in the Southwest area of campus. If you have trouble finding it, you can locate it using the search box, because it is one of the few buildings on campus that has an actual address: 318 Old Main Cir, Murfreesboro, TN 37130. Type the address into the search box, and click the magnifying glass. My Maps will show its location with a green marker and add a separate "Smith Hall" layer for it over in the map editing box. You can delete the green marker by clicking the "x" next to the "318 Old Main Cir, Murfreesboro, TN 37130" address in the "Smith Hall" layer.
- Click the upside-down-teardrop-shaped "Add marker" icon on the map's tool bar. Your mouse pointer will turn into a " + " symbol.
- Position the pointer over Smith Hall, and click. My Maps will place a blue marker on the point you clicked and open the marker's detail window in "edit" mode.

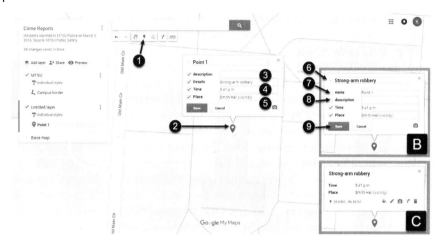

Figure 3.30 Adding a map marker and formatting the detail window. Zoom in on the first map marker's location, then click the "Add marker" tool (1). Place the marker on the map by clicking where you want it to go (2), and type the incident information into the detail window's fields (3, 4 and 5). Click the down arrow next to the title field (Inset B, 6) and select "Details" as the new title field. Uncheck the "name" (7) and "description" (8) fields, and click "Save" (9). Inset C shows the edited detail window. Google and the Google logo are registered trademarks of Google Inc., used with permission.

- Type the incident's "Details" (Strong-arm robbery), "Time" (5:41 p.m.), and "Place" (Smith Hall vicinity") into the detail window's fields.
- While you're here, go ahead and rearrange the detail window's fields into the view you want map users to see when they click on a map marker. Click the down arrow next to the detail window's title and change it from the default "name" field to the "Details" field that you added. Now, the incident detail, like "Strong-arm robbery," will show up both as the detail window's title and as the marker's label over in the map legend. Also uncheck the "name" and "description" fields, which are empty and have no reason to appear in the detail window. But leave the "Time" and "Place" fields checked, so they will show.
- Click "Save" to save both the data you entered and the revised detail window layout.

Use the same process to add a map marker for each of the other incidents. If you are replicating our map, MTSU's latest parking map (see www.mtsu.edu/parking/documents/parking-map.pdf) might help you find your way around. Or you could use these techniques to map reported crimes around your own campus or city. By the way, the MTSU police log from March 3, 2016 was unusually dramatic. Strong-arm robberies and car thefts aren't the norm on campus. When you are done, you can style the map using the layer-styling techniques already described. We chose red "x" markers for the incidents to make them stand out on the map. We thickened the line showing the campus borders. We also edited the map's title and subtitle, as well as each layer's title and labels. You'll also want to share and publish your map, again using the techniques described earlier.

Consider how useful these "on the fly" map-making techniques could prove in what journalists call a "spot news" situation. For example, on Dec. 14, 2016, residents of Rutherford County, Tennessee, where we live, awoke to news that a tractor trailer carrying chlorine had crashed and caught fire on Interstate 24 in the Southeastern part of the county, producing a potentially dangerous cloud of chlorine gas. Initial reports indicated that the cloud was threatening the entire county. As more details emerged, it became clear that while emergency personnel had scrambled to evacuate a subdivision downwind of the fire, most other areas in the county were perfectly safe. Police closed the stretch of interstate where the crash had occurred and set up a detour. The Rutherford County Sheriff's Department set up a command post at a nearby Subway restaurant and began providing updates that local news media broadcast live or streamed on the Web. An emergency shelter opened at a Murfreesboro community center for anyone displaced by the incident. In the end, nobody got seriously hurt, and things returned to normal by that evening.

The incident generated extensive local news coverage, but none of it included the kind of online, interactive map that an enterprising reporter with a Web-connected laptop or mobile device could have made in a few minutes using the techniques described above. The "Draw a line" tool could have outlined the official evacuation zone. The line could have been adjusted, or even redrawn, as details about the danger zone's parameters became clearer. Markers could have shown the locations of the crash, the Sheriff Department's command post, and the emergency shelter. The "Add directions" tool, which we didn't demonstrate here, could have plotted the detour route. And while editing the map marker detail window (see Figure 3.30), you might have noticed the camera icon. Clicking it could have added photos and video to each of the map features' detail windows. Sharing the map's editing privileges with every member of a reporting team would have let each member add points, information, photos and video from whatever scene he or she was covering, all in real time.

Recap

This chapter has shown you how to use Google Sheets and Google My Maps to make online, interactive maps. You've seen how to place things on the map by defining their borders with a. kml file, their latitude and longitude coordinates, or their addresses. You've also seen how to generate a map on the go by simply using My Maps' built-in tools. Other, better online mapping tools are available, and more might have become available by the time you open this book. But learning to use My Maps is a good place to begin.

References

"Media Log (March 2016)." 2016. Middle Tennessee State University Police Department. Accessed April 30, 2016. www.mtsu.edu/police/media-log.php.

U.S. Department of Energy. "Alternative Fuels Data Center." Accessed Dec. 30, 2018. https://afdc.energy.gov/stations/#/analyze.

U.S. Environmental Protection Agency. 2015. "Factors to Consider when Using Toxics Release Inventory Data." Accessed Dec. 30, 2018. www.epa.gov/toxics-release-inventory-tri-program/factors-consider-when-using-toxics-release-inventory-data.

U.S. Environmental Protection Agency. "TRI Basic Data Files: Calendar Years 1987–2017." Accessed Dec. 30, 2018a. www.epa.gov/toxics-release-inventory-tri-program/tri-basic-data-files-calendar-years-1987-2017.

U.S. Environmental Protection Agency. 2018b. "TRI Basic Data Files Guide." Accessed Dec. 30, 2018. www.epa.gov/toxics-release-inventory-tri-program/tri-basic-data-files-guide.

4

Microsoft Excel and PivotTables

It's time to set Google apps like Sheets and My Maps aside and look at other data tools capable of doing useful things Google apps can't do as efficiently, or can't do at all. This chapter will introduce you to Microsoft Excel, the spreadsheet program typically included in Microsoft Office. Excel's capabilities overlap considerably with those of Google Sheets. Everything you learned in Chapter 1 about columns, rows, cell addresses, formulas and functions will work the same way in Excel as in Google Sheets. Excel can't make Web-based interactive graphics and maps as easily as Google Sheets and Google My Maps can. But handling a larger dataset with Excel usually will require less time than handling the same dataset in Google Sheets, because the speed of Google Sheets depends upon the speed of your Internet connection. In practice, you may typically find yourself crunching your data in Excel, then transferring the results to Google Sheets or Google My Maps for graphing or mapping.

This chapter focuses on turning data into a table of totals, statistics and other values called a "pivot table" that can help you spot newsworthy or otherwise meaningful patterns and associations in your data. Google Sheets has a pivot table tool, and it is getting better all the time. We'll take a brief look at it toward the end of the chapter. But it presently doesn't operate as smoothly as the corresponding tool in Excel.

Introducing PivotTables

Figure 4.1 shows an Excel file containing itemized individual contributions during the year 2015 to Rep. Scott DesJarlais, a Republican who held Tennessee's Fourth District seat in the U.S. House of Representatives throughout that year. We picked the Tennessee Fourth because it's the district we live in. We'll be referring to DesJarlais frequently in this chapter, so let's dispense with a potential distraction right up front: His last name is pronounced "DAY-zhar-lay."

Data Skills for Media Professionals: A Basic Guide, First Edition. Ken Blake and Jason Reineke.
© 2020 John Wiley & Sons, Inc. Published 2020 by John Wiley & Sons, Inc.

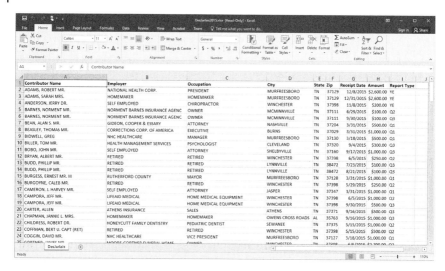

Figure 4.1 An Excel file containing information about itemized individual donations to Tennessee Rep. Scott DesJarlais during 2015. Used with permission from Microsoft.

One of his early campaign ads focused on helping district voters distinguish the sound of his last name from "Dijon mustard," "Dijonnaise sauce," and "déjà vu" (DesJarlais4TN, 2012).

Anyway, you can download such data from the U.S. Federal Election Commission for any U.S. federal candidate during any recent federal election cycle. We'll show you how a bit later. In the figure, each row gives information about a donation the candidate received, including the donor's name, employer, occupation, city, state, and zip code, and the donation's receipt date and amount. The "Report type" column shows whether the candidate reported the donation in the 2015's first-quarter, second-quarter, third-quarter, or year-end report.

Figure 4.2 shows one example of the kind of information a pivot table can produce. To make the table, Excel combined all donations from each city and calculated, for each city, how much money the donations added up to and how many donations were made. Finally, it sorted the cities by donation total, so that the city with the largest donation total appeared at the top of the list.

If you compare the two figures while thinking like a media professional whose job is to tell an understandable, interesting story, you'll perhaps realize that Figure 4.2 makes telling such a story much easier than Figure 4.1 does. For example, a news story based on Figure 4.1 could start, at best, with something like, "A lot of people from various places donated varying amounts of money to U.S. Rep. Scott DesJarlais during 2015, data from the U.S. Federal Election Commission show. Donors included Robert Adams of Murfreesboro, Tennessee, president of National Health Corp., who gave $2,600 on Dec. 8, and Sarah Adams, a Murfreesboro homemaker, who gave another $2,600 later the

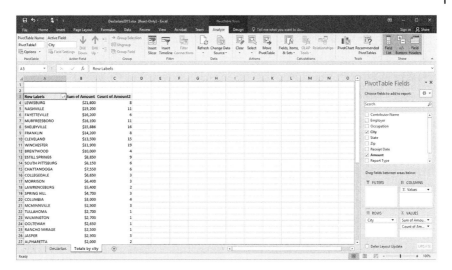

Figure 4.2 An Excel PivotTable showing totals and counts, aggregated by city, for donations to Tennessee Congressman Scott DesJarlais during 2015. The records have been sorted in descending order by donation totals. Used with permission from Microsoft.

same month." But a news story based on Figure 4.2 could start with something like, "Lewisburg, Tennessee, proved to be U.S. Rep. Scott DesJarlais' most lucrative fundraising territory during 2015, data from the U.S. Federal Election Commission show. The South Pittsburg, Tennessee, Republican picked up eight donations in Lewisburg totaling $21,600. Nashville, Tennessee, the state capital, ranked second, producing 11 donations totaling $19,200. In all, DesJarlais raised $10,000 or more in nine cities, including Murfreesboro, the largest city in his district, where he received 11 donations totaling $16,000."

It's not that individual donations are uninteresting. In fact, if you double-click on the $21,600 cell in Figure 4.2, Excel will produce the tab shown in Figure 4.3, which lists details about those eight donations from Lewisburg. As you can see, all eight came from four individuals who appear to be members of the same family and who all appear associated with the same die-casting business. That's potentially very interesting, indeed. But until you've combined the data somehow – for example, until you've combined contributions by city – it's difficult to know where the story might begin, let alone how to tell it.

This demonstration illustrates how to decide whether a pivot table might be a useful tool for analyzing a given dataset. Look for at least one column in your dataset that repeats information. In Figure 4.1, for example, the "City" column contains multiple occurrences of "Murfreesboro," "McMinville," "Winchester," and so on. The same is true of several other columns. The "Contributor name" column contains repeating entries for "Barnes, Norment Mr.," "Budd, Philip Mr.," and "Campora, Jeff Mr." And the "Employer," "Occupation," "City," "State"

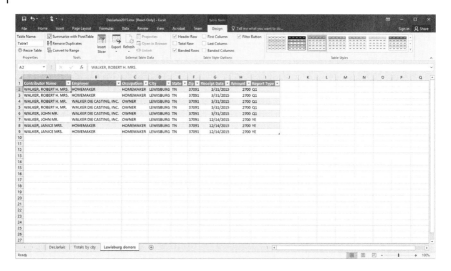

Figure 4.3 The results of clicking Cell B4 in Figure 4.2, after expanding the columns and relabeling the tab name from "Sheet3" to "Lewisburg donors." Used with permission from Microsoft.

and "Zip" information for those individuals naturally duplicates as well. If such repetition is present in your dataset, ask yourself whether combining the duplicates into totals, counts or even averages might reveal some newsworthy patterns, help you gain a better understanding of the data, or provide a better way to tell the story. If so, then consider using a pivot table.

A few caveats are in order. First, note that repeating values may not always be as obvious as they are here. The data in Figure 4.1 have been sorted alphabetically by last name, so rows showing multiple contributions from the same person ended up next to one another. Had the data been sorted by, say, the "Receipt Date" column, you would have had a much more difficult time realizing that Barnes donated twice, because his first donation, received on June 29, 2015, might have been listed far from his second donation, received three months later, on Sept. 30, 2015. So, even if duplicates aren't obvious at first, checking for them with a pivot table, or at least a sort or two, can be wise.

And here's a second, equally important caveat: repeating values aren't always a good thing. Look, again, at the two records in Figure 4.1 showing $100 donations by Barnes. The records are identical except for their dates. Had their dates been identical as well, you would have good reason to suspect that someone had accidentally recorded the donation twice. It's also possible, although less likely, that somebody accidentally recorded the same donation with two different receipt dates. Like a lot of data you'll encounter, Federal Election Commission datasets are notoriously "dirty," meaning they often contains errors. Checking for obvious, or at least likely, duplication errors is a good habit to develop.

We hope, though, that this demonstration has interested you in learning to use Excel's pivot table tool. If it has, let's take a closer look at how to get the most out of it. A quick note about the figures in this chapter: Microsoft's guidelines don't allow us to mark up Excel screen images the way we marked up Google Sheets, Google MyMaps and QGIS screen shots in the preceding chapters. We'll do our best to keep the figures understandable whenever they depict multiple steps.

Getting Started: Aggregating Contributions by City

If you like doing things the hard way, or if you just can't wait to see who's giving money to the federal candidate of your choice, feel free to skip ahead to the "Downloading campaign finance data from the Federal Election Commission" section, grab a dataset that interests you, and use it while working through the techniques below. We recommend, though, that you download and use the same dataset we're using, at least until you feel confident about your pivot table skills. We've put the file into Excel 2016 format, deleted some unnecessary columns, and set the spreadsheet to keep the column headers and the first column of data in view as you scroll around in the file. There's even a file suitable for earlier versions of Excel. You'll find download URLs in the References section of this chapter (Blake, 2016a). We're using Excel 2016 on a Windows 10 PC. Other versions of Excel, including those designed for Macs, differ somewhat.

Download the file to a computer that has a copy of Excel installed. Open Excel, click "File / Open," browse to the data file, and double-click on the file. Your computer screen should look something like Figure 4.1. Depending on your computer's setup, you might have to click "Enable Editing" once the file opens in Excel. Also, if you opened the data file straight from the Web, save the file on your computer before proceeding. In some versions of Excel, the PivotTableTool won't work until you've saved the file locally – that is, on your computer's hard drive or on an attached flash drive. Also, you'll be making some changes to the file as we go along, so you'll probably want to save your work.

Time to do some analysis. First, combine the data by "City," as in Figure 4.2:

- **Click on a cell that is part of the data you want to include in the pivot table**. For example, Cell A1. Doing so helps Excel know what data to use. If you click on a blank cell, Excel won't be able to locate any data to include in the pivot table, and you'll end up with a "Data source reference not valid" error message.
- **Click the "Insert" tab, then click "PivotTable" on the far left of the ribbon**. The "Create PivotTable" dialog box will open. By default, "Select a table or range" will be selected, and the range of cells holding the data will be shown in the "Table/Range" box. Also, by default, "New Worksheet" will be

selected under "Choose where you want the PivotTable report to be placed." Both defaults are just fine. Click "OK."

- **Excel will open a new sheet**. The left side will be blank except for a "PivotTable1" box showing the message, "To build a report, choose fields from the PivotTable Field List." On the right, under "PivotTable Fields," you'll see a scrollable list of the column labels from the data, like "Contributor name," "Employer," "Occupation," and so on. Below the list, you'll see four empty boxes labeled "Filters," "Columns," "Rows" and "Values." The "PivotTable Fields" area will open any time you click within the "PivotTable1" box. Click outside the "PivotTable1" box, and Excel will hide the "PivotTable Fields" area.

- **Using your mouse, click on the "City" label, hold the mouse button down, drag the "City" label to the "Rows" box, and release the mouse button**. On the left side of the screen, a list of all cities in the dataset's "City" column will appear in Column A, with one city occupying each row in the list. Notice that the list, in addition to being alphabetized, contains no duplicate entries. Remember how there were multiple entries for "Murfreesboro" in the "City" column? Scroll down, and you'll see that there is now only one "Murfreesboro" on the list.

- **Next, drag the "Amount" label into the "Values" box**. A "Sum of Amount" column will appear in Column B. Each row will contain the total, or sum, of all donations given by people in the row's city. For example, a total of $250 was given in Alexandria, $2,000 in Alpharetta, $500 in Athens, etc.

- **Drag the "Amount" label into the "Values" box a second time**. A "Sum of Amount2" column will appear in Column C containing values that are identical to the values in the "Sum of Amount" column in Column B. Don't worry about the redundancy; we're going to do something interesting with Column C on the next step.

- **Click the second "Sum of Amount2" label in Column C, then click "Value Field Settings ..."** The "Value Field Settings" dialog box will appear.

- **On the "Summarize Values By" tab of the dialog box, choose "Count," then click "OK."** Column C will change to "Count of Amount2," and the values in the column will show you how many contributions there were from each city. Figure 4.4 shows the results. So, for example, all $250 from Alexandria came from one donation, but the $2,000 from Alpharetta came from two separate donations, and Cleveland's $13,500 in donations is the sum of 15 separate donations.

- **Click the down arrow next to the "Row labels" heading in Column A, and choose "More sort options."** The "Sort (City)" dialog box will open.

- **Choose the radio button beside "Descending (Z to A) by:," click the down arrow, select "Sum of Amount" from the drop-down list, and click "OK."** Excel will sort the entire pivot table report by the figures in the "Sum of Amount" column (Column B) so that the city with the largest contribution total – Lewisburg, which had eight contributions totaling $21,600 – will

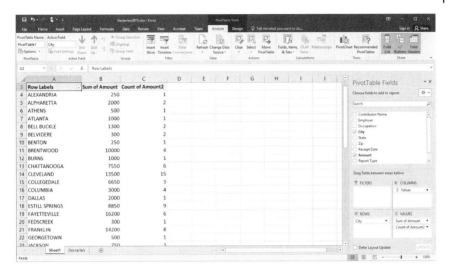

Figure 4.4 The PivotTable, right after aggregating the "Amount" column by the "City" column twice, then changing the second "Amount" aggregation to summarize by "Count" rather than "Sum." Used with permission from Microsoft.

appear at the top of the list, and the other cities will be listed in descending order by their contribution totals. Nashville should be second, with $19,200 from 11 contributions, Fayetteville, third, with $16,200 from six contributions, and so forth. By the way, if you scroll all the way to the bottom of the pivot table, you'll see a "Grand Total" row that gives you the sum of both the "Sum of Amount" column ($223,686) and "Count of Amount2" column (174).

- **Double-click the $21,600 given by donors in Lewisburg (Cell B4).** Excel will open a new tab, shown in Figure 4.3, showing you all available information for the eight contributions that made up the $21,600 total. You may need to expand the columns by selecting all of the data and double-clicking the boundary between any two columns.

Think back to what you learned how to do in Chapter 2, and you might see an opportunity, here. Remember learning how to use Google Sheets to make an online, interactive column chart showing the unemployment rate data for each metro area in Tennessee? Suppose you copied the data from Cell A3 (the "Row labels" cell) to Cell B12 (the cell showing Brentwood's 10,000 contribution total) into a Google Sheet, then changed the column labels to "City" and "Contribution total." If you did, you could make and publish a nice-looking, online, interactive column chart summarizing the donation totals for each city that gave DesJarlais $10,000 or more in itemized individual contributions during 2015. That graphic could help illustrate a news story about where DesJarlais' individual contributions tended to come from. The example illustrates how

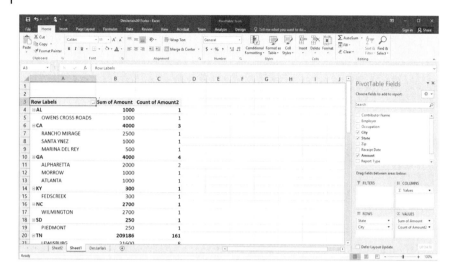

Figure 4.5 The PivotTable, after aggregating the donation totals and counts first by state, then by city. Used with permission from Microsoft.

you can switch back and forth between Excel and Google Sheets to conduct and present an analysis.

You've probably noticed by now that the pivot table tool operates in real time. In other words, the moment you change something in the "PivotTableFields" area on the right side of the screen, the results show up immediately in the pivot table on the left side of the screen. For example, go back to the "Sheet1" tab – the one with the pivot table in it – use your mouse to grab "City," drag it out of the rows box and to the left, and release it anywhere in the spreadsheet. The "City" column will disappear from the pivot table, and you'll be left with only the sum of all contributions ($223,686) and the total number of contributions (174). Now, drag "State" into the "Rows" box. Immediately, you'll get donation totals and counts for each state. Drag "City" back into the "Rows" box and release it just underneath "State," and you'll have totals and counts for each city again, but the cities will be grouped by state, and you'll also have counts and totals for each state. Figure 4.5 shows the results. Because the pivot table tool responds immediately like this, you can look for a lot of different patterns in your data in a short amount of time.

Using the PivotTable Tool's "Filters" Box

To see what the "Filters" box is for, grab the "State" field out of the "Rows" box (if you left it there) or from the list, and drop it into the Filters box. Now, scroll all the way to the top of the pivot table. There, in cell B2, you'll see the word

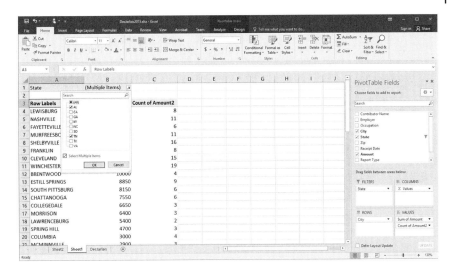

Figure 4.6 Setting a filter to show only donations from Tennessee and Alabama. First, drag the "State" field into the "Filters" box in the "PivotTable Fields" area. On the filter's drop-down menu, check the "Select Multiple Items" box, then check both "AL" and "TN." Used with permission from Microsoft.

"All" next to a down-pointing arrow. Click the arrow, click on "TN," for Tennessee, and click "OK." Excel will filter out all cities except those in Tennessee. If you ever want to select two or more filter criteria at once – both "TN" and "AL," for example – check the "Select Multiple Items" box, then check as many criteria as you like. Figure 4.6 shows the "State" field in the "Filters" box and the filter menu open, with the filter set to show donations from both Tennessee and Alabama.

There are even more ways to filter a pivot table's results. Suppose, for example, you wanted to see only the cities with contribution totals of $10,000 or more. Beside the "Row Labels" cell (A3), click the down-arrow, choose "Value Filters," then "Greater Than Or Equal To …" Then, on the "Value Filters (City)" box, use the drop-down menus to specify a filter in which "Sum of Amount" "is greater than or equal to" "10000." Then click "OK." You'll end up with nine cities that have donation totals of $10,000 or more. Furthermore, all nine will be cities in Tennessee, because the "TN" filter is still in place. Also note that, because you specified a descending sort based on the "Sum of Amount" field, the pivot table is still sorting the city totals from greatest to smallest, even though you are altering other aspects of the original pivot table. Figure 4.7 shows the "Value Filters (City)" box settings, as well as the filter's results.

Following the same steps, but choosing "Label Filters" rather than "Value Filters," will let you specify a text-based filter and apply it to the city names. Such a filter isn't especially useful in the situation at hand, unless, for some

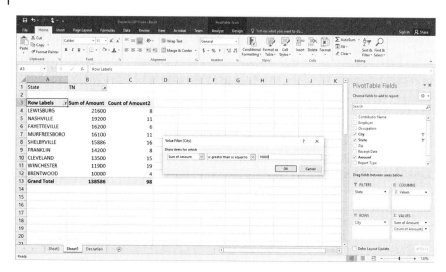

Figure 4.7 The results of filtering the data for "Sum of Amount" values equal to, or greater than, 10,000, with the Value Filter menu open to show the filter setup. To create the filter, click the down arrow next to "Row Labels" in Cell A3, choose "Value Filters / Greater Than or Equal to …," complete the "Value Filter (City)" box as shown, and click, "OK." Used with permission from Microsoft.

reason, you wanted to filter for all city names that contain "ville," like Nashville, Fayetteville, Shelbyville, etc. But if you were using a pivot table to aggregate the data by contributor name, it could be pretty handy to be able to filter the table's data for people with the same last name. Recall, here, the Walker family, from Lewisburg, Tennessee, whose collective $21,600 contribution put Lewisburg at the top of DesJarlais' most lucrative fundraising cities.

Using the PivotTable Tool's "Columns" Box

There is one, last box to explore in the PivotTable Fields area: the "Columns" box. To see what it can do, grab the "Report Type" field and drop it into the Columns box. The "Report Type" field indicates whether the contribution was received during the first quarter of the year (Q1), second quarter (Q2), third quarter (Q3), or fourth/year-end quarter (YE). Excel will show each city's contribution totals by quarter. For example, the $21,600 contributed from Lewisburg consisted of $13,500 given in the first quarter and another $8,100 given in the year-end quarter. No contributions came from Lewisburg in the second and third quarters, so those cells are blank.

To the right of the city-by-quarter totals, the pivot table gives you the same kind of breakout for the contribution counts (five from Lewisburg in the first quarter, none in the second and third quarters, and three in the year-end quarter). The last

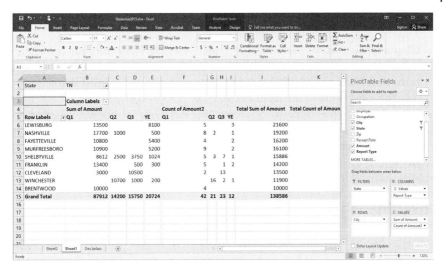

Figure 4.8 The results of dragging the "Report Type" field into the "Columns" box in the "PivotTable Fields" area. Excel will break down each city's contribution totals and counts by the categories in "Report Type," which are the first-quarter report (Q1), second-quarter report (Q2), third-quarter report (Q3), and fourth-quarter, or "Year End," report (YE). Used with permission from Microsoft.

two columns give you the totals and counts for each city. Figure 4.8 shows the results of putting "Report Type" in the "Columns" box with all of the filters described above still in place. Note the small funnel-shaped icons to the right of both the "City" and "State" fields in the list under "PivotTable Fields" on the right of the screen. You can modify or remove the filters by clicking these icons.

If you are able, it's wise avoid putting a field in the "Columns" box if the field has more than three or four categories. The "Report Type" field, for example, had only four categories: Q1, Q2, Q3, and YE. The more categories there are in a field you place in the "Columns" box, the wider the table will be, and the farther right you'll have to scroll to see the right end of the table. For most people, pivot tables with many horizontal rows and just a few vertical columns – that is, long-but-skinny pivot tables – are easier to understand than pivot tables that are both long and wide, or short and wide.

One last tip before we switch to a different dataset: If it has been bothering you that the "Sum of Amount" figures are showing as plain numbers, even though they represent dollar figures, Excel offers a trick that will let you format the amounts as dollar figures.

- **Head to the "Sum of Amount" entry in the "PivotTable Fields" area's "Values" box, click the down-arrow, and choose "Value Field Settings …,"** just like you did when you changed the second "Sum of Amount" entry from "Sum" to "Count." The "Value Field Settings" window will open.

- **Click the "Number Format" button** on the "Value Field Settings" window. The "Format Cells" window will open.
- **Choose "Currency"** from the list under "Category" in the "Format Cells" window, choose "Currency," and, if you like, change "Decimal places" to a zero, which will round off the donation amounts to the nearest whole number. You can choose a different currency symbol, too, if you like.
- **Click "OK" twice**, once to close the "Format Cells" window, and again to close the "Value Field Settings" window. Excel will display the donation totals as dollar currency amounts, complete with commas and the currency symbol you selected.

Investigating Relatedness

Patterns like the ones we've been looking at often suggest that one thing might be related to another. In Figure 4.2, for example, we see statistical evidence that both the amount and the number of contributions to DesJarlais are related to the geographic location of the contribution's donor. The amounts and numbers of donations were substantially larger in cities like Lewisburg, Nashville, Fayetteville, and Murfreesboro than in cities farther down the list. Figure 4.8 reveals what looks like an additional relationship: At least in cities with contributions totaling $10,000 or more, the amount and number of contributions appeared related to the time of year. Except in Cleveland and Winchester, donations tended to be more numerous and to total more in the first quarter than in later quarters. The tables wouldn't be nearly as newsworthy if they didn't show these relationships. Imagine, for example, that Figure 4.2 showed about eight to 12 contributions in every city, with contribution totals ranging from $2,500 to $3,000. Or imagine that Figure 4.8 showed nearly identical contribution counts and totals for all quarters in each of the cities. The main conclusions to be drawn would be that location and time of year had nothing to do with – that is, no relationship with – contributions. The lack of relatedness would have little news value unless it was somehow unexpected or surprising.

Never make the mistake, though, of assuming that an apparent relationship between two things proves that one of the things caused the other. Figure 4.2, for example, might seem to show that living in Lewisburg, Tennessee, caused people there to be unusually generous toward DesJarlais' campaign. After all, contributions from Lewisburg totaled $21,600, more than the contributions from any other city. As Figure 4.3 shows, though, it's likely that the generosity in Lewisburg toward DesJarlais had more to do with belonging to the Walker family than with residency in Lewisburg. The Walkers just happened to call Lewisburg home. In fact, nobody else in Lewisburg, a city with a population of just over 11,000, donated any money at all to DesJarlais in 2015.

Proving that one thing causes another is actually pretty difficult. Evidence of a relationship between the two things is only one of several requirements. Additional requirements include demonstrating that the cause preceded the effect in time. A journalist might notice, for example, that four city council members who frequently play golf together on weekends also tend to vote the same way on controversial issues. But do they vote together because they golf together, golf together because they vote together, or just happen to like both golf and similar policy positions? It would be difficult to say without evidence that they started golfing together before they started voting together, or started voting together before they started golfing together. Another requirement involves eliminating, or at least minimizing, the possibility that something other than the presumed cause can do a better job of explaining the effect. As noted earlier, Figure 4.2 might suggest "City" caused both the amount and number of contributions to DesJarlais' campaign, until Figure 4.3 reveals that "Family" offers a better explanation. Finally, it's a good idea to have some sort of plausible, evidence-based understanding of a process by which the cause could bring about the effect. Figure 4.3 certainly suggests that belonging to the Walker family causes generosity toward DesJarlais. But what process connects the two? The "Employer" column in Figure 4.3 suggests the Walkers run a die-casting business. Is supporting DesJarlais somehow advantageous to their business? Or do they support him for some other reason, or reasons? The donation data can't say. But other information sources, such as the Walkers themselves or people who know them or at least know about them, probably could.

Despite these principles, people make unsubstantiated claims about causality pretty frequently. An example involving DesJarlais' campaign finances illustrates the point and shows how a pivot table can help you question at least some aspects of such claims.

In January of 2016, the FEC's website released campaign contribution data from the final quarter of 2015 for the campaign of Murfreesboro, Tennessee, attorney Grant Starrett, DesJarlais' opponent in the Fourth District's August, 2016, Republican primary. Starrett ("STARE-et," since we helped you with "DesJarlais" earlier) had raised $654,381 in itemized contributions from individuals and from political action committees, according to the report, including $23,400 Starrett had kicked in out of his own pocket. DesJarlais had raised only about half as much: $326,406. Starrett's campaign manager, Tommy Schultz, said Starrett's fundraising success showed "that conservatives continue to rally behind Grant Starrett's visionary campaign for Congress." But DesJarlais campaign spokesman Robert Jameson countered that nearly all of Starrett's money had been raised from donors living outside the Fourth District. That fact, he said, indicated that Starrett had managed to gain no support inside the district. "Now, his plan is to use huge sums of out-of-state money to try and buy a congressional seat," Jameson said. "Unfortunately for him, the Fourth District is not for sale" (Sher, 2016).

Both spins on the facts at hand included unsubstantiated causal claims. The data showed only that Starrett had received more donation checks than DesJarlais had, and that those checks added up to more money than DesJarlais' total. The rest amounted to guesses. Donors can write multiple checks of varying amounts, so check counts and contribution totals don't necessarily equate to votes in the ballot box. Also, research shows that the relationship between political fundraising and political success involves a lot of factors that neither analysis took into account, including incumbency, how much candidates spend, and what they spend it on.

But let's focus on a claim central to the interpretation offered by Jameson, DesJarlais' campaign spokesman. Jameson claimed that contributions to Starrett had come disproportionately from sources outside of Tennessee. Was Jameson's claim correct? Yes – and no. More on that in a moment. First, let's look at the available data and how a pivot table could use it to investigate Jameson's claim. To work along with what you're about to read, you'll need an Excel file we've created that combines the 2015 itemized individual and campaign contributions for both DesJarlais and Starrett. You'll find a download link in the references (Blake, 2016b). Below are names and descriptions of the fields in the data file:

- **ID:** A unique ID code for each contribution.
- **Recipient:** The name of the candidate who received the contribution. Possible values are "DesJarlais" or "Starrett."
- **Contributor Name:** The name of the donor who made the contribution.
- **Contribution Type:** Two values are possible. "Individual" means the donor was an individual person. "Committee" means the donor was a political action committee.
- **Employer:** The name of the donor's employer, if provided. Some individual donors do not provide an employer name. Also, "Committee" donors do not have employers, so "N/A," for "not applicable," is shown in this field if the donor was a committee.
- **Occupation:** The donor's occupation. This field may be blank for individual donors. "N/A" is shown if the donor was a committee.
- **City:** The donor's city of residence.
- **State:** The donor's state of residence.
- **Source Type:** Two values are possible. "In state" is shown if the "State" field contained "TN." "Out of state" is shown in the "State" field contained anything else.
- **Zip:** The ZIP code of the donor's residence.
- **Receipt Date:** The date on which the candidate received the contribution.
- **Amount:** The amount of the donation, in dollars.
- **Report Type:** Four values are possible, each indicating the quarter in which the contribution was received. "Q1" means "First quarter;" "Q2," second quarter; "Q3," third quarter; "YE," year-end/fourth quarter.

To make this file on your own, you would have to download and combine four different files from the FEC: the itemized individual and itemized committee donor files for DesJarlais, and the same two files for Starrett. It's not difficult, but it does involve some carefully planned copying and pasting. Again, we'll show you at the end of this chapter how to download files from the FEC's Web site.

Returning to Jameson's claim, let's translate it into a statement that a basic pivot table can verify. A pivot table can tell you whether some value, compared across two or more types of one thing, is related to two or more types of a second thing. Put another way, a pivot table can investigate a claim if you can re-express the claim in a way that fills in every blank in this statement:

The value of ___, compared by ___, is related to ___.

Re-expressed in this form, Jameson's claim reads:

- "The value of <u>total money contributed</u>, compared by <u>candidate</u> (Starrett or DesJarlais), is related to <u>the type of source</u> (in-state or out-of-state)."

The next question to ask is whether the available data can provide reliable measures of each of the things that went into the statement's blanks: total money contributed, the candidate who received each contribution, and the type of source. Fortunately, the answer is "yes." Among the variables in the dataset:

- The "Amount" variable, summed, can tell us the total money contributed.
- The "Recipient" variable can tell us which candidate, Starrett or DesJarlais, received each donation.
- The "Source Type" variable can tell us whether each contribution came from an in-state or out-of-state donor.

Let's plug these three variables into a pivot table and see what we can learn. Start by opening the pivot table dialog box the same way you learned to earlier: Click any cell in the data (we clicked Cell A1), then click "Insert," then click "PivotTable," then click "OK." Excel will open a new sheet on a tab labeled "Sheet1." The "PivotTable Fields" dialog box will be visible on the right, and an empty pivot table will be visible on the left. As for which variable to drag to which box: The results will be easiest to understand if you put the variable in the statement's first blank into the pivot table's "Values" box, the variable in the second blank into the pivot table's "Columns" box, and the variable in the third blank into the pivot table's "Rows" box. One way to remember what goes where is to match up the first letter of each information type from the statement with the first letter of each pivot table area's name. Specifically:

- Put the "<u>v</u>alue of" variable (Amount) in the pivot table's "<u>V</u>alues" box.
- Put the "<u>c</u>ompared by" variable (Recipient) in the "<u>C</u>olumns" box.
- Put the "<u>r</u>elated to" variable (Source Type) in the "<u>R</u>ows" box.

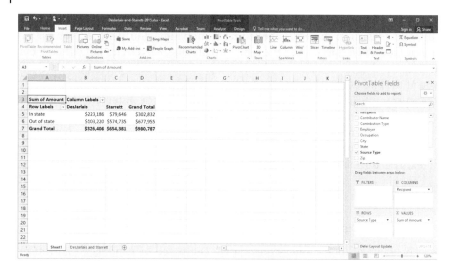

Figure 4.9 Using a PivotTable to investigate whether the value of total money contributed, compared by candidate (Starrett or DesJarlais), is related to the type of contribution (in-state or out-of-state). Drag "Amount" to the "Values" box, "Recipient" to the "Columns" box, and "Source Type" to the "Rows" box. Used with permission from Microsoft.

Figure 4.9 illustrates the setup and the resulting pivot table. To make the results easier to read, we took the additional step of formatting the table's values and dollar amounts, using the "Number format" button on the "Value Field Settings" window for the "Sum of amount" variable in the pivot table's "Values" box. We described the process in detail earlier.

The resulting pivot table shows that Starrett received quite a bit more out-of-state money than DesJarlais did. You can tell by picking one amount and comparing it with its counterpart in the same row. For example, Starrett took in $574,735 from donors outside Tennessee, compared to $103,220 for DesJarlais. Comparing values from the same row, by the way, is a good strategy for keeping your head straight while you are reading a pivot table, assuming you've followed our recommendation of putting the "compared by" variable in the "Columns" box and the "related to" variable in the "Rows" box. Looking at values in the same column can tell you about only one of the things you're comparing. For example, looking at the $223,186 and $103,220 figures in Column B can tell you that DesJarlais raised more money from in-state donors than from out-of-state donors, and that can be interesting. But it can't tell you how either amount compared to those for Starrett. Meanwhile, looking at diagonal figures is generally the least helpful of all approaches. For example, knowing that DesJarlais raised $223,186 from in-state donors (Cell B5) and that Starrett raised $574,735 from out-of-state donors (Cell C6) won't tell you much of anything about either of them or about how they compare. In fact, you'll probably just get confused.

As informative as these dollar amounts are, though, they don't provide enough information to conclude that out-of-state donors provided substantially more of Starrett's money than of DesJarlais' money. Starrett's out-of-state total is certainly larger than DesJarlais' out-of-state total, but Starrett's overall total is also larger than DesJarlais'. What we really need to know, here, is whether the percentage of Starrett's money that came from out-of-state sources is greater than the percentage of DesJarlais' money that came from out-of-state sources. One way to get those percentages would be to pull out a pocket calculator and divide each candidate's out-of-state total by his grand total. For example, punching in Starrett's $574,735 from out-of-state, then dividing by his $654,381 grand total would show that about 88 percent of Starrett's money (that is, 88 cents out of every dollar) came from out-of-state sources. Do the same calculation for DesJarlais, and you'll find that only 32 percent of his money, or 32 cents out of every dollar, came from out-of-state sources.

Excel can easily produce these percentages for you, though. To get it to do so:

- **Drag "Amount" into the "Values" box a second time.** A second "Sum of Amount" item, labeled "Sum of Amount2," will appear in the box.
- **Click the down-arrow beside "Sum of Amount2" in the "Values" box, and choose "Value field settings" on the pop-up window.** The "Value Field Settings" window will open.
- **Change the default "Sum of Amount2" to "Percent of Amount"** In the window's "Custom Name:" box. This isn't an essential step, but it will make the resulting table easier to understand.
- **Choose the "Show values as" tab.**
- **Choose "% of Column Total"** from the drop-down list under "Show values as," then **click "OK."**

The steps tell Excel to do the same thing you would have done with your pocket calculator: Divide DesJarlais' "In state" total by his "Grand Total," then do the same for his "Out of state" total, then do the same thing for Starrett's in-state and out-of-state totals, and even the overall in-state and out-of-state totals. Excel will display each result as a percentage in a column that Excel will insert next to the totals the percentages are based on. Excel will display them under the label you typed into the "Custom Name" box on the "Value Field Settings" window. Figure 4.10 shows the setup and the results.

What does the pivot table show now? Again, stick to the rule about picking one figure and comparing it to its counterpart in the same row. For example, you could observe that about 68 percent of DesJarlais' money came from in-state sources, compared to only about 12 percent of Starrett's money. Or you could observe that about 88 percent of Starrett's money came from out-of-state sources, compared to only about 32 percent of DesJarlais' money. Either finding – or both, if you like – indicates a relationship consistent with what Jameson, the DesJarlais spokesman, said about Starrett raising most of his

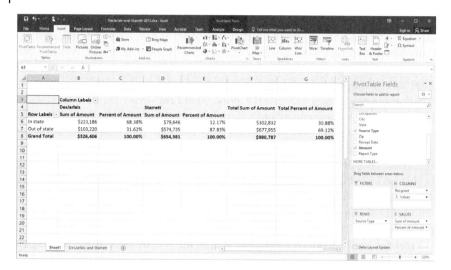

Figure 4.10 Calculating percentages. Drag "Amount" into the "Values" box a second time, click the down arrow beside it, and choose "Value Field Settings." Change "Custom Name" to "Percent of Amount," click the "Show Values As" tab, and choose "% of Column Total" from the drop-down list. Finish by clicking "OK." Used with permission from Microsoft.

money from out-of-state sources, and more, by comparison, than what DesJarlais raised from out-of-state sources.

So that's it, then? Jameson was right? Well, not so fast. Jameson's comment on Starrett's finances didn't draw attention to the fact that some contributions came from individual donors, while other contributions came from political action committees. Political action committees are often regional or national organizations, with headquarters in places other than Tennessee. And DesJarlais, having been in Congress for two terms by 2015, might have been more likely than political newcomer Starrett to attract money from such organizations. Donations from them wouldn't necessarily indicate the kind of home-grown support Jameson was suggesting his candidate, DesJarlais, had more of than Starrett. What we're talking about, here, is another "related to" variable, one we might want to consider in addition to the "In-state or out-of-state" characteristic we're already considering as a "related to" variable. The dataset's "Contribution Type" variable, which indicates whether each contribution came from an individual or a political action committee, offers exactly the information we need. Figure 4.11 shows what happens when you drag the "Contribution Type" variable into the "Rows" box and drop it above the "Source Type" variable. Placing "Contribution Type" above "Source Type" tells Excel to divide each candidate's contributions first according to whether they came from a committee or an individual, then, within each type of contribution, according to whether the donor resided inside the state or outside the state.

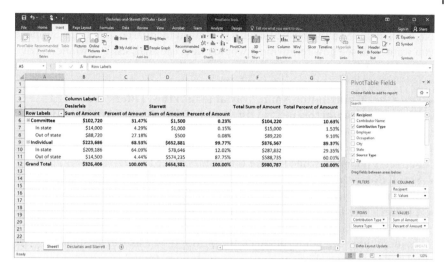

Figure 4.11 Adding "Contribution Type" as a "related to" variable to examine how in-state and out-of-state donations compared among donations from political action committees and among donations from individuals. Drag "Contribution Type" into the "Rows" box and drop it above the "Source Type" variable. Used with permission from Microsoft.

The results show that, among committee contributions only, the relationship reverses direction. DesJarlais raised far more committee money ($102,720, or 31 percent of his total) than did Starrett ($1,500, or 0.23 percent of his total). That, alone, puts a bit of a dent in Jameson's "man of the people" characterization of DesJarlais. Perhaps more notably, out-of-state money from committees accounted for more than a quarter (27 percent) of DesJarlais' total funds, compared to far less than 1 percent (0.08%) of Starrett's total funds.

Nothing about this more detailed analysis changes the fact that most of Starrett's money came from outside the state, while most of DesJarlais' money came from inside the state. But the analysis somewhat blunts the DesJarlais campaign's criticism of Starrett for taking in "huge sums of out-of-state money." Moreover, a look at committee contributions during 2015 to Tennessee's other members of the U.S. House of Representatives shows that all but one raised more out-of-state dollars than DesJarlais did, both in total money and percentage of money raised. If Starrett's heavy reliance on donors from outside the district raised questions about Starrett's support inside the district, perhaps DesJarlais' heavy reliance on donors from inside the district raised similar questions about DesJarlais' support outside the district. More broadly, the results demonstrate that you often can produce a more nuanced explanation of a relationship by examining how the relationship behaves under different conditions.

One last detail is worth mentioning, if only to demonstrate the flexibility of Excel's pivot table tool. We mentioned that Starrett had given his campaign

$23,400 out of his own pocket. Starrett was living in Tennessee, so that $23,400 has been included all along in Starrett's in-state individual contribution. Suppose you wanted to see how removing it would affect the analysis. You wouldn't have to set the entire pivot table up all over again. All you would have to do is:

- **Drag the "Contributor Name" variable into the "Filters" box.**
- **Click the down-arrow next to the "Contributor Name (All)" box.** The box will appear above the pivot table.
- **Check the "Select Multiple Items" box.** This step will allow you to exclude Starrett's donation while leaving the rest included.
- **Scroll down the list of names until you find "Starrett, Grant."** The list will be in alphabetical order, so finding Starrett's entry shouldn't take long.
- **Uncheck the box next to Starrett's name.** Note that there are donations from two other people with the last name "Starrett." They are probably family members. You could uncheck those too, if you like, given that they are related to Starrett. Both are out-of-state donors, though.
- **Click "OK."**

Figure 4.12 shows the results as well as the configured filter menu. Applying the filter raises Starrett's percentage of money Starrett received from individual out-of-state donors from 88 percent to 91 percent.

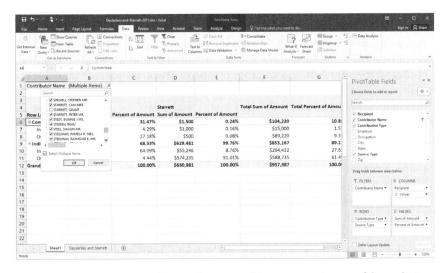

Figure 4.12 Filtering Starrett's $23,400 donation to his own campaign out of the analysis. Drag "Contributor Name" into the PivotTable's "Filters" box, click the down arrow next to the "Contributor Name" filter that will appear above the PivotTable, check the "Select Multiple Items" box, uncheck the box beside Starrett's name, and click "OK." Used with permission from Microsoft.

Remember, too, that you can double-click on any cell in the pivot table and get a look at the individual records the cell represents. For example, double-click on Cell B7, which contains the total for DesJarlais' contributions from in-state political action committees, and a new tab will open showing details about the eight donations. You'll see that two of the eight donations came from the National Health Corporation PAC, two from the Frog Jump PAC (yes, that's a real name), and two from the Advancement of Cotton Committee. The capability offers yet another way to explore the data quickly and efficiently using a pivot table.

Spotting the Absence of a Relationship

Relationships are evident in several of the figures above. But what, exactly, would an absence of relationship look like? A chief of police in Murfreesboro, Tennessee, recently asserted that installing red-light cameras had dramatically reduced crashes at the city's signalized intersections. The private company operating the cameras for the city had installed them at six of the city's busiest intersections. Sensors connected to the cameras at a camera-equipped intersection caused the cameras to photograph each vehicle that ran a red light at the intersection. If an officer who reviewed the photographs confirmed that the photograph showed a violation, the vehicle's owner would receive a traffic citation in the mail. In a letter to city council members who were considering whether to renew the city's contract with the company providing the cameras, the chief wrote:

"For the fiscal year of 2007–2008, there were 1,692 crashes reported at all signalized intersections in Murfreesboro. For the most recent fiscal year, 2013–2014, there were 797 crashes at all signalized intersections, a decrease of 895 crashes or 52.8 (percent decline). At the six intersections where red-light cameras would later be installed, there were 173 crashes in 2007–2008. In 2013–2014, there were 88 crashes at those intersections, a decrease of 85 crashes or 49.1 (percent decline.) Despite increased traffic counts on Murfreesboro streets, the addition of more signalized intersections and an increase in population, the success of this program is clear and supported by crash data" (Broden, 2014 November).

Expressed in our "Value of / compared by / related to" form, the chief's claim that installing the cameras reduced the number of crashes could be expressed this way:

- "The value of the number of crashes, compared by time period (before cameras/after cameras) is related to intersection type (intersections with cameras/without cameras)."

The raw data file that produced the chief's summary figures was not readily available. But a pivot table can be built manually from the summary figures given. Table 1 in Figure 4.13 shows the four figures the chief provided. As the chief said,

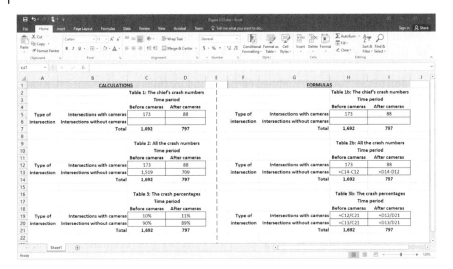

Figure 4.13 Manual construction of a PivotTable from the Murfreesboro police chief's vehicle accident statistics. Table 1 shows the number the chief provided. Table 2 shows the missing numbers, calculated using the Excel formulas shown in Table 2b. Table 3 shows the totals expressed as column percentages, using the Excel formulas shown in Table 3b. Used with permission from Microsoft.

1,692 crashes occurred at signalized intersections in fiscal year 2007–2008, before cameras had been installed at any of the city's intersections. Furthermore, 173 of these crashes happened at intersections that would later receive cameras. Meanwhile, 797 crashes took place at all signalized intersections in fiscal year 2013–2014, after six of the city's busiest intersections received cameras. Of these 797 crashes, 88 occurred at the six camera-monitored intersections.

The chief did not say how many crashes had occurred in each fiscal year at intersections that did not receive cameras. But it's easy to calculate the missing numbers for each year by subtracting the number of crashes at camera intersections from the total number of crashes. Table 2 shows the results of the calculations, and Table 2b shows the Excel formulas for performing the calculations. Having determined the counts for each cell in the pivot table, the final step is to translate them into column percentages. Table 3 shows the percentages, and Table 3b shows the Excel formulas for producing them.

If you compare the row percentages in Table 3, you'll see that the chief's assertion about the cameras' effectiveness at reducing crashes just doesn't hold up. The chief emphasized – correctly – that the number of crashes at camera intersections and at all intersections had dropped dramatically since the cameras had been installed. But Table 3's percentages show that he omitted a key fact: The share of crashes at camera intersections before and after the cameras arrived remained almost exactly the same. Before the cameras arrived, the six intersections destined to get cameras accounted for 10 percent of all crashes. After the cameras arrived, those six intersections accounted for 11 percent of all crashes. If anything, the percentage of crashes happening at camera-monitored intersections actually increased. Whatever prompted the considerable city-wide decline in crashes, there is no evidence in these numbers that it had any connection with the arrival of the red-light cameras.

Downloading Campaign Finance Data from the Federal Election Commission

This chapter can make you a hotshot at using pivot tables. It can't, unfortunately, make you a hotshot at analyzing campaign finance data downloaded directly from the FEC. The FEC's files are considerably larger and more complex than the simplified versions we've provided to help you try out the techniques we've shown. Our file of itemized individual contributions to DesJarlais contained nine fields. The full version from the FEC contains 77. It also contains less-than-obvious pitfalls, such as the fact that if you don't filter out records that contain an "x" in the dataset's "memo_code" field, you might end up erroneously counting some contributions twice. Accordingly, before you dive head first into wrangling FEC data yourself, you might see whether a site like OpenSecrets.org, maintained by the Center for Responsive Politics, has what you're looking for. Of course, if you use data from a third party in a published news story, you should cite the data's source.

If you want to work directly with FEC data, the FEC publishes a "Resources for journalists" page (www.fec.gov/press/resources-journalists/) and various guides for candidates and committees who must file reports with the FEC (www.fec.gov/help-candidates-and-committees/). The FEC's "Download bulk data" page also offers helpful data file descriptions www.fec.gov/data/browse-data/?tab=bulk-data).

Here's a step-by-step guide to downloading a candidate's individual contribution records:

- **Open a Web browser and head to the Federal Election Commission's home page.** The home page's URL is https://www.fec.gov/.
- **Navigate to the page that allows you to search for a candidate by his or her name.** The FEC Web site undergoes occasional redesigns. By the time you open this book, the path to the page might have changed. Presently, though, the page's URL is www.fec.gov/data/candidates/. To get there from the FEC's main page:
  - **Click "Campaign finance data" in the main page's top navigation menu.** The drop-down menu includes "Candidates," where you will find data for individual federal candidates, and "Committees," which offers data for federal candidates' fundraising committees as well as for political action committees. For this demonstration, choose the "Candidates"

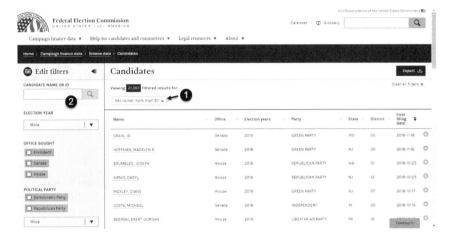

Figure 4.14 The Federal Election Commission's "Candidates" search page, available at www. fec.gov/. If you arrive by navigating from the FEC's home page, this page loads with a preset filter for candidates who have raised at least some money. You can remove the filter, if you like, by clicking the filter's "x" (1). To search for a candidate, type the candidate's name or committee ID into the search box (2).

option. A "Browse data" page will open that offers you links to search all candidates, just presidential candidates, just U.S. Senate candidates, or just U.S. House of Representative candidates.

- **Click "All candidates."** This option offers the broadest search. You should arrive at something like the page shown in Figure 4.14.

- Use the page's search tools to find your candidate's Financial Summary Page. Figure 4.15 shows the "Total raised" area of the Financial Summary Page for Congressman Scott DesJarlais, whose 2015 campaign donations we examined earlier in this chapter. Searching for a more common name than "DesJarlais" may return multiple records. You may have to scroll through them to find the one you want. If a candidate has run for two or more different offices, the search will return a result for each office. For example, searching for "Clinton, Hillary Rodham" will produce results both for her U.S. Senate campaigns and for her U.S. presidential campaigns.

- Click the total for the candidate's "Itemized individual contributions." A scrollable listing of individual donations to the candidate will open, showing each donation's contributor name, election cycle, contributor state, receipt date, and amount. Figure 4.16 shows the itemized individual records page for DesJarlais. By default, the FEC will show you only records that it has "Processed," meaning categorized and coded. If you prefer, you can click the "Raw" button on the left side of the screen and retrieve records including data that has not yet been coded and categorized by the FEC.

Figure 4.15 The "Total raised" area of the FEC's "Financial summary" page for Rep. Scott DesJarlais. Note the drop-down menu that lets you select data for earlier election cycles, (1) if the candidate has run for office previously. Many of the totals for different donation types (2) are clickable links that lead to individual-level donation records. Scroll down for similar summaries of types of spending, many of which, again, link to individual-level expense records.

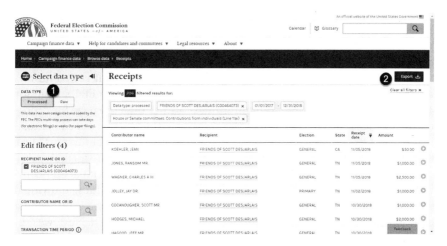

Figure 4.16 The first page of the FEC's individual donation records for DesJarlais. Note the "Processed / Raw" button (1), which toggles between including raw data not yet categorized and coded by the FEC. The "Export" button (2) will download all retrieved records as a comma-separated value file readable in Excel.

- **Click the "Export" button in the page's upper-right corner.** The site will prepare your file and show you a "Download" link.
- **Click the "Download" link.** Your browser will download the file in comma-separated value format.
- **Save the file to a subdirectory on your computer**. Be sure to make a note of where you put it.
- **Open the file using Microsoft Excel**. The process for opening the file in Excel will vary, depending on your computer's configuration. Often, your computer will automatically recognize the comma-separated value file as one that Excel can open. In such cases, simply double-clicking on the file will open the file in Excel. You can then save the file as an Excel file. If your computer does not automatically recognize the file as compatible with Excel, open Excel, click "File / Open," navigate to the subdirectory you saved the file to, and change "All Excel Files" to "All files," so that the downloaded file, with its.csv extension, will be available to click on. Double-click the file to open the file in Excel, then save the file in Excel format by clicking "File / Save As," navigating to where you want to save the file, and changing "Save as type" to "Excel Workbook (.xlsx)."

After you open the data file in Excel, you'll probably need to widen some of the columns so that their values will display in their entirety. Remember that you can adjust all column widths at once by clicking the upper-left corner of the data – the square above the "1" row label and to the left of the "A" column label – to highlight all of the data, hovering your mouse cursor over the border between any two column labels – like the "A" and "B" column labels – and double-clicking.

The same approach will allow you to download data about contributions to, and by, political action committees. Just navigate to the FEC's page for committees, www.fec.gov/data/committees/, rather than the page for candidates. The search function works the same way there, as do the "Financial summary" table, with its links to individual-level data, and the "Export" link that will let you download the data in comma-separated value format.

To make the combined file of DesJarlais' and Starrett's individual and committee contributions, we separately downloaded four .csv files: individual contributions to DesJarlais, committee contributions to DesJarlais, individual contributions to Starrett, and committee contributions to Starrett. Next, we created a blank Excel file, labeled the blank file's first column as "ID," and the blank file's second column as "Recipient." Then, we manually assembled the combined dataset by copying and pasting data from the four separate files, using the "Recipient" column to keep track of which candidate received each block of donations copied. Once the assembly was done, we used Excel's "Auto Fill" capability to add a unique ID number for each donation. Specifically, we:

- Typed "C1," short for "Contributor 1," in Cell A1, the first cell of the "ID" column.
- Typed "C2" in Cell A2, the ID column's second cell.

- Used the mouse to highlight Cell A1 and A2.
- Double-clicked the small square in the lower-right corner of Cell A2.

Follow these steps, and Excel will fill Cell A3 with "C3," A4 with "C4," and so on, until it encounters the blank row after the final donation record in the dataset. We used "C1" and "C2" instead of simply "1" and "2" so that Excel would automatically treat the ID codes as text rather than numbers. By default, Excel pivot table analyses try to count the frequency of text information but try to add numerical information. It is possible to override this default by telling Excel to format numbers as text, and also to format numbers stored as text into actual numbers that can be analyzed quantitatively. But for purposes of introducing pivot tables, we thought setting up the data to align with Excel's defaults would be best.

Another tip: You may have noticed that each cell in the "Source Type" column of our file combining contributions to DesJarlais and Starrett contains an Excel function that checks the contents of the adjacent cell in the "State" column and displays "In state" if it sees "TN" and "Out of state" if it doesn't. You may recall from Chapter 1 that a "function" in Excel is like a miniature program that performs a particular task. Here is the version of the function in Cell I2 in the first row of data:

$$=IF(H2 = "TN", "In state", "Out of state")$$

The function tells Excel to look next door in Cell H2, display "In state" if Cell H2 contains "TN," and display "Out of state" if Cell H2 contains anything else. You can modify and use this function any time you need to create a column of categories based on the information in some other column. We set up the function in Cell I2, then just copied it down the column. An alternative approach would be to fill the "Source Type" column with "Out of state," sort the entire dataset by "State," scroll down until you see all of the records that have "TN" in the "State" column, and, for just those records, replace the "Out of state" phrase with "In state" in the "Source Type" column.

Excel vs. Google Sheets

To continue a point we made at the opening of this chapter: The capabilities of Google Sheets and Microsoft Excel overlap considerably. We began this book with an emphasis on Google Sheets because the application's ubiquity, consistency across computer operating systems, and accessibility made it, to us, a good tool for introducing you to data analysis. The ease with which Google Sheets produces online data visualizations and Google Sheets' seamless integration with Google My Maps' map-making capabilities were pluses, too. But for many, and maybe most, data analysis tasks you will face, we suspect you will

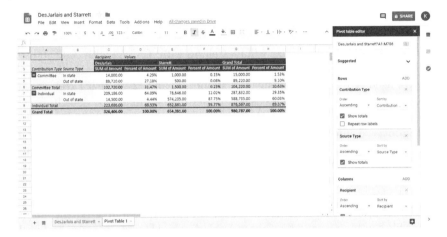

Figure 4.17 A Google Sheets PivotTable comparable to the Excel PivotTable shown in Figure 4.11. To insert a PivotTable in Google Sheets, click "Data / Pivot table …," then set up the table by using the "Add" buttons for the "Rows," "Columns," "Values" and "Filters" buttons in the "Pivot table editor" area on the right side of the screen. The interface isn't as smooth yet as Excel's drag-and-drop PivotTable editor, but it is rapidly improving. Google and the Google logo are registered trademarks of Google Inc., used with permission.

find Excel to be a more polished, more reliable tool. Still, many of our students tell us they prefer Google Sheets. The choice is yours, of course.

Figure 4.17, for example, shows the Google Sheets version of the Excel pivot table shown in Figure 4.11. To create a pivot table in Google Sheets, click a cell in the data you want to include in the pivot table, then choose "Data / PivotTable …," and use the pivot table editor's "Add" buttons to place variables in the "Rows," "Columns," "Values" and "Filters" boxes. Google Sheets' pivot table editor, the top part of which is visible toward the right side of Figure 4.17, presently lacks the Excel editor's "drag and drop" capabilities. But with a little experimentation, you can get it to produce the same results as an Excel pivot table. Remember, though, that the larger the dataset, the faster and more reliably Excel will perform compared to Google Sheets. The bottom line, here, isn't that you should pick one application or the other and use it exclusively. It's that you should be prepared to use whichever application is best suited for the task at hand.

Recap

You've seen in this chapter how to use Excel's powerful pivot table tool to analyze patterns in campaign finance data. We used data from the campaigns of two competitors in a local U.S. House of Representatives District primary campaign, but we've shown you how to download similar data for any federal candidate or candidates you like. You've also understood, we hope, how the pivot table tool's powerful features could be used in other types of analyses. We'll use it more in the next chapter, where we look at the record matching capabilities of Excel's VLOOKUP function.

References

Blake, Ken. 2016a. "Individual Contributions to Congressman Scott DesJarlais During 2015." *Demonstration Files.* Excel 2016 file. Accessed March 30, 2016. http://thedatareporter.com/demonstration-files/.

Blake, Ken. 2016b. "Individual Contributions to Congressman Scott DesJarlais and Candidate Grant Starrett during 2015." *Demonstration Files.* Excel 2016 file. Accessed March 30, 2016. http://thedatareporter.com/demonstration-files/.

Broden, Scott. 2014, November 12. "Police Chief Recommends Keeping Red-light Cameras." *Daily News Journal.* Accessed April 25, 2016. www.dnj.com/story/news/2014/11/12/police-chief-recommends-keeping-red-light-cameras/18948073/.

DesJarlais4TN. 2012. "Scott DesJarlais for Congress." *YouTube.* Accessed Jan. 3, 2018. www.youtube.com/watch?v=0EjOW9UDfsU.

Sher, Andy. (2016, January 30). "4th Congressional District's Grant Starrett and Scott DesJarlais Clash over Fundraising." *Chattanooga Times Free Press,* Politics State. Accessed April 5, 2016. www.timesfreepress.com/news/politics/state/story/2016/jan/30/4th-congressional-districts-starrett-and-desj/347505/.

5

Matching Records with Excel's VLOOKUP

Fairly soon after you start looking for news in data, you'll find yourself asking a question that you can answer only be combining information from two or more different sources. For example, a recent search of the Federal Election Commission's online database of campaign finance records retrieved 942 donations by federally registered political action committees to Republican Marsha Blackburn during her 2018 campaign to represent Tennessee in the United States Senate. A similar search retrieved 163 donations by federally registered political action committees to her opponent, Democrat Phil Bredesen (Blake, 2018). Blackburn, a seven-term member of Tennessee's delegation to the U.S. House of Representatives, won the election after capturing 55 percent of the statewide vote in the Nov. 6, 2018 election compared to 44 percent for Bredesen, a former mayor of Nashville, Tennessee, and also a former Tennessee governor.

Using the pivot table skills you learned in Chapter 4, you could aggregate Blackburn's donations by source, learn how much each PAC had given her in total, and sort the totals to learn which PACs had given her the most. You could do the same with PAC donations to Bredesen. You even could combine and compare them, just like, in the last chapter, we combined and compared records of donations to Tennessee Congressman Scott DesJarlais and his Republican primary rival, Grant Starrett. You would be stuck, however, the moment you asked, "Which PACs gave money to both candidates, to Blackburn exclusively, or to Bredesen exclusively?" It would be a newsworthy question. PACs often represent companies that are publicly traded, do business with the general public, or both. Tennessee voters, whom the hard-fought election had polarized, might want to know which company PACs had chosen a side in the election, and which side.

Arranging the combined data into a pivot table could get you close to the answer you would need. Figure 5.1 shows some results of a pivot table created from a combined file of PAC donations to Blackburn and Bredesen. To use the language of pivot table creation we introduced in Chapter 4, we examined how

Data Skills for Media Professionals: A Basic Guide, First Edition. Ken Blake and Jason Reineke.
© 2020 John Wiley & Sons, Inc. Published 2020 by John Wiley & Sons, Inc.

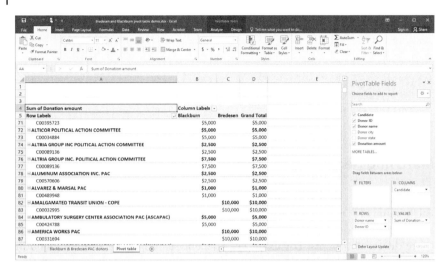

Figure 5.1 Data comparing donations to Blackburn and Bredesen, produced using PivotTable skills like those covered in Chapter 4. But note the duplicate entries for the Altria Group PAC in rows 73 through 76. The VLOOKUP function offers a better strategy. Used with permission from Microsoft.

the value of the amount of money given (represented by the "Donation amount" field), compared by candidate (Blackburn or Bredesen, represented by the "Candidate" field), is related to the donation source (represented by the "Donor ID" field). The "Donor ID" field is just an FEC-assigned code, like the "C00395723" code in Row 71 of Figure 5.1., so we added the "Donor name" field, which contains the PAC's name as reported by the candidate. The "C00395723" code, for example, corresponds to the Alticor Political Action Committee, which represents Amway Corporation, a U.S.-based direct sales company. Adding the field allows you to see from the table that PAC C00395723, the Alticor Political Action Committee, gave $5,000 to Blackburn and no money to Bredesen. Meanwhile, PAC C00489948, Amalgamated Transit Union – Cope," which represents the ATU-COPE transit worker union, gave $10,000 to Bredesen and no money to Blackburn.

There's a problem, though. PAC C00089136, the Altria Group PAC, appears twice. Look closely, and you'll realize that it appears twice because Blackburn's campaign, when recording the PAC's name, sometimes included and sometimes omitted the period after the "Inc." abbreviation. It's not much of a difference, but it's enough of a difference to make Excel treat the period and no-period entries as different donation sources. You could go through the records and standardize the PAC names, of course, but doing so could take a lot of time, and you'd always wonder whether you missed one. Alternatively, you could leave the "Donor name" out of the pivot table, because Donor IDs tend to be entered more consistently. But omitting the "Donor name" field from the table would leave your pivot table showing no PAC names, only cryptic ID codes.

Excel's VLOOKUP function offers a better, more flexible solution. This chapter will show you how to use it. The demonstration will use Excel 2016 running on a Windows 10 PC, but VLOOKUP will work the same way in Mac versions of Excel and also in Google Sheets. We're sticking with Excel, because the demonstration involves using pivot tables, and we like Excel's smooth "drag-and-drop" pivot table interface. To follow along with the demonstration, download the "Bredesen and Blackburn 2018.xlsx" file from the link in the references. As with the demonstration file in Chapter 4, these are real records. We imported them from the "Other committee contributions" area of each candidate's "Financial summary" page on the Federal Election Commission Web site, using the techniques described in Chapter 4. However, we filtered out records irrelevant to the demonstration, such as those flagged with an "X" in the original download's "memo_code" field to indicate that they should not be included in donation totals, and those for donations for committees with no federal ID number. We also deleted all but the columns most relevant to the demonstration and renamed several of the columns with labels we considered more descriptive than the original ones.

The file contains three tabs. The first two contain records of individual PAC donations to Bredesen and Blackburn and are named accordingly. Each contains the following fields:

- **Donor ID:** A 9-character alphanumeric code assigned to a committee by the Federal Election Commission. The original column name in the downloaded data was "contributor_id."
- **Donor name:** The name of the committee that donated the money, as recorded by the candidate. Originally "contributor_name."
- **Donor city:** The "city" portion of the donating committee's address. Originally "contributor_city."
- **Donor state:** The "state" portion of the donating committee's address. Originally "contributor_state."
- **Donation amount:** The amount of money donated, in dollars. Originally "contribution_receipt_amount."

Each row in the tabs represents a single donation, and many donors gave two or more separate donations. As a result, some rows represent separate donations from the same donor.

The third tab, labeled "FEC Committee List," contains official FEC information about each committee registered with the FEC during the 2018 election cycle. We downloaded the data from the FEC's "Committees" page. The original file contained information about each political committee, group or individual registered with the Federal Election Commission. We kept the following fields, retaining the original field names because we considered them both succinct and reasonably descriptive:

- **CMTE_ID:** Each committee's 9-character alphanumeric code assigned by the FEC. If a given committee donated to Bredesen or Blackburn, the code in the donation's "Donor ID" field will match the code in this field.
- **CMTE_NM:** Each committee's official name, according to the FEC. If a given committee donated to Bredesen or Blackburn, the name in the donation's "Donor name" field may, or may not, exactly match the name in this field. For example, the official FEC name for the Altria Group PAC, "ALTRIA GROUP, INC. POLITICAL ACTION COMMITTEE (ALTRIAPAC)," differs from the versions of the committee's name found in Bredesen's and Blackburn's records.
- **CMTE_CITY:** The "city" portion of the donating committee's address.
- **CMTE_STATE:** The "state" portion of the donating committee's address.

Overview

Figure 5.2 illustrates the results we'll be working to produce. Notice the three additional columns, E, F and G, on the "FEC Committee List" tab. If a row represents a donation to Bredesen, the row's cell in Column E shows the amount of the donation. If the row does not represent a donation to Bredesen,

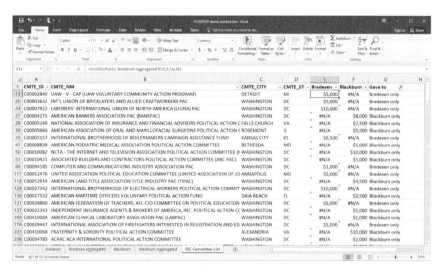

Figure 5.2 Result of using VLOOKUP functions to display donation amounts to Bredesen, Blackburn or both, in Columns E and F, paired with the PACs that contributed them. Column G categorizes each PAC based on whether it donated to one candidate, the other, both, or neither. The results are shown filtered for PACs that contributed exclusively to one or the other. Used with permission from Microsoft.

the cell contains, "#N/A." Column F does the same for donations to Blackburn. The cells in these columns contain VLOOKUP functions like the one in Cell E11, which is visible in the formula bar above Column B. The function reads:

- =VLOOKUP(A11,'Bredesen Aggregated'!D:E,2,FALSE)

We'll explain each part of the function later. The important thing to understand for now is that donation amounts showing in Columns E and F are visible because VLOOKUP functions are finding and retrieving those values from elsewhere in the spreadsheet and displaying them. When no donation occurred, VLOOKUP shows the "#N/A" code.

Each cell in Column G, meanwhile, is showing "Blackburn only" if the row's PAC donated exclusively to Blackburn, "Bredesen only" if the row's PAC donated exclusively to Bredesen," "Both" if the row's PAC donated to both Blackburn and Bredesen, and "Neither" if the row's PAC donated to neither Blackburn nor Bredesen. A filter applied to Column G is hiding all except "Bredesen only" and "Blackburn only" rows. You can tell the column is filtered, because a tiny funnel-shaped icon is visible to the right of the "Gave to" label in Column G, and the record count in the screen's lower-left corner reads, "621 of 12116 records found." We created the designations in Column G with a process involving systematically applying filters to Columns E and F.

Producing the results shown in Figure 5.2 involves three steps, each of which we will describe in detail:

- Aggregating each candidate's donations by source, using a pivot table.
- Creating the VLOOKUP functions.
- Using filters to create a classification column.

Aggregating each Candidate's Donations by Source

Essentially, a VLOOKUP function works like an information directory. Go to the online directory for members of Congress at www.congress.gov/members directory, for example, and type your representative's name into the "Members" search box. Assuming you accurately typed a real name, the directory will show you the representative's photo, home state, party, time in office, and a link to even more information, such as the representative's website, mailing address, phone number, and recently sponsored or cosponsored legislation. In a spreadsheet, a VLOOKUP function does the same thing. Suppose, for instance, that the spreadsheet included a tab that had a row for each member of Congress and columns like "Representative's name," "Web site URL," "Office phone number," "Mailing address," and so on. From anywhere in the spreadsheet, or even from anywhere in another open spreadsheet, a VLOOKUP command, if given a representative's name, could come to the tab and scan through the first column (the "V" in "VLOOKUP" stands for "vertical") until it found a name matching the name it had been given. Having found a match, it then could retrieve and display the web site URL, office phone number, mailing address, or any other information in any other cell from the matched name's row. In fact, that's exactly how we're going to get Excel to show, in Columns E and F of the "FEC Committee List" tab, how much, if anything, each committee donated to each candidate.

Imagine, though, how confused you would feel if you typed your representative's name into the online congressional directory and came up with a dozen different directory entries, each showing your representative's name but each containing different information. You'd have been expecting to find only one phone number – specifically, the right one – not a dozen different ones. Being a human, you might be smart enough to figure out which of the available options is the phone number that will actually put you in touch with your representative's office. But VLOOKUP isn't that smart. It will simply start at the top of the column of names, find the first one that matches, and go with it, regardless of whether it's the correct one. It won't even tell you that there were other matches available. About the only thing a VLOOKUP function can do besides bring you some piece of information from the first match it finds is tell you that it found no matches, which it does by showing "#N/A" in the cell you put it in.

It's perhaps easy to see, now, why you're asking for trouble if you use VLOOKUP on data that contains two or more potential matches for whatever information you send it in search of. And the "Bredesen" and "Blackburn" tabs of the demonstration file are both full of such trouble. On both tabs, each row of data represents a donation to a candidate by a PAC. As noted earlier, some PACs made two or more donations to the same candidate during the time period covered by the data. For example, the League of Conservation Voters Action Fund donated to Bredesen's campaign seven separate times between July 26, 2018 and Nov. 5, 2018, in amounts ranging from $37.67 to $4,000. A VLOOKUP command sent to the "Bredesen" tab to look for the Conservation Voters Action Fund row and return the amount of the PAC's donation to Bredesen won't find and report all seven, or even the sum of all seven. It will return the first amount it finds, then quit. And it will make the same mistake 43 more times, because 44 of the 108 PACs that donated to Bredesen donated twice or more. That's 41 percent. Blackburn's donors also frequently chose to write two or more smaller checks instead of one big one. Of her 541 donor PACs, 244, or 45 percent, donated twice or more.

There's a practical way to solve this problem, though: Use pivot tables. We told you those things would come in handy. Click the demonstration file's "Bredesen" tab, then do this:

- **Click on Cell A1.**
- **Click "Insert / PivotTable."** The "Create PivotTable" window will open. Leave the "New Worksheet" radio button selected.

- **Click "OK."** Excel will open a new tab, you will see the "PivotTable Fields" area on the right side of the screen.
- **Drag the "Donor ID" field into the "Rows" box in the "PivotTable Fields" area.** Doing so will add one row per donor ID number to the spreadsheet's Column A.
- **Drag the "Donor amount" field to the "Values" box.** The "Donor amount" field contains numbers – specifically, donation amounts in dollars – so Excel will automatically select "Sum" as the aggregation method and add the resulting totals to Column B, one per Donor ID.
- **Copy the pivot table's data, click Cell D2, and paste the data as "values."** Pasting data as "values" discards any formatting and functions from the original cells and pastes only the values themselves. The point of this step is to get the aggregated donation totals out of the pivot table and into a couple of columns as just plain, unformatted data. Writing formulas and functions that reference data within a pivot table can produce unexpected results. Also, it will be helpful, on an upcoming step, to have the data begin in Row 1 instead of in Row 3, which is where Excel puts pivot tables by default.
  To paste the data as values:
  – Use your mouse to highlight all of the data in the pivot table. That should be all of the data from Cell A3 to Cell B112.
  – Right click, and choose "Copy." Or press Ctrl/c or Cmd/c on your keyboard.
  – Right click on Cell D1.
  – On the pop-up menu, choose the icon under "Paste options" that looks like a tiny clipboard with a "123" across its lower-right corner. Alternatively, you can click on "Paste Special …" under the pop-up window's "Paste Options …" heading, click the radio button next to "Values" on the "Paste Special" window, and click "OK."
- **Double-click on the tab's "Sheet1" name, change it to something more descriptive, and press "Enter."** We changed the tab's name to "Bredesen Aggregated," indicating that the figures represent Bredesen's donation amounts, aggregated by the Donor ID field. Another way to rename a tab is to right click on the tab's name and choose "Rename" from the pop-up menu.
- **Click the "Bredesen Aggregated" tab and drag it to the first position after the "Bredesen" tab.** This step is optional. It just makes sense to us for the "Bredesen Aggregated" tab to appear after the tab containing the data it came from.

When you have finished, click on the "Blackburn" tab and repeat the process there. Figure 5.3 shows the results of the process on the "Blackburn Aggregated" tab, with the "Bredesen Aggregated" tab already produced. Essentially, you've turned Columns D and E of the "Blackburn Aggregated" tab into a simple directory that you can use a VLOOKUP function to search. In the next section, you'll see how to give a VLOOKUP function a PAC's ID number, send the

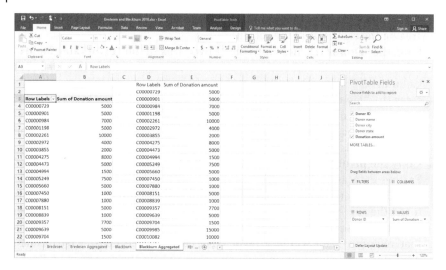

Figure 5.3 Aggregating Blackburn's donations by Donor ID and pasting the results as values. The PivotTable Fields area to the right shows the correct PivotTable setup. The PivotTable's data have been pasted as values starting in Cell D1. Bredesen's donations have already been similarly aggregated and pasted on the "Bredesen Aggregated" tab. Used with permission from Microsoft.

function to the "Blackburn Aggregated" tab, have it look for a matching ID number in the directory's first column, Column D, and, if it finds a match there, return with the donation total from the directory's second column, Column E. You'll be able to do the same thing with Columns D and E on the "Bredesen Aggregated" tab. The next section will show you how to tell a VLOOKUP function where to search and what to bring back.

Using VLOOKUP

Switch to the "FEC Committee List" tab and look at Row 2, which contains information about the tab's first PAC, C00659441, more commonly known as the Jason Ortitay for Congress PAC, based in Canonsburg, Pennsylvania. What you want to know, here, is whether this PAC gave money to Bredesen and, if so, how much. In a moment, we'll put a VLOOKUP function in Cell E2 that will find out for us. Then we'll copy it down the column to learn the same things about each of the other PACs on the list. Then we'll do the same thing for Blackburn. First, though, let's examine the parts of a VLOOKUP function and learn what each part does.

Here's the general form of a VLOOKUP function:

- =VLOOKUP(lookup_value, table_array, col_index_num, [range_lookup])

And here's the specific version of the function that, if put in Cell E2 of the "FEC Committee List" tab, will determine whether, and how much, Ortitay's PAC donated to Bredesen:

- =VLOOKUP(A2,'Bredesen Aggregated'!D:E,2,FALSE)

Both probably look like gobbledygook to you, unless you've had at least a little computer programming experience. Don't worry. We'll explain. Also, while you could type the function into your spreadsheet manually, it's a lot easier to build it through a combination of typing and using your mouse. We'll show you how in a moment.

- The "**=VLOOKUP**" part is just the name of the function, "VLOOKUP," preceded by a " = " symbol that tells Excel to read "VLOOKUP" as instructions to be followed. Type "VLOOKUP" without the " = " in front of it into a cell, and Excel, thinking that "VLOOKUP" is just text you want displayed in the cell, will do exactly that.
- The "(" symbol tells Excel that you're about to give it each piece of information that a VLOOKUP function requires, with a comma separating each piece of information.
- The "**lookup_value**" is the first piece of required information. It's the cell address of whatever text or value you want Excel to use when looking for a matching value in the directory's first column. In the version that will search for a donation to Bredesen from the Ortitay PAC, the "lookup_value" would need to be "A2," the location of the Ortitay PAC's ID number.
- The "**table_array**" is the location of all the cells in whatever directory you want the VLOOKUP function to search. In our Ortitay/Bredesen version, the table array is "'Bredesen Aggregated'!D:E," which is Excel speak for "Go to the 'Bredesen Aggregated' tab and look at Columns D through E."
- The "**col_index_num**" indicates which column of the directory you want Excel to bring information back from if it finds a match for the "lookup_value" in the directory's first column. The Ortitay/Bredesen version specifies "2" as the column index number, because the information we want to retrieve, the donation amount, is in the directory's second column, Column E. You might expect VLOOKUP to ask for the specific column letter, like "Column E." But it doesn't work that way. Incidentally, directories can have as many columns of information as you need. Ours just happens to have only two.
- The "**range_lookup**" which is basically a word, either "true" or "false" (without the quote marks) that tells Excel whether you want it to keep searching until it finds an exact match for "lookup_value" or search only until it finds an approximate match. In the Ortitay/Bredesen version, we specified the range_lookup value as "false" (again, without the quotes). We recommend always telling Excel to find an exact match. If you ever want to search for an

approximate match for some reason, type "false" instead. The "[" and "]" characters enclosing range_lookup in the function's general form mean that you can omit the range_lookup specification if you want to. But if you omit it, Excel will assume you meant to type "true" and settle, as a result, for approximate matches. That could mess up your analysis if you intended Excel to look for exact matches, so watch out.

Now that you have at least an idea of what each part of the function is doing, let's look at how to let Excel help you create the Ortitay/Bredesen version of the function and put it in Cell E2 of the "FEC Committee List" tab:

- **Start typing "=VLOOKUP(" into Cell E2.** Don't include the quote marks, and don't press "Enter" yet. Once you've typed the "(" character, you can start using your mouse and let Excel handle most of the remaining typing for you.
- **Click on Cell A2.** Note that, up in the formula bar, Excel has added the cell address, "A2," to the function for you.
- **Type a comma.** Doing so tells Excel you're done providing the "lookup_ value" information and are ready to specify the next required piece of information, the "table_array."
- **Click the "Bredesen Aggregated" tab.** Remember: This tab contains the directory you want the VLOOKUP function to search. Note Excel has added the tab's name, "Bredesen Aggregated," to the function.
- **Click on the "D" of Column D and keep holding down the mouse button.** If you've clicked in the right place, a moving, dotted line will surround Column D. Column D, of course, is the first column of the directory, the one with the PAC ID numbers.
- **Drag your mouse right until the highlighting includes Column E.** Excel will add the "table_array" information to the function for you: "!D:E," meaning "everything in Column D, and on through everything in Column E." If at some future time you are working with a directory that has more than two columns, highlight every column in the directory, or at least the first column, the column you want to retrieve information from, and all columns in between the two.
- **Release the mouse, then type another comma.** The comma, again, signals that you're moving on to the next required piece of information, "col_index_num."
- **Type "2," with the comma, but without the quote marks.** The "2" tells the function to retrieve the information from the directory's second column from the left, the one containing the donation amount, if it finds a value in the first column, the column of donor ID numbers, that matches the value in the cell address you specified for the "lookup_value" part of the function. Adding the comma, meanwhile, tells Excel you're ready to specify the function's final part, the "range_lookup" value.

- **Type "false," without the quote marks, and without the comma.** Recall that the "false" range value tells Excel to search the directory's first column for an exact, rather than an approximate, match to the information specified by the "lookup_value" part of the function.
- **Press the "Enter" key on the keyboard.** Technically, you should have finished the function by typing a ")" before pressing "Enter." But if you go ahead and press "Enter," Excel will add the ")" for you without complaining in the slightest.

After all of that typing and clicking, you'll get an anticlimactic "#N/A" in Cell E2, because, alas, Ortitay, being, at the time, a Republican state legislator representing a district in the Pittsburgh area of Pennsylvania, opted not to donate to the campaign of a Democratic candidate for U.S. Senate. But here comes the possibly exciting part: Find the small, green square in the lower-right corner of Cell E2, and double-click on it. Excel will copy your VLOOKUP function to each of the remaining rows in Column E, and the function in Row 11 will spot the first match: A $5,000 donation total to Bredesen from UAW - V - CAP (UAW VOLUNTARY COMMUNITY ACTION PROGRAM). The PAC represents the UAW, which is short for the International Union, United Automobile, Aerospace and Agricultural Implement Workers of America. Scroll down the column, and you'll see still more matches. For every row that produced no match, meanwhile, Column E will display a "#N/A" message.

You might take a moment to marvel at how much time and headache you just saved yourself. There were 108 donation totals on the "Bredesen Aggregated" tab. Assuming you could check them all against the FEC Committee List and record the results at a rate of two per minute, the job would take you close to an hour of tedious, eye-crossing work. You would make mistakes; the only question is how many. And the next item on your agenda would be repeating the task for each of Blackburn's considerably longer list of 541 donation totals. As you can see, the VLOOKUP function did the work perfectly, and in a fraction of a second. It probably took you a while to get the function set up, but you'll get faster with practice.

Speaking of practice, do it again, but this time for Blackburn. This time, we'll skip all the explanatory asides, and perhaps you'll see that it's really not that complex of a process. Figure 5.4 shows the process about half way through, right after dragging across Columns D and E, and right before typing a comma and adding "2" as the column index number. Starting, again, on the "FEC Committee List" tab:

- In Cell F1, type: Blackburn
- In Cell F2, type: =vlookup(
- Click Cell A2
- Type a comma
- Click the "Blackburn Aggregated" tab
- Drag across Columns D and E

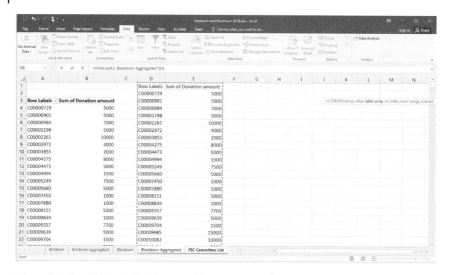

Figure 5.4 Specifying the "table_range" for a VLOOKUP function that will search Blackburn's aggregated donation amounts by the PAC ID numbers in Column D and return the Column E donation total if the function finds a matching record. The figure shows the middle of the process, right after specifying the table range and right before typing a comma and then specifying the column index number. Used with permission from Microsoft.

- Type a comma
- Type: 2
- Type another comma
- Type: false
- Press "Enter"
- Copy the function down the column

Not too bad, right? Ortitay's PAC didn't donate to Blackburn, either, so a "#N/A" will show in cell F2. But you'll get a hit in Row 27, which will show that the AMERICAN BANKERS ASSOCIATION PAC (BANKPAC) gave Blackburn a total of $8,000 and gave Bredesen exactly nothing. You'll see more hits further down – many more, in fact, seeing as Blackburn received more PAC donations than Bredesen did, both in terms of the number of donations and the donation total.

Your journalistic senses might be starting to buzz at this point. Bredesen seems to have attracted a lot of donations from labor interests, specifically unions. Blackburn, at least so far, has attracted none. Instead, her donors seem to represent business interests. In fact, why keep looking around all those "#N/A" codes when you know how to use filters? Try this:

- **Click Data / Filter.** Excel will put a down-pointing arrow at the top of each column. The "Filter" button looks like a big funnel.

- **Click the arrow next the "Bredesen" in Column E.** Excel will open a menu. Scroll down until you see "#N/A."
- **Uncheck the box next to "#N/A" and click "OK."**

Excel will hide each of Bredesen's "#N/A" rows, letting you easily see not only which PACs donated to Bredesen but also which ones donated to Blackburn as well. In Row 287, for example, you'll see that the PAC for SunTrust Bank, a popular banking choice among Tennessee voters, gave $1,000 to Bredesen but also donated to Blackburn and, interestingly, gave Blackburn more: $5,000. Ruby-red Republican voters in Brentwood, Tennessee, where SunTrust's Web site (SunTrust, 2019) says the company has three branches, might be upset that SunTrust's PAC gave any money at all to Bredesen. But Democrats just north of Brentwood in deep-blue Nashville, where SunTrust maintains 18 branches, might be equally dismayed at the SunTrust PAC's apparent favoritism toward Blackburn. If you click the down arrow next to Blackburn's name and uncheck the box next to "#N/A" in her filter, you'll be left with a filtered list of the 11 PACS that gave money to both Bredesen and Blackburn. Two of them, the PACs for Morgan Stanley and Unaka Company, gave the two candidates exactly equal amounts of money. The rest, though, favored one or the other, even if by only $200, as in the case of the PAC for LifePoint Health, Inc. Of course, we collected these data before the FEC had finished processing end-of-year campaign finance reports from either Bredesen or Blackburn. It is possible that SunTrust's PAC, and perhaps others, balanced their donations by the end of the election cycle, or at least got them closer to balancing.

Using Filters to Create a Classification Column

Applying filters to Bredesen's and Blackburn's donation amounts more systematically will allow you to produce a handy "classification column" in Column G indicating whether each PAC donated exclusively to Bredesen, exclusively to Blackburn, to both, or to neither. Learn the technique for making the column, and you'll be able to apply it any time you need to classify records into two or more categories.

It is possible to perform such classification with an "=IF" function. You might remember that we used an "=IF" function in Chapter 4 to distinguish between in-state and out-of-state donors to the campaigns of Scott DesJarlais and Grant Starrett, rivals in the 2016 Republican primary for Tennessee's Fourth Congressional District. Excel's relatively new =IFS function, which also works in Google Sheets, allows you to specify three or more alternatives. But for all their flexibility, these functions could become more trouble than they're worth if you tried to use them to classify the PACs in the way we're describing. Here's a better way:

- Click the big, funnel-shaped "Filter" button on the "Data" menu to remove all filters. Make sure the arrows disappear from the top of the columns.

- Type "Gave to" in Cell G1. The text will serve as the categorization column's label.
- Type "Unclassified" into Cell G2 and press "Enter." You can use some word other than "Unclassified," if you like, even something as simple as a single "X." The point is to choose something that won't be a part of the category names you'll be using in the column.
- Click the funnel-shaped "Filter" button. The filter arrows at the top of each column should reappear.
- Click the filter arrow at the top of Bredesen's column, Column E. A list of donation amounts in the column will appear. Scroll down until you see the "#N/A" item at the bottom of the list.
- Uncheck the box next to the "#N/A" item. You're telling Excel to hide all rows that have "#N/A" in the "Bredesen" column. Figure 5.5 shows the process at this step.
- Click OK. Doing so will apply the filter. Scroll down, and you'll see that Bredesen's column contains only numbers and no "#N/A" items.
- Click the filter arrow for Blackburn's column. That would be Column F.
- Uncheck the filter menu's "Select all" box. All the check marks on the filter menu will disappear.
- Check the "#N/A" item's box. Then click OK.

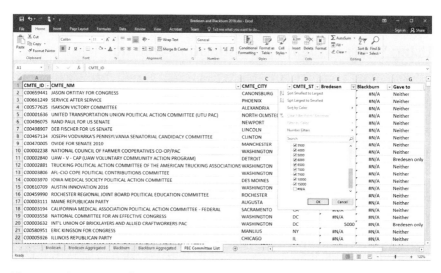

Figure 5.5 Getting started on creating the classification column. The filter for Bredesen's column is open, and the check beside the "#N/A" item has been removed. Clicking "OK" will hide all PACs that gave Bredesen no money. Simultaneously setting a filter for the Blackburn column that shows only "#N/A" records will display all PACs that donated exclusively to Bredesen. Used with permission from Microsoft.

You should be looking at 97 rows that have both an amount in Bredesen's column and "#N/A" in Blackburn's column. The first will be the $5,000 UAW-V-VCAP PAC donation we looked at earlier. In other words, these are PACs that gave money to Bredesen only. To categorize them as such, click on the first cell in the "Gave to" column, Column G, and type "Bredesen only." Then, copy the phrase "Bredesen only" to each of the other cells showing in the column. You can do so by double clicking on the small square in the lower-right corner of the first "Bredesen only" cell.

Next, clear all the filters by clicking the funnel-shaped "Filter" button. Then click the button again to make the filter arrows reappear. Now, specify one of the remaining three classifications. If you clear and reset the filters each time (which we highly recommend), the order in which you specify the classifications doesn't matter. The important thing is to make sure you cover all possible classifications. This time, let's set the filters (again) to display the 11 PACS that donated to both Bredesen and Blackburn. Set each candidate's donation column filter to show all amounts but hide all "#N/A" items, and you'll be looking at the 11 PACS that donated to both candidates. Over in the "Gave to" column, type "Both" into the column's first cell and copy it into the remaining 10 cells.

Clear and reset the filters, then set Bredesen's column to show only "#N/A" records and Blackburn's to show everything except "#N/A" records. Mark the selected records as "Blackburn only" in the "Gave to" category. Finally, clear and reset the filters a final time, set both Bredesen's and Blackburn's columns to show only "#N/A" entries, and mark all displayed records as "Neither" in the "Gave to" column.

Did you get everything covered? Better check. To do so, clear and reset the filters, then click the filter arrow for the "Gave to" column. There should be no "Unfiltered" records available. If there are, you somehow missed them when you were filtering and categorizing the PACs. Click the box next to "Unfiltered," and show those records so you can figure out what happened, or at least categorize them correctly.

VLOOKUP Pitfalls

You'll find VLOOKUP a useful and reliable tool, but only if you know its limitations. We've mentioned a few of them already. For example, the column you want to match has to be the first column on the left in whatever range of data you want VLOOKUP to pull data from. That doesn't mean it always has to be Column A. In the example above, we pulled data from two ranges, each of which started in Column D of their spreadsheet tabs.

Also, remember that, unless you have a clear, thoroughly tested reason for doing otherwise, always specify the "range_lookup" part of you VLOOKUP functions as "false," which directs VLOOKUP to find an exact match. If you forget to do so, VLOOKUP will default to "true," meaning VLOOKUP will settle for an approximate match. In particular, Excel will assume you have sorted your data by the matching column. It will compare the lookup value to the values in the lookup column, starting at the top, until it finds a value that exceeds the lookup value you gave it. The moment it does, it will stop in its tracks and pull its information from the previous row. This method has utility in some situations, but if you turn it loose in your data without knowing that's what it's going to do, disastrous mismatches could result.

To remind you of another problem we've already mentioned: There should be no duplicate values in the first column of the lookup range you specify in the VLOOKUP function's second argument. If there are, VLOOKUP simply won't see them, because it will stop at the first match it comes to. That's why, in this chapter's example, we aggregated Bredesen's and Blackburn's donation totals by PAC before using the VLOOKUP function.

As for potential problems we haven't yet mentioned: Avoid adding columns of data to a range of columns you've specified in the "table_array" portion of some earlier VLOOKUP function. If, somewhere earlier in your analysis, you told Excel to scan the first five columns on Tab 1 and give you a value from the third column, Excel will do that without complaint or error right up until you go back and stick a new column between the range's first and second ones. When you do, that third column your original VLOOKUP function was pulling data from will shift to the right and become the fourth column, and your VLOOKUP function will start pulling results from what used to be the second column and has now become the third column.

A fourth tip: Make sure you count the lookup range's columns correctly when you're telling your VLOOKUP function which one to pull data from. Each of our example VLOOKUP functions pulled from a directory of only two columns, so it wasn't difficult to remember that the "col_index_no" value was "2." But if the directory you're pulling from contains many columns, it's easy to miscount.

The last potential problem we'll talk about involves numbers that have been stored as text. Suppose you had employee IDs and six months' worth of weekly overtime amounts in one worksheet, had employee IDs and names in another worksheet, and wanted to use VLOOKUP to match each ID from the first sheet with an ID on the second sheet and retrieve the associated name from the second sheet. You program the VLOOKUP as needed but get a column of solid "#N/A" indicators. What happened? One possibility is that the employee IDs have been stored as numbers on one worksheet and as text on the other. If you send VLOOKUP searching for the number 1234567, but all it finds is the text string 1234567, it won't consider the two a match. A tip-off, here, can be the fact that, by default, Excel left-aligns text but right-aligns numbers. So, if you see a column of numbers in which the numbers are all hugging the left side of their cells, they might have been stored as text. A solution is to turn the numbers-as-text back into numbers-as-numbers. In Excel, you can highlight the column, click "Data / Text to Columns," which opens Step 1 of the "Convert Text to Columns Wizard." You don't need the remaining steps if all you're doing is converting text to numbers, so just click the "Finish" button.

Recap

You've seen in this chapter how to combine data from two or more different sources using Excel's VLOOKUP function. You've also learned a technique for using filters to categorize rows based on the contents of two or more different columns.

Our example dealt with data more or less designed to be put together. Some outstanding journalism can be done, though, by using VLOOKUP to put together data that shouldn't go together. For example, suppose you got your hands on a spreadsheet of delinquent local parking tickets, with columns for the amount of each unpaid ticket plus the name and address of the person cited. Now suppose you also happened to have a separate spreadsheet including the name and address of each city employee. There ought to be no overlap between those two spreadsheets. City employees, especially, ought to pay their parking tickets promptly, and the city should have little trouble collecting overdue parking fines from the people whose paychecks it writes. Nonetheless, VLOOKUP functions could help you look for matches between the two spreadsheets.

In short, VLOOKUP offers powerful capabilities for putting together datasets that nobody thought to put together for you, or that at least some people are hoping nobody will ever put together. We hope you enjoy knowing how to use it.

References

Blake, Ken. 2018. "Committee Contributions to Phil Bredesen and Marsha Blackburn During the 2018 U.S. Senate Election in Tennessee." *Demonstration Files*. Accessed Jan. 5, 2019. http://thedatareporter.com/demonstration-files/.

SunTrust. "Tennessee Branches." Accessed Jan. 5, 2019. www.suntrust.com/branch/tn.

6

Google Sheets and Inferential Statistics

Many media professionals who eventually see their work published in some form on the web or social media live by the mantra "don't read the comments." While we certainly understand the desire to avoid some of the less affirming feedback that may come from the audience, we have to admit that we haven't always adhered to this rule when it comes to our work.

For more than two decades, we conducted a public opinion poll of people in the state where we work, Tennessee, twice each year. We were always happy to see our work picked up and reported by news media outlets. But there were almost always people who were unhappy with the results in some way and who wrote things in the comments section along the lines of, "Well, they didn't ask me!" Part of the implication of a comment like this one is that the views of this particular person were not represented in our findings. We can probably take such a person at her or his word, because we didn't ask our questions of everyone in the state of Tennessee, which, at the time, had a *population* of about 6.5 million people; in fact, only a *sample* of about 600 people typically responded to our poll.

However, because of the methods we used, we knew some things about our data that made claims about people in the state as a whole possible. Even if the commenter wasn't a respondent to our poll, she or he had at least the same chance as everyone else of being a participant. We can also say with a high degree of certainty that our samples were pretty good representations of the population of the state. Furthermore, we can have a high degree of confidence that the relationships between variables in the data we collected from those samples were probably pretty similar to the relationships between those variables in the population.

This knowledge comes from sampling and inferential statistics. In this chapter, we'll tell you about some analyses you can conduct when dealing with a sample, and how you can make confident claims about the population the sample represents by analyzing data from the sample.

Data Skills for Media Professionals: A Basic Guide, First Edition. Ken Blake and Jason Reineke.
© 2020 John Wiley & Sons, Inc. Published 2020 by John Wiley & Sons, Inc.

Sampling and Assumptions of Inferential Statistics

This section of the chapter discusses some of the principles that allow us to be confident that inferential statistics calculated from a random sample of a population are a valid representation of the same quantities in the population as a whole. This does get a little abstract, so if you are more interested in the *how to* of analysis, you can take our word for it that analyses conducted using these techniques are representative, and you can move on to the next section, where we show you how to analyze some data. We think it is important to include this information, though, so you can understand *why* we can make the claims that we do about what comes next.

Inferential statistics, as the name and example at the beginning of the chapter suggest, allow us to infer things about a population from observations taken from a sample of that population. Our example commenter implicitly questioned such an inference. Essentially, he asked how we could claim to know something about everybody in the state if he lived here and we didn't ask him about it?

Random samples of greater size allow us to make increasingly accurate inferences about the population they are drawn from. Randomness is defined, in the context of sampling, as a means of selecting units from a population such that each unit has an equal probability of selection. This means that with a poll like ours, any person who lives in Tennessee, is 18 years of age or older, and has access to a cell or "landline" telephone (or both) has the same chance of being selected as any other person who meets the same criteria. For ethical and methodological reasons, our samples always excluded people who didn't live in the state, were under 18 years old, or who didn't have telephones. But among those who did live in the state, were over 18, and did have telephones, no individual had a greater or lesser chance of being contacted by us than any other. There have been many academic papers, chapters, and books written on the processes and principles of random sampling. You can find some examples in the references at the end of this chapter. We don't want to get bogged down in that discussion here. Suffice it to say that for us to be sufficiently confident that inferential statistics are valid representations of a population, they have to be calculated from a sufficiently large, random sample of that population. It is important to understand how the population is defined, and that the sample was collected in a random manner that gives every unit of that population the same chance of being selected.

At this point, if not before, you are probably wondering how big a random sample has to be to represent a population. We wish there were a single, simple answer to this question, but there is not. Larger random samples represent populations better. But the returns, in terms of better representation, of larger and larger random samples diminish. In other words, we can expend a lot of time, energy, and money to collect a larger random sample, but not have much to show for it. There are a number of freely-available online resources that will allow you to calculate an appropriate random sample size or, conversely, determine how representative a random sample is of the population it was selected from if that information is not provided to you by the source of the data, or if for some reason you feel the need to verify a claim of representativeness made by the source of the data. We've included a couple of these calculators in the references at the end of this chapter.

Adequate sample size depends on how much error you are willing to tolerate in the match between observations of your random sample and the same observations if they were of the population as a whole. Statisticians have mathematically established that this random sampling error can be accurately quantified using two numbers. The first is the confidence level, which tells you how often unobserved population measures will fall within the second, the margin of error, of your observed sample measure. A confidence level is easy to understand. It is just a percentage. The most commonly accepted and used confidence level is 95 percent, meaning that 95 percent of the population observations would be within the margin of error of our sample observation. Conversely, though, this means we also know that 5 percent of population observations will be outside of the margin of error of the sample observations. The problem is that we don't know which 5 percent of our sample observations are unacceptably different from the population. We accept this as a risk of sampling rather than expending the additional time, effort, and money necessary to observe the entire population (a census).

The margin of error is the amount of discrepancy we are willing to accept between our sample observations and population observations. Usually we are willing to accept somewhere between ±2 percent and ±5 percent margin of error when it is quantified as a percentage. The "±" ("plus or minus") is important, because it means that the observation in the population will be within the margin of error *above* or *below* the observation in the sample 95 percent (the confidence level) of the time. So, for example, if we observe that 70 percent of the Tennesseans sampled in our poll say that they approve of the job the governor is doing, and if we have a ±4 percent margin of error at the 95 percent confidence level, that means we expect the percentage of the Tennessee population who say they approve of the governor to be between 66 percent and 74 percent. It also means that if we conducted a hundred data collections like this one, the population percentage would be within ±4 percentage points of the percentage observed in the sample 95 times out of 100.

However, despite the familiarity of percentages, many statistics aren't usually quantified that way. And as you may have discerned already, using two numbers to quantify the confidence we have in our results can get a little confusing. Most of us would probably prefer a single metric that we can say "yea" or "nay" with when it comes to deciding whether our observation is valid or not. Fortunately, there is such a metric. All substantive inferential *test statistics*, which in some way quantify the strength of relationship between two variables in data from a random sample, have an associated statistic called a *probability value*, or p-value, or "p" for short. One of the most respected statisticians in our field, Andrew F. Hayes, defines a p-value as "…the probability of the obtained result or one even more discrepant from the null hypothesis than what we found if the null hypothesis is in fact true" (Hayes, 2005, p. 163). This sounds complicated and scientific, but heuristically, a p-value is a very easy statistical tool to use. The "null hypothesis," as Hayes puts it, is simply the proposition, for our purposes anyway, that two variables are not related in the population. Thus the p-value tells us how probable it is that we would get an observation as strongly, or more strongly, indicative of a relationship between two variables in the data from our random sample if there is no relationship between those variables in the population.

Similar to the decisions we make about the confidence level and margin of error, we decide how much of a probability we are willing to accept that our observation indicates a relationship that does not actually exist in the population. Typically, social scientists are willing to accept up to a 5 percent chance that their observation is, essentially, wrong. P-values are quantified between 0.000 and 1.000, rounded to three decimal places, so when the p-value associated with a test statistic is 0.050 or less, a social scientist is typically willing to reject the assumption that there is no relationship between the two variables in the population, and accept that she or he has evidence of a relationship between variables. This is the rule we'll use going forward in this chapter. However, the convention of using a cut-off, or α-level, of $p \leq .05$ has little justification – it is really just what most social scientists agree most of the time is a small enough chance of being wrong. If that is not good enough for you, you can lower your α-level to $p \leq .01$ (a 1% chance), or $p \leq .000001$ (a 1 in one-million chance) that your data is essentially wrong. But there is always some chance, no matter how small, that we are wrong.

The metaphorical rabbit hole of sampling and inferential statistical theory goes a lot deeper than what we have covered here in what we admit is certainly a very rudimentary, but perhaps also somewhat esoteric, introduction. Research methods and statistical mathematics, let alone mathematical proofs and the laws that they demonstrate, are beyond the limits of our discussion in this text. You can easily spend several years in graduate school studying the science and mathematics that underpin these analyses if you are interested, or some of the references at the end of this chapter can help you take your first steps in that direction. For our purposes, the discussion above is more than enough to introduce you to the kind of data and analyses we'll be working with from here on in this chapter, and what it means for data to be sufficiently representative and evidence to be sufficiently strong for us to make confident inferences about the population.

Getting the Data and Installing the XLMiner Google Sheets Add-on

We're going to switch from Microsoft Excel back to Google Sheets for this chapter, for reasons we'll explain in a moment. If you want to follow along, you'll need to download the data file we'll be working with and import it into a

Google Sheet. The file, "Professor salaries.csv," is available for download in comma-separated value format at http://thedatareporter.com/demonstration-files/, the same page offering demonstration data files for Chapters 4 and 5. You can import the file using the same process you used to import the Toxics Release Inventory data in Chapter 3. In particular, see Figure 3.21. We'll tell you more about the file's contents later.

Excel and Google Sheets have similar capabilities for handling inferential statistics. Both programs do so through a combination of built-in functions and additional tools that are free but which you have to activate or install before you can use them. For example, in Excel 2016 for Windows, the additional tools are included in the Data Analysis ToolPak. You activate it by opening Excel, clicking "File / Options / Add-ins," choosing "Excel Add-ins" from the drop-down list next to "Manage," clicking "Go," checking the boxes beside "Analysis ToolPak" and "Analysis ToolPak – VBA," and clicking "OK." Run through that process once, and, from then on, you'll be able to access the tools in Excel by clicking "Data / Data Analysis." In this chapter, though, we will be using the XLMiner add-on for Google Sheets. It works similarly to Excel's Data Analysis ToolPak. In fact, if you want to use Excel's Data Analysis ToolPak instead of XLMiner, you'll be able to do so with minimal adaptation. But XLMiner offers the important advantage of running entirely within Google Sheets and, as a result, running the same way regardless of whether you are using a PC, like we are, a Mac, or even some other operating system. XLMiner shares the disadvantages of Google Sheets, too, of course. Like Google Sheets in general, XLMiner requires an Internet connection, and the larger the dataset you're working with is, the faster the Internet connection needs to be. On balance, though, we think XLMiner probably will be the best choice for most users of this book.

To install XLMiner:

- **Open the Google Sheet containing the "Professor salaries.csv" data you've imported.** You can install XLMiner from any Google Sheet, including a blank one, if you like. You also have to do it only once. After you do, it will be available in every Google Sheet in your drive, both pre-existing ones and each new one you create.
- **Choose "Add-ons" from the menu, then select "Get add-ons…"** The "Add-ons" window will open.
- **Type "XLMiner" into the "Search add-ons" box and press "Enter."** The search will retrieve the add-on install button for XLMiner.
- **Click the "+Free" installation button.** A "Sign in with Google" window will open.
- **Select a Google account.** If you have multiple Google Drive accounts, select whichever one you want to use when using Google Sheets and the XLMiner add-in. We're pretty sure XLMiner is a reasonably safe add-in. But if you have a main Google / Gmail account that contains your entire life, and you're nervous about giving XLMiner access to it, you can easily create a Google

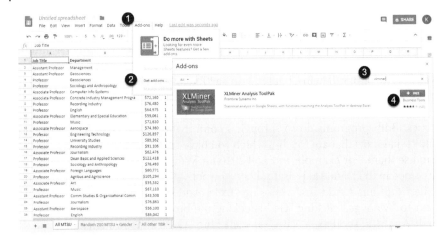

Figure 6.1 Installing the XLMiner add-on, Part 1. In an open Google Sheet, click "Add-ons" (1), then "Get add-ons …" (2). The "Add-ons" window will appear, displaying a scrollable list of add-ons (not shown). Type "XLMiner" into the "Search add-ons" box (3) and press "Enter." Click the "+ Free" button (4). Google and the Google logo are registered trademarks of Google Inc., used with permission.

Account and Google Drive specifically for running XLMiner. That's what we did for this book. Whatever you decide to do, a window will appear asking you to grant XLMiner access to your Google account.

- **Click the "Allow" button.** You are installing the add-on in your Google Drive, not on the local hard drive of the computer you are using. As a result, the add-on will be available regardless of which computer you are using while you are using Google Sheets.

That's all there is to the installation. Figures 6.1 and 6.2 illustrate the steps. From now on, you can use the XLMiner add-on by opening a Google Sheet and clicking "Add-ons / XLMiner Analysis ToolPak / Start." XLMiner's interface will appear on the right side of the screen.

Computing and Understanding Basic Inferential Statistics

For our analysis examples in this chapter, we randomly sampled records on 150 professors at Middle Tennessee State University (MTSU), where we work, from the Tennessee Board of Regents Salary Database during 2015. The database is publicly available. After obtaining all of the data from the website using some scraping techniques and filtering out any employees who weren't full time, tenured faculty at MTSU, we were left with a population of 548 tenured faculty members at MTSU. Of these, we randomly sampled 150

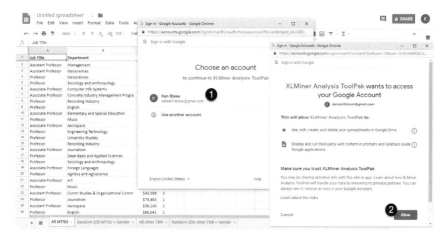

Figure 6.2 Installing the XLMiner add-on, Part 2. Choose the Google account for which you would like to activate the add-on (1). On the next window, choose "Allow" (2). Google and the Google logo are registered trademarks of Google Inc., used with permission.

for the data set. We know of no single, nationally comprehensive source of such data for universities, or even for other types of institutions. Generally, though, salaries for government employees, including public university faculty, are public record. Some cities have begun sharing employee salary data via online data portals. New York City's is available at https://opendata.cityofnewyork. us/. Chicago's is at https://data.cityofchicago.org/. Nashville's is at https://data. nashville.gov/. If you wanted to replicate our analysis using data from a local university or government agency, you probably could. But here is a list of our data file's columns and some information about each one:

- **Count.** An alphanumeric ID number for each professor. We removed the professor names. University employee salaries, with employee names (including ours, if you're curious) remain publicly available on the web at www.mtsu.edu/hrs/salary/employee-salary-database.php. But the salary amounts have changed since we acquired the data, and some of the individuals listed probably no longer work at the university. Finally, names aren't essential for what we're going to demonstrate. Accordingly, we thought it fair to omit the names from the data.
- **Gender.** Before we deleted the names from the dataset, we used the names to determine the gender of each faculty member, either by inferring gender from the name or, if gender could not reasonably inferred from the name, by looking the faculty member up in the university directory and inferring gender from the faculty member's picture. In some cases, we sought information from other sources, such as online student evaluations that referred to the faculty member as "he" or "she."

- **Certainty of gender.** This column indicates whether we assumed gender based solely on the professor's name or verified it by looking up information about the professor online.
- **Job title.** This column's "Associate Professor" and "Professor" job titles both refer to tenured faculty members. But a "Professor" is, by university policy, one promotion rank higher than an "Associate Professor" and typically earns more.
- **Department.** The university academic department in which the faculty member teaches.
- **College.** We added this variable in order to simplify each professor's affiliation within the university. Departments are housed within colleges, so the "Department" column represents subsets of the "College" column.

Descriptive Statistics and Confidence Intervals

Since we are primarily interested in faculty salaries, it will be useful to first establish a baseline of what faculty salaries are overall. We can do this with descriptive statistics. Furthermore, we can estimate how close our sample's descriptive statistics are to the population statistics using confidence intervals. XLMiner makes calculating descriptive statistics easy. Figure 6.3 illustrates the steps, which are:

- **Activate XLMiner, if you haven't already.** To activate XLMiner, click "Add-ons / XLMiner Analysis ToolPak / Start." The XLMiner area will open on the right side of your screen.

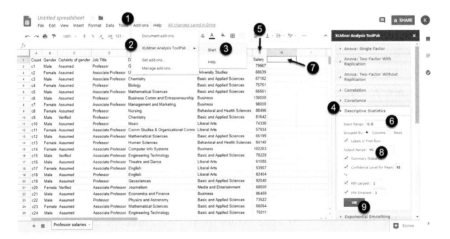

Figure 6.3 Getting descriptive statistics for the "Salary" amounts. Activate XLMiner by clicking "Add-ons" (1) "XLMiner Analysis ToolPak" (2), and "Start" (3). The XLMiner area will open on the right. Click "Descriptive Statistics" (4), then click the "G" in Column G to highlight the entire "Salary" column (5). Click the Input Range box (6) to deposit the range notation for the "Salary" column. Click Cell H1 (7) as the destination for the descriptive statistics output, and click the Output Range box (8) to deposit the cell's address. Finish by clicking "OK" (9). Google and the Google logo are registered trademarks of Google Inc., used with permission.

- **Click "Descriptive Statistics."** You will find the "Descriptive Statistics" button listed alphabetically in the XLMiner area. Clicking the button will open a drop-down menu.
- **Click the "G" at the top of Column G.** Column G contains the salary figures we want descriptive statistics for. Clicking the "G" at the top of the column will highlight the entire column.
- **Click on the box beside "Input Range."** Doing so will put the range notation for Column G into the box. The notation should read "G:G." By the way, if you are accustomed to doing such things in Excel, you will find this process to be backwards. Excel typically asks you to click the dialog box field first, then specify the value range to put in the box. XLMiner, as you can see, uses the reverse process. You specify the desired range first, then click the box where you want to specify the range.
- **Make sure the "Labels in first row" radio button is checked.** XLMiner presently checks the box by default. The check tells XLMiner to ignore the "Salary" text, in Cell G1, that serves as the column's label.
- **Click Cell H1.** What you're doing, here, is telling XLMiner where to put the descriptive statistics after it has calculated them. You can put them anywhere in the spreadsheet. We just chose to put them close by. Note that they will overwrite anything in their way. Accordingly, don't use, for example, cell A1 as the output location. If you do, you will wipe out a good chunk of the data in the "Count" and "Gender" columns.
- **Click the "Output Range" box.** Doing so specifies the address of the cell you just clicked on, H1, as the destination for the output.
- **Click "OK."**

Figure 6.4 shows the descriptive statistic output for the sample MTSU tenured faculty salaries after we copied the output to a new tab called "Descriptive Statistics" and expanded each column so it could be fully read. You could leave the output exactly where XLMiner put it, if you wanted to. We just like keeping things organized by tabs. By the way, we also gave the spreadsheet the name "Professor salaries."

There are several statistics reported in the output, but a few are of particular interest while a few others are outside our present analytical scope. First, there are two important statistics of *central tendency* shown in the table. Central tendency describes what the center value of a variable is. First is the *mean*, or an average, which is computed by adding all the values up and then dividing by the number of values. The sample mean tenured faculty salary is $79,129.94. We also obtained the confidence interval for the 95% confidence level of the mean, which rounds to the penny to ± $3,038.76. This means that for 95% of samples like this one, the population mean will be within $3,038.76 above or below the sample mean. We can be pretty confident that the population salary mean is probably somewhere between $76,090.24 and $82,168.70 ($79,129.94 − $3,038.76 and $79,129.94 + $3,038.76, respectively).

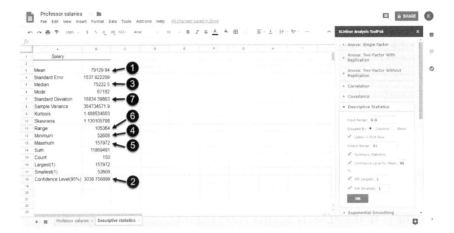

Figure 6.4 The descriptive statistics output, shown copied to a new tab, includes measures of central tendency, like the mean (1) along with its 95 percent confidence level (2), and the median (3). Measures if dispersion includes the minimum (4), maximum (5) and range (6), and standard deviation (7). Google and the Google logo are registered trademarks of Google Inc., used with permission.

When dealing with income in particular it is also, and some would argue more, important to look at the *median* as an indicator of central tendency. Means are relatively easily distorted by small numbers of extreme values, or *outliers*, which are common in income data. In other words, for example, a single income that is much higher than all the others can make the mean income higher than we would typically be comfortable using as a description of the center value of the variable. The median, in contrast, is simply the value of the variable with an equal number of values above and below it in the data when the data are ordered from the lowest value to the highest. If there are an even number of cases, the median is the average of the two values with equal numbers of values above or below them. In our data set, with 150 cases, the median salary is the average of the salaries in the 125th and 126th places when all salaries are ordered from lowest to highest. As you can see in the output, the sample median salary is $75,222.50. This is a little lower, but not too different from, the sample mean salary ($79,129.94), so we wouldn't worry too much about misrepresenting the center of the variable by reporting the mean. However, when it comes to income, or other variables where the mean could be influenced by outliers, the more different the median is from the mean, the more reason we would have to report the median as the central tendency statistic.

Suppose that our university's highest-paid employee, the head football coach whose salary at the time we collected these data was $721,704.00 per year, were named a tenured professor and added to this data set. Adding that salary to the ones in the dataset and rerunning the descriptive statistics would produce a much higher sample mean, $83,385.40, while the median would be $75,225.00, practically unchanged. In this example, the median would probably be the better indicator of central tendency to report.

There are a few important statistics indicating *dispersion* in the table as well. Dispersion statistics describe how the data are spread out, or distributed from each other. First, we can look at the *minimum*, which is the lowest salary in the sample, $52,608.00, and the *maximum*, which is the highest salary in the sample, $157,972.00. The difference between the minimum and maximum, obtained by subtracting the minimum from the maximum, is the *range*. The sample range is $105,364.00 ($157,972.00 – $52,608.00).

From a statistician's perspective, the most important descriptive statistic indicating dispersion is probably the *standard deviation*. The standard deviation can be thought of as the average of the absolute (meaning always positive) differences between the values and the mean. To compute the standard deviation, XLMiner takes each salary in the data set and subtracts the mean from it. Then, it makes each of these values positive. Then, it computes the average of these values (the sum of all the values divided by the number of values). The standard deviation for our sample of tenured faculty salaries is $18,834.40, rounded to the penny. This means that on average, individual salaries in the sample are $18,834.40 different from the mean salary of $79.129.94. This gives us an idea of how spread out salaries are around the mean. However, as you might have already noticed, the standard deviation can be a little difficult for non-statisticians to understand, so in many cases you might want to report the minimum, maximum, and perhaps the range as indicators of dispersion.

Descriptive statistics give us an idea of what a single sample variable looks like simplified down to relatively few numbers. With the confidence level and confidence interval, we can get an idea of about what the population value for the variable probably is. Next, we will move on to an examination of how the values of a sample variable can be compared to some standard, and whether we can say whether the difference between the values in the sample are different from that standard in a statistically significant way.

By the way, it is possible to generate many of these descriptive statistics with Google Sheets (or Excel) functions. As you saw back in Chapter 1, for example, the =average function will calculate a mean. But producing each of these statistics individually, using a function, would take quite a bit of time compared to the time it takes to calculate them in XLMiner.

The One-sample T-test

Suppose that we wanted to see from our sample how tenured faculty at MTSU compare to others in terms of their income. We know from our descriptive statistics what the mean of salaries in the sample is, but how would we compare that to Americans in general?

First we need to identify our standard of comparison. How will we quantify what Americans in general make? The U.S. Census Bureau calculates a statistic that might be useful to us in this regard – the median household income. At the time we collected the data, the U.S. Census Bureau's most recent median household income estimate for the United States was $53,657.00 (Census, 2015, p.5). It is important to note that there are some differences between this number and our tenured faculty salaries. First, the tenured faculty salaries are for individuals, while the household income estimate is based on totals for everyone who lives in a given home. Second, the household income estimate is described with a median, while we describe our tenured faculty salaries with a mean. Despite these differences, the household median income estimate gives us a reasonable point of comparison for the MTSU tenured faculty salaries in our sample. Do MTSU faculty make more than the typical U.S. household?

We already know that the sample mean tenured faculty salary, $79,129.94, appears to be quite a bit more than the national median household income estimate of $53,657.00. And the highest tenured faculty salary in the sample is a lot more, at $157,972.00. However, the lowest tenured faculty salary in the sample, $52,608.00, is less than the median household income estimate. Plus, we have to remember that we're dealing with a sample, and the sample might be a little different from the population (all faculty salaries at MTSU). So how can we determine whether we can say with confidence whether MTSU tenured faculty salaries are different from national household incomes?

To answer these questions, we can use a statistic called a *one-sample t-test*, which allows us to compare a single sample mean for a continuous variable to some other number and see whether there is a statistically significant difference between them. XLMiner has no procedure for computing a one-sample t-test. It does, however, have a procedure for computing a two-sample t-test, something we'll talk about a bit later. However, we can trick XLMiner into using its two-sample t-test procedure to compute a one-sample t-test. The first step is to add the median figure to a cell in each row of the data. We could use any available column for the purpose, but it makes sense to use Column H, which happens to be both blank and conveniently right next to the professor salary figures in Column G. To add the column of median figures:

- **Type "U.S. median" into Cell H1.** It will serve as the column's heading.
- **Enter the median figure, 53657, into Cell H2,** right under the "U.S. median" column heading. Don't worry that the 53657 hasn't been formatted as currency – that is, doesn't look like "$53,657." All we really need right now is the number.
- **Click on the 53657 you just typed into Cell H2.** This step ensures that you have selected Cell H2. A blue outline should surround the cell, and there should be a tiny, blue square visible at the outline's lower-right corner.

- **Double-click the tiny, blue square.** To help you aim accurately, your mouse pointer will turn to a larger " + " symbol when it is directly over the square. The double-click should automatically copy the 53657 figure to every cell from Cell H3 through Cell H151. The copy process automatically stops at Cell H151, because Cell G151, right next door, was the last cell in Column G to contain data. If you don't like the double-click approach to copying, you can get the same thing done by clicking Cell H2, pressing "Ctrl/c" or "Cmd/c" on the keyboard, highlighting cells H3 through H151, and pressing "Ctrl/v" or "Cmd/v."

Having copied "53657" into each dataset cell of Column H, we can ask XLMiner to run the t-test. Figure 6.5 shows the process and the results. If the XLMiner add-on isn't already running, start it by clicking "Add-ons / XLMiner Analysis ToolPak / Start." The XLMiner area will open on the right side of your screen. Then:

- **Click "t-Test: Two-Sample Assuming Unequal Variances" in the XLMiner area.** Choose carefully; there are three different "t-Test" procedures available in XLMiner. The "Paired Two Sample for Means" version is for an entirely different type of situation, one not covered in this book.

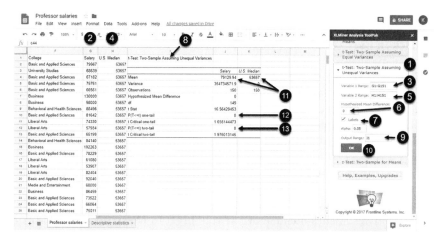

Figure 6.5 Setup and results of a one-sample t-test in XLMiner. To run the procedure, click the "t-Test: Two-Sample Assuming Unequal Variances" tab (1). Highlight all of the values in the "Salary" column (2), then click the "Variable 1 Range" box (3). Highlight all of the values in the "U.S. Median" column (4), and click the "Variable 2 Range" box (5). Type a zero into the "Hypothesized Mean Difference" box (6), and check the "Labels" box (7). Click Cell I1 (8) and click the "Output Range" box (9). Then click "OK" (10). Key values in the output are the "Salary" and "U.S. Median" column averages (11), the one-tailed p-value (12), and the two-tailed p-value (13). Google and the Google logo are registered trademarks of Google Inc., used with permission.

The "Two-Sample Assuming Equal Variances" version assumes that the two columns of data you are comparing have equal levels of variability. That's rarely the case, and it's certainly not the case here. Column H has no variability whatsoever. Every value is the same: 53657. By contrast, the values in Column G, as we saw by looking at their standard deviation, vary from their mean by an average of nearly $19,000. Even if Column H's values varied at least a little bit, using the "Assuming Equal Variances" version would require statistically testing whether the variation levels in each column are the same, or at least similar enough. The test for doing so isn't available in XLMiner, so we advise that you just plan on always using the "Unequal variances" version.

- **Select all of the data in Column G.** That's the faculty salary data. A quick way to get it done is to click on Cell G1, hold down the keyboard's "Ctrl" and "Shift" keys, and press the down arrow. Alternatively, you can drag across the cells with your mouse.
- **Click in the "Variable 1 Range" box.** Doing so will deposit the cell range information in the box: "G1:G151," meaning "Every cell in Column G from Cell 1 through Cell 151."
- **Select all of the data in Column H.** That's the column consisting solely of the U.S. median figure: 53657. Again, you can do so by clicking on the first cell in the column, Cell H1, and pressing and holding the "Ctrl" and "Shift" keys, then pressing the down arrow.
- **Click in the "Variable 2 Range" box.** Again, doing so will deposit the cell range in the box.
- **Type a zero into the "Hypothesized Mean Difference" box.** Remember the "null hypothesis" discussion above? This step tells XLMiner to test the null hypothesis that there is zero difference, or no difference at all, between the average tenured faculty salary and 53657, given the data in columns G and H. The "Hypothesized Mean Difference" will always be zero, unless you have a very good reason for setting it at some other value.
- **Check the box beside "Labels."** This step tells XLMiner to bypass the "Salary" and "U.S. Median" labels in cells G1 and H1 when performing its calculations. Here, the box isn't checked by default the way it was in the descriptive statistics menu above. If you forget to check the box, XLMiner will produce an error message reading, "Input range contains non-numeric data." That's XLMiner's way of saying, "You asked me to average data that include text. It's impossible to average text. Therefore, I can't do what you asked me to do."
- **Click Cell I1, then click the "Output Range" box.** XLMiner will put "I1)" into the box and, when you run the test, display the output starting in Cell I1.
- **Click OK.**

The output's first row shows the means that we compared to each other. The "Salary" mean, which landed in Cell J4 in Figure 6.5, is the same as we initially calculated, $79,129.94. The "U.S. Median" mean, in Cell K4, is the average of the values we entered for every case in the data set, $53,657.00. Unsurprisingly, when you average 150 occurrences of the same number, you get the number. By the way, that's how we tricked XLMiner into giving us a one-sample t-test. We make one of the "samples," the "Variable 2 Range," nothing but repeated occurrences of the value we wanted it to compare to the first sample, the column of tenured faculty salaries in the "Variable 1 Range."

Our test statistic, in this case called a t-statistic ("t Stat" in the table; see Cell J9) is 16.564, rounded to 3 decimal places. This statistic quantifies the difference between the two means, though it is not readily interpretable on its own without going into the mathematics that underlie its calculations. The *degrees of freedom*, or df (Cell J8), are also important from a mathematical and statistical perspective, but for our purposes it suffices to note that for a test about a single mean (like our sample mean salary of $79,129.94), df is simply equal to one less than the sample size, here 149 (150 − 1).

Crucially for our purposes, we should look at the p-value, shown in Cell J12. Recall that we asked whether the sample mean salary is *different from* the national household income. In the language of statistics, this is a *non-directional hypothesis*, meaning we didn't specify whether the sample mean salary might be more than, or less than, the national household income. To answer this question, we look at the *two-tailed p-value*, or in the table "P(T<=t) two-tail." In the table, the two-tailed p-value is shown as "0." It's not actually absolutely zero. It's just so small that XLMiner rounded it off to zero. Run the same procedure in the Data Analysis ToolPak for Excel, and Excel will show this value in scientific notation, specifically as: 1.31384E-35. Note the "E," which indicates the number is being expressed in scientific notation. What this means is that the number represents a zero, followed by a decimal place, followed by 34 more zeros, followed by "…131384." Written out in full, in other words, the number is:

0.00000000000000000000000000000000131384

Perhaps you can see why XLMiner decided to just go ahead and call it zero. But what does this mean? For our purposes, heuristically, recall that we are really only interested in whether $p \leq 0.05$. This obtained p-value is certainly less than 0.05. What this means is that we can confidently say that MTSU tenured faculty salaries are *different* from the median national household income.

Suppose we want to be more specific, and ask whether MTSU tenured faculty salaries are *greater than* national household income. In the language of statistics, this is a *directional hypothesis*, which specifies the way in which we expect salaries to differ from national household income. To answer this question, we first look at the direction of the difference between the standard and the sample observation. Indeed, our sample observation is a larger number than the standard, so the difference is in the hypothesized direction. Next, to see if that difference is statistically significant, we simply look at the *one-tailed p-value*, or in the table "P(T<=t) one-tail." See Cell J10. XLMiner has rounded this figure off to zero as well. The comparable Excel procedure gives it as "6.56922E-36," or:

0.00000000000000000000000000000000000656922

Again, what is really important here is that this obtained p-value is less than 0.05. So we can confidently say that MTSU tenured faculty make *more* than the median national household income. Reporting this result in an academic publication would require providing several of the statistical values from the output, including some of the more esoteric ones. Reporting it in a news story or press release intended for a general audience would require only some kind of indication that you tested the difference statistically. Ways to do so would include:

- "Statistically, the salary for a tenured faculty member averages to about $79,130, significantly more than the median figure for U.S. households, $53,657."
- "On average, a tenured faculty member earns about $79,130. Statistically, the figure is significantly higher than the median U.S. household income of $53,657."
- "A tenured faculty member earns about $79,130 on average, exceeding the $53,657 median U.S. household income by a statistically significant amount."

Other sentence structures are possible, of course. The common characteristic among the three examples above is that they all work in the words "statistically" and "significantly." Used together, the two words can serve as a sufficient cue that you applied some kind of statistical test to the difference and found the average faculty salary differed from the median household figure to a degree that random sampling variation alone could not reasonably account for.

The One-sample Chi-square Test

The fact that tenured faculty are comparably well off probably doesn't seem all that newsworthy. But gender-based inequity and underrepresentation probably do. Suppose we wanted to know for a story whether the percentages of men and women among the tenured faculty at MTSU more or less match those in the country overall, or one gender appears more represented among the tenured faculty than among the population, and thus the other less represented among the tenured faculty than among the population.

To answer this question, we can use a *one-sample chi-square test*, which allows us to see whether the percentages of values for a single, categorical variable in a sample differ significantly from some standard percentages that we define.

As with the one-sample t-test, for the one-sample chi-square test we have to determine what our standard of comparison is. The most recent United States

Figure 6.6 Setup and results of a one-sample chi-square test. After clicking on a cell in the salary data, click "Data / Pivot table ..." to open the "Pivot table editor" on a new tab. Click "Add" in the "Rows" area (1), and choose "Gender" from the drop-down list of variables (not shown). Click "Add" in the "Values" area and choose "Gender" from the drop-down list of variables (not shown). Change "Default" (3) to "% of column" if you want to temporarily change the counts to percentages, but change the setting back to "Default" before proceeding. Type "Expected counts" as a heading (4), although this step is optional. Put the formula =0.51*B4 into Cell C2 (5) and the formula =0.49*B4 into Cell C3. Put the formula =chitest(B2:B3,C2:C3) into Cell A6. Google and the Google logo are registered trademarks of Google Inc., used with permission.

Census estimates as of our data collection told us that 51% of the population was female, and that 49% was male (Census, 2016). We also need to know the percentages of males and females in our sample of tenured faculty. You could count and percentage them manually, of course. But a pivot table could do the job much faster, and probably more accurately. You might recall learning in Chapter 4 how to create pivot tables in Excel. We mentioned that Google Sheets offers a pivot table tool as well, one that, although not quite as polished as Excel's, is still pretty good. We'll incorporate its use here, given that we're already working in Google Sheets. Below are the steps for creating a Google Sheets pivot table and calculating the chi-square test. Figure 6.6 shows the steps and the results. Before proceeding, by the way, we copied the one-sample t-test output to a new tab.

To create a pivot table in Google Sheets:

- **Close the XLMiner add-on,** if it is still running. Click the "x" to the right of "XLMiner Analysis ToolPak." If you leave XLMiner open, it will cover up the pivot table editing area you will need access to in order to create the pivot table.
- **Click on any cell in the data you want to include in the pivot table.** We clicked on Cell A1.

- **Click "Data / Pivot table ..."** Google Sheets will automatically open a new tab, show you a blank pivot table on the left side of the screen and the "Pivot table editor" on the right side of the screen.
- **Click the "Add" button next to "Rows" in the pivot table editor.** A drop-down list showing every variable in the dataset will appear.
- **Click the "Gender" variable.** A box for "Gender" will appear under "Rows." By default, the box will be set to show the gender categories in ascending alphabetical order by the "Gender" category names, "Female" first, then "Male." The "Show totals" box will be checked, too. As with Excel, anything you do in the pivot table editor produces real-time results in the actual pivot table on the left side of the screen. For example, adding "Gender" to the "Rows" area will create a row for each "Gender" category.
- **Click the "Add" button next to "Values" in the pivot table editor.** Like last time, a menu of variables will drop open.
- **Choose "Gender" (again) from the list of variables.** Google Sheets will add a "Gender" box to the "Values" area. By default, it will count the number of times "Female" appears in the "Gender" column and display the count (69). It will do the same for "Male" (81), and also show you the grand total (150).

Time for a pause. You might have difficulty figuring out how close the percentages of men and women among the tenure faculty sample are to the percentages of men and women throughout the U.S. population, because the pivot table is showing you counts, not percentages. You can easily take a peek, though. Just go to the "Gender" box under "Values" and choose "% of column" under "Show as." Google Sheets will change the counts of men and women into percentages of the 150-faculty-member total. The results show that the sample of faculty members is 46 percent female and 54 percent male. That's about five percentage points in favor of men, compared to the national figures of 51 percent female and 49 percent male.

But the percentages really aren't all that far off, are they? How confident can we be that there is a real difference between the gender composition of MTSU tenured faculty and the U.S. population? After all, this is just sample of MTSU tenured faculty, not the population of MTSU tenured faculty, and it is possible that we are only seeing this difference due to sampling. If we looked at all tenured MTSU faculty, we might see less, and maybe even no, difference between the tenured faculty and national population in terms of gender. Broadly speaking, there are two possible explanations for the difference between our sample's gender percentages and the U.S. population's gender percentages, assuming no flaws in our sampling method or in our calculations so far. One is that MTSU's tenured faculty members really do include a higher percentage of men than the general U.S. population does. The other is that our one-time, random sample of the MTSU tenured faculty members just happened to include an abnormally high percentage of men. It could have happened for the same reason that a random handful of marbles grabbed from a bag containing exactly 50 white marbles and 50 black marbles won't necessarily be exactly half white and half black. A one-sample chi-square test can help us assess the probability of this latter explanation – that is, the explanation that random sampling variation is responsible for our sample's difference from the general population. If the test can all but rule out the latter explanation, then we can assert the former explanation more confidently. After all, it will be the only explanation left.

Now, promise not to panic when we tell you this: XLMiner can't do a one-sample chi-square test. You'll have to do it on your own. But you'll get a huge assist from a built-in Google Sheets function, =CHITEST. Relax. It's really not a big deal. Here's what to do:

- **Switch the pivot table back to showing counts.** Under "Show as" in the "Gender" box in the "Values" area of the pivot table editor, change "Show as" back to "default." The pivot table should go back to showing you that the sample contains 69 females and 81 males.
- **Type the word "Expected counts" into Cell C1.** Below it, we'll calculate the counts we would have expected to see in the sample had the sample contained 51 percent women and 49 percent men, just like the general U.S. population.
- **Calculate what each expected count would be.** You can do it with a simple formula like the ones you learned to write back in Chapter 1.
  - Click on Cell C2, the one right next to the 69 showing the number of females in the sample.
  - Type this, without the quote marks: "=.51*" and then click Cell B4, the cell containing the 150-person total for the sample.
  - Press "Enter." Google Sheets will show "76.5," which is 51 percent of the 150-person sample size. That's our expected count for women.
  - Do the same for the men by putting the formula "=.49*B4" into Cell C3. Again, don't include the quote marks in the formula. Google Sheets should show the expected count for men as 73.5.
- **Click on a nearby empty cell.** We used Cell A6, two cells down from the pivot table's "Grand Total" label.
- **Type "=chitest(" with no quote marks.** Doing so starts the =chitest function, which will calculate the chi-square test for you if you give it the information it needs.
- **Use your mouse to highlight cells B2 and B3.** These are the cells in the pivot table that contain the counts we observed of women and men in the sample, the ones we got using the pivot table.
- **Type a comma.** The comma signals that you have finished entering one piece of required information (the "observed count" cell addresses) and are about the enter a second piece of required information.
- **Use your mouse to highlight cells C2 and C3.** These are the cells that contain the counts you just calculated by multiplying each of the U.S. population percentages by 150, the size of our sample.
- **Press "Enter."**

Now in cell A6, we can see the probability that the difference between what we observed in the sample and what we expected based on census figures was due to chance alone. The p-value we obtained is 0.2205790283 (see Figure 6.17). Recall that as a rule of thumb, we look for whether the p-value is less than or equal to 0.050. The p-value we obtained here is not. This means that, despite the differences between the gender counts we observed and what we expected according to the census, we can't confidently rule out the explanation that those differences resulted from the chances associated with random sampling. In the language of statistics, we would say that there is not a statistically significant difference between what we observed and what we expected. The gender composition of our sample does not significantly differ from what we would expect based on the gender composition of the United States according to the Census. In the language of a journalist, you could write any of the following:

- "The sample's proportion of men, 54 percent, differed from the 49 percent share of men in the U.S. population, but not enough to be statistically significant, given the sample's size."
- "Men made up 54 percent of the sample compared to 49 percent of the U.S. population. But considering the sample's size, the difference was not statistically significant."
- "The sample overrepresented males, compared to the U.S. population. But not to a statistically significant degree for a sample of its size."

Again, including some version of the words "statistical" and "significant" can help signal that you checked the difference out using inferential statistics. We recommend adding a reference to the sample's size, too. Had these same proportions shown up in a random sample of 600 tenured faculty, the observed values would have been 276 women and 324 men, the expected values would have been 306 women and 294 men, and the chi-square probability associated with the difference would have been a statistically significant 0.014 percent. Put another way, MTSU's faculty really might include proportionally more men than the U.S. population does, just like in our 150-member sample of MTSU's faculty does. It is possible our 150-member sample just isn't large enough to rule out random sampling variation as an explanation for the overrepresentation in our sample. Adding a caveat about the sample's size is probably a good idea if your sample size is smaller than 600 and represents less than about 5 percent of the population you drew the sample from.

Knowing which Test to Use

This is a good time to point out something important that might not be obvious. A one-sample t-test and a one-sample chi-square test do essentially the same thing, in that they each compare a statistic from a sample to a known value of the same statistic in some population. Students of ours who realize this point sometimes ask why two different tests are needed. What such students usually haven't noticed yet is that each test deals with a different kind of data. Data like "gender," measured as either "male" or "female" is an example of what statisticians call "categorical data." As the name implies, categorical data simply categorize things. The variable "gender" categorizes people as "male" or "female," or perhaps "male," "female," and perhaps "non-binary/other." The variable "class rank" categorizes people as "freshman," "sophomore," "junior" and "senior." A percentage is about the most sophisticated descriptive statistic you can compute from such data. Even in the case of something like "class rank," where the categories have a clear numeric order (freshmen have earned the fewest credit hours, sophomores have earned more, juniors even more, and seniors the most of all), about the most you can do is describe the percentage of all students who fall into each of the categories. That's the kind of data you have to use a chi-square test on, because a chi-square test is designed specifically to work with percentages.

Meanwhile, something like "salary," measured in dollar amounts, is an example of what statisticians call "continuous data." The defining characteristic of continuous data is that the amount of "stuff" between any two adjacent values in the data is fixed, or constant, and easily countable. In salary data, for example, the difference between one dollar and two dollars is the same as the difference between 100 dollars and 101 dollars, 1,000 dollars and 1,001 dollars, and so on. It's one dollar every time. This property makes "salary" countable. And because we can count the dollars in every salary, it becomes possible to add up the dollars in a sample of salaries, divide by the number of salaries, and report the result as an average. That's the kind of data you have to use a t-test on, because t-tests are designed specifically to work with averages.

Try the same process with "class rank," and things get confusing. One freshman might be 30-some credits away from being a sophomore, while another freshman might be only one credit away from being a sophomore. The number of credit hours earned isn't always the same between "freshman" and "sophomore," between "sophomore" and "junior," and between "junior" and "senior." As a result, averages don't work all that well, and you're better off relying on percentages. Try it with something like "gender," and things make even less sense. The amount of "gender" between "male" and "female" isn't the same as the amount of "gender" between "female" and "non-binary/other." In fact, "gender" isn't an amount at all. It's a social construct we can describe only in terms of categories.

One last thing you might have noticed: You can turn continuous data, like "salary in dollars," into categorical data by simply dividing it into groups, like "lower income, middle income, and upper income." After you divide it into groups, you can describe each group in terms of percentages. Once you have described each group in terms of percentages, you can use a chi-square test. But it doesn't work the other way. You can't take a categorical variable like "gender" and re-express it as a continuous variable, because it's not about amounts at all.

Bottom line: Which test you should use depends on the type of data at hand. Use a chi-square with categorical data described using percentages, and use a t-test for continuous data described using averages.

Computing and Understanding Basic Bivariate Statistics

So far, we've looked at how we can use statistics in Excel to describe single variables in a sample using just a few numbers, and how we can compare continuous and categorical variables in a sample to some standard. What if we want to examine whether differences across cases on two variables in our sample are associated with each other in a non-random way, and determine whether we can be confident that those associations are not due to the chances inherent in sampling alone? The following *bivariate statistics* allow us to answer this type of question. Fortunately, the first two tests are very similar to what you have just learned about. They utilize the t-test and chi-square statistics. The third test is a new one, used to determine whether we have evidence in our sample of an association between two continuous variables. This is called a *regression*.

Two-sample T-tests

As we mentioned previously, gender equity is a topic that receives a lot of attention and discussion in the media these days. One of the most commonly-discussed issues within the topic is the oft-cited pay discrepancy between men and women, such that men tend to be paid more money than women in general and for the same amount of work in the same jobs. Is there a difference in pay between males and females in our sample of MTSU tenured faculty? Are male tenured faculty paid more than female tenured faculty at MTSU? To answer these questions, we use a slightly modified technique of applying the t-test that we already looked at, since gender is a dichotomous categorical variable and salary is a continuous variable.

The last time we ran a t-test, the data involved appeared in two columns. One column contained the salaries of each of the faculty members in the sample, one per cell. The other column, right beside it, contained the U.S. median household income, repeated for every cell in the column. The first column became the "Variable 1 range" in the XLMiner setup window, and the second column became the "Variable 2 range" in the setup window. See Figure 6.5. For a two-sample t-test comparing the average salaries of men and women, we again need two columns of data, one of which we'll specify as "Variable 1," and the other of which we'll specify as "Variable 2." But this time, we're comparing the salaries of the sample's men with the salaries of the sample's women. To do that, one column must contain all of the salaries for men, and the other must contain all of the salaries for women. We'll put these two columns on a new tab in the spreadsheet, then work with them there.

There are a couple of ways you could get the data arranged in the way described, but one of the fastest and easiest ways is to use a filter. You've already learned about filters, first in Chapter 1, when you filtered the metro areas for those in Tennessee, then again in Chapter 5, when you used filters to categorize donors has having given money to one candidate, the other, or both. As a result, most of what comes next should be a review.

- **Make a new spreadsheet tab.** To do so, click the "Add sheet" plus sign in the lower-left corner of your Google Sheet. Google Sheets will open a new tab and show you a blank spreadsheet.
- **Type "Males" in Cell A1 of the new tab.** This text will serve as the column label for the male salaries.
- **Type "Females" in Cell B1 of the new tab.** This text will be the column label for the female salaries.
- **Name the new tab "Two-sample t-test."** Just double-click on the tab's default name, then type the new name.
- **Switch back to the "Professor salaries" tab.** That's the tab containing the original data, including each tenured faculty member's salary.
- **Filter the data to show only the salaries for male faculty.** Click Cell A1, or any cell in the data, and choose "Data / Create a filter." You might want to re-expand all the columns so that the full name of each column will be visible.
- **Click the down arrow next to the "Gender" label in Column B.** Column B, of course, is the column that indicates each faculty member's gender.
- **Remove the check next to "Female" by clicking once on it, then click "OK."** Google Sheets will hide all of the female records and display only the male ones.
- **Highlight and copy all of the salary figures showing in the "Salary" column.** The "Salary" column is Column G. One quick way to copy the figures is to click on Cell G2, the first figure, hold down the "Ctrl" and "Shift" keys on the keyboard ("Cmd" and "Shift" keys on a Mac), and press the down-arrow key. Google Sheets will highlight all visible cells in the column that contain data. With the cells highlighted, press "Ctrl/c" or "Cmd/c" to copy the highlighted figures.
- **Paste the salary figures under the "Males" heading on the "Two-sample t-test" tab.** Just click Cell A2 and press "Ctrl/v" or "Cmd/v."
- **Use the same process to paste the salaries for female faculty members under the "Females" heading in the "Two-sample t-test" tab.** Switch back to the "Professor salaries" tab, click the funnel-shaped icon next to the "Gender" heading in Cell B1, uncheck "Male" and check "Female," then click "OK." Copy the visible salaries, which should be salaries only for female faculty, and paste them into Cell B2 under "Females" in the "Two-sample t-test" tab.

- **Go back to the "Professor salaries" tab and click "Data / Turn off filter" so that all of the salaries are visible again.** Of course, two seasoned data wranglers like us are much too experienced to ever absentmindedly leave a filter in place, then fail to notice all the errors the lapse caused in subsequent analyses. Nope, not us. But you might, so we thought we'd better mention it to you.

The "Two-sample t-test" tab should now show a "Males" column containing all the salaries for male faculty, and a "Females" column containing all the salaries for female faculty. All you have to do now is set the analysis up in XLMiner in much the same way you did for the one-sample t-test. The only difference is that you'll be comparing the average of the men's salaries with the average of the women's salaries, rather than the average of all salaries with the U.S. median household income. Here's what to do:

- **Open XLMiner, if it isn't already running.** Click "Add-ons / XLMiner Analysis ToolPak / Start."
- **Choose "t-Test: Two-Sample, Assuming Unequal Variances" from the XLMiner menu.** Again, it's near the bottom, so you'll probably have to scroll down.
- **Deposit the cell addresses for the "Males" salaries into the "Variable 1 Range" box.** Use the same procedure you did when setting up the one-sample t-test: Click Cell A1, the column's label, hold down "Ctrl / Shift" or "Cmd / Shift," and press the down arrow. Then, with the data highlighted, click in the "Variable 1 Range" box. The box should read, "A1:A82."
- **Do the same for the "Females" salaries and the "Variable 2 Range" box.** When you're done, the "Variable 2 Range" box should read, "B1:B70."
- **Set up the rest of the analysis the way you did before.** Put a zero in the "Hypothesized Mean Difference" box, check the "Labels" box, click on the cell you want the output to start in (we picked Cell C1), click the "Output Range" box to deposit the cell address there, and click "OK."

Figure 6.7 show the test's XLMiner setup and results. Cells D4 and E4 contain the means that we compared to each other. The mean of females' salaries is $75,700.74, rounded to the penny. The mean of males' salaries is $82,051.11, also rounded to the penny. So there appears to be a difference. But can we be confident that this difference in our sample is not just due to chance?

The t-statistic ("t Stat" in the output table) is 2.071, rounded to three decimal places, and the degrees of freedom ("df" in the output table) are 141. As before, these are not too informative for non-statisticians, but they essentially quantify the difference between the salary means and the size of the sample, respectively, in statistical terms. For our purposes, we are more interested in the p-values. The two-tailed p-value, or "P(T< =t) two-tail" in the table, is 0.040, rounded to three decimal places. Since 0.040 is less than 0.050, the figure indicates we can be confident that the observed *difference* in salaries in the sample is not due to chance alone.

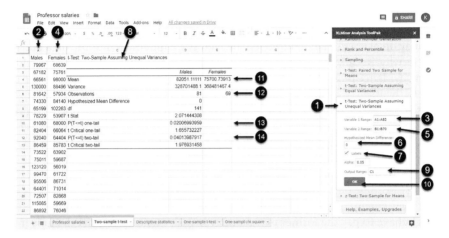

Figure 6.7 Setup and results of a two-sample t-test. With the salaries for male and female faculty members copied into side-by-side columns on a new tab, open XLMiner's "t-Test: Two-Sample Assuming Unequal Variances" menu (1), use the mouse to select the "Males" label and all the salaries in the column (2). Click in the "Variable 1 Range" box to deposit the cell addresses (3). Do the same to put the "Females" salaries (4) into the "Variable 2 Range" box (5). Set the "Hypothesized Mean Difference" to zero (6), check the "Labels" box (7). Select a starting cell for the output (8), click the "Output Range" box to deposit the cell's address (9), and click "OK" (10). Key parts of the output include the means of the two columns (11), the number of salaries counted in each column (12), the one-tail p-value (13), and the two-tail p-value (14). Google and the Google logo are registered trademarks of Google Inc., used with permission.

Are male tenured faculty paid *more* than female tenured faculty? Since the observed salary difference is in the direction expected (the mean salary for males is $82,051.11, which is more than the mean for females, $75,700.74), we can use the one-tailed p-value, or "P(T< =t) one-tail" in the table, to answer this question. Since the one-tailed p-value, 0.020 rounded to three decimal places, is less than 0.050, we can be confident that our evidence of *males being paid more than females* is not due to chance alone.

We have statistically significant evidence from our sample that there is a difference in tenured faculty pay associated with gender such that male tenured faculty at MTSU are paid more than female tenured faculty. To phrase the same conclusion like a journalist might, you could write any of the following:

- "Male tenured faculty make $82,051 on average, a statistically significant $6,350 more than the $75,701 average for women."
- "Salaries among male faculty average $82,051, significantly more than the $75,701 average among women, a statistical analysis of the data shows."
- "Male faculty make significantly more money than females do, a statistical analysis of the data shows. Salaries average about $82,051 among men compared to only $75,701 among women."

What's not said, here, is as important as what is said. The data provide compelling evidence that tenured male faculty members at MTSU make more money on average than tenured female faculty members do. But the data don't tell us why. Recall, here, our discussion in Chapter 4 about causality. As we said then, evidence of a relationship between two things, like gender and pay, can't prove, by itself, that one of the things caused the other. Additionally, the supposed cause has to precede the supposed result in time, and the relationship has to persist independently of other things that might contribute to the effect. Lots of factors influence how much money the university pays a tenured faculty member. Gender bias built into the university's hiring and advancement systems could be one such factor. But there could be others, too. For instance, faculty in some departments could command larger salaries in the private sector than faculty in some other departments could. As a result, the university might have to pay the former more money in order to keep them at the university. Pay among tenured faculty is also related to rank. As mentioned earlier, tenured professors rank higher than tenured associate professors. Moving up the to rank of professor requires meeting teaching, service and scholarship requirements that are more demanding than those met by associate professors. Accordingly, professors earn more than associate professors do. In the next section, we'll look for evidence that male tenured faculty are more likely than female tenured faculty to hold the rank of professor. But it's important to understand that identifying the cause, or causes, of pay differences between men and women at MTSU or any other institution will take more than a few quick analyses of whether pay and rank differ by gender. The effort will require regular journalism, too, the kind that involves posing carefully chosen questions to key information sources and double checking and cross-validating their responses. Data journalism can't replace regular journalism. But it can bolster regular journalism. For example, evidence that male tenured faculty make more than female tenured faculty can help you move past the question of whether the disparity exists and on to the question of why.

Chi-square Analysis of a PivotTable

As we mentioned a moment ago, rank helps determine pay among tenured faculty. We have found evidence that male tenured faculty earn more than female tenured faculty do. But what if we also found evidence that a higher percentage of males than of females held the rank of professor? Such a finding would suggest that the pay disparity between male and female tenured faculty has at least something, and maybe everything, to do with rank, apart from gender. The explanation would become especially plausible if we found that salary differences between men and women disappeared in comparisons of men and women of the same rank. Of course, such a finding also would raise the question of why a greater share of men than of women hold professor rank.

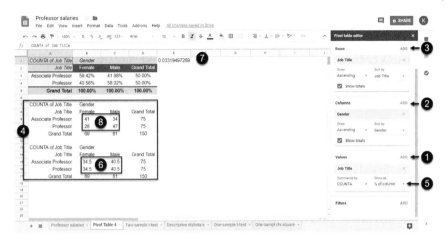

Figure 6.8 Setup and results of a two-sample chi-square test on a PivotTable. Add "Job Title" to the "Values" area (1), "Gender" to the "Columns" area (2), and "Job title" to the "Rows" area (3). Copy the resulting PivotTable and paste it twice, in "values only" format, below the original (4). Change "Show as" to "% of column" (5), then replace the values in cells B15, B16, C15 and C16 with expected values (6). Each expected value can be calculated by multiplying the "Grand Total" percentage for its type of range by the "Grand Total" count of its gender type. Finally, use the " =chitest" function to compute the chi-square probability (7). Using the function involves highlighting the "observed values" in cells B9, B10, C9 and C10, (8) typing a comma, then highlighting the expected values. Google and the Google logo are registered trademarks of Google Inc., used with permission.

Perhaps institutional discrimination against women affects women's pay chiefly by affecting their opportunities for promotion to professor rank.

But getting back to this section's initial question: Is the percentage of men who hold professor rank in our sample greater than the percentage of women who hold professor rank? And, if so, is the difference large enough to rule out random sampling variation as a plausible explanation for the difference? We can't answer this question with a two-sample t-test, because a t-test is designed to compare averages. Nothing about this question can be averaged. A faculty member's gender is either "male" or "female," and a faculty member's rank is either "associate" or "full." To use a term we introduced earlier, both "gender" and "rank" are categorical variables. Accordingly, we need an inferential procedure designed to work with two variables that are both categorical. A chi-square test, applied to a pivot table, is just such a procedure. It involves a more elaborate pivot table than the one you made to count the number of men and women in the tenured faculty sample and a more elaborate version of the chi-square test you used to evaluate the results. Figure 6.8 illustrates the process.

First, let's look at setting up the pivot table. Using the pivot table language we introduced in Chapter 4, we can phrase the statement we're evaluating as,

"The value of <u>the number of faculty members</u>, compared by <u>gender</u> (male or female), is related to <u>the type of rank</u> (associate professor or professor)."

- **Close XLMiner, if the add-on is still running.** Left running, XLMiner will cover up the pivot table editor.
- **Click Cell A1 of the "Professor salaries" tab.** As usual, this step helps Google Sheets know what data you want to include in the analysis.
- **Click "Data / Pivot table ..."** A new tab will open, as will the pivot table editor.
- **Add "Job title" to the pivot table editor's "Values" area.** All we need for the "value of" variable, "number of professors," is some categorical variable that will indicate how many faculty members end up in each cell of the pivot table. The "Job title" variable will do just fine. So would any of the other categorical variables in the dataset.
- **Add "Gender" to the "Columns" area of the pivot table editor.** We're comparing the number of male and female faculty members. In keeping with the approach described in Chapter 4, the "<u>c</u>omparison" variable should go in the "<u>C</u>olumns" box.
- **Add "Job title" to the "Rows" area of the pivot table.** As the "<u>r</u>elated to" variable, "Job title" goes in the "<u>R</u>ows" box.

It's always wise to transform the pivot table's counts into column percentages in order to better see any patterns in the table. But in this case, you can see a pattern even before you do so. Of the 69 women, the majority (41) are associate professors, and a minority (28) are full professors. Among the 81 male faculty, the pattern is reversed. The majority (41) are professors, and the minority (34) are associate professors. To see the pattern more clearly, or at least differently, click the down arrow under "Show as" in the "Job title" box under "Values" and change "Default" to "% of column." Now you can see that 58.02 percent of the male faculty are at the higher "professor" rank, compared to only 40.58 percent of the females. Or, looking at the other side of the pattern, 59.42 percent of the female faculty are at the lower "associate professor" rank, compared to only 41.98 percent of the male faculty.

So, a larger share of male than female faculty in the sample have made it to the higher "professor" rank. But could it be that there is no such gender difference among all MTSU tenured faculty, and the difference in our sample showed up purely due to random sampling variation? Applying a chi-square test to the pivot table can answer that question for us. The pivot table is a little more complex than the pivot table involved in the one-sample chi-square test discussed above, so a little more complex version of the test will be needed. But we think you'll find the adaptations easy to make. Here's what to do:

- **Change the "Show as" option for the "Job Title" box under "Values" back to "Default."** Doing so will revert to showing you counts for each pivot table cell rather than column percentages. What comes next won't work correctly if you leave the pivot table showing percentages.

- **Make two "values only" copies of the pivot table, and paste each of them underneath the pivot table.** You eventually might develop your own way of doing this part, but this is the approach that works best for us and the students we've taught to do it.
  - Use your mouse to highlight the pivot table, Cell A1 through Cell D5.
  - Press "Ctrl/c" or "Cmd/c" on the keyboard to copy what you've highlighted.
  - Click on Cell A7, which is two rows beneath the bottom of the pivot table.
  - Press "Ctrl/Shift/v" or "Cmd/Shift/v" on the keyboard to paste the pivot table's contents as "values only," meaning just text and data, with no formatting or formulas. If you'd rather use your mouse than use the key combination, right click on Cell A7, then choose "Paste special / Past values only."
  - Click on Cell A13, and repeat the process. Doing so will paste a second "values only" copy of the pivot table one blank row beneath the first "values only" copy of the pivot table.
  - At this point, some students like to highlight the pivot table and both "values only" copies, then choose "Format / Align / Center" to center the contents of all three tables. Doing so can make it easier to match table contents with their labels. There's also a center-align button on the menu that you can use instead, or you can use the "Ctrl/Shift/E" or "Cmd/ Shift/E" key combination. It's an optional step, though.
- **Return the original pivot table to showing column percentages.** Click the table, then change "Default" under "Show as" to "% of column." Now you'll be able to keep the percentages in front of you for reference as you perform the chi-square test on the counts in the two copied tables.
- **Highlight and delete the four counts in the center of the second copied table.** That would be the 41 in Cell B15, the 34 in Cell C15, the 28 in Cell B16, and the 47 in Cell C16.
- **Fill Cell B15 with the "expected count" for women at the associate professor rank.** This expected count is the number of female associate professors you would expect there to be in the sample if there were no relationship whatsoever between gender and rank.
  - This step sounds hard, but it isn't, if you take a moment to think about it. Fifty percent of all faculty members in our sample hold the rank of associate professor. You can tell by looking at the pivot table's "Grand total" percentage in the "Associate Professor" row (that is, the percentage in Cell D3). So if gender made no difference at all in rank, you would expect the percentage of women at the associate rank to be exactly the same as the percentage of all faculty members at the associate rank: 50 percent.
  - There's an easy way to calculate this "expected value." Click on Cell B15, the one for female associate professors, then type a " = " symbol to begin writing a formula.

- Click Cell D3, the 50 percent "Grand total" percentage for all associate professors, regardless of gender.
- Press the "*" symbol on the keyboard, to signal multiplication.
- Click Cell B17, the one containing the total number of female faculty in the sample (69).
- Press "Enter."
- You've just calculated that 50 percent of the 69 female faculty would be 34 and a half female faculty members. Don't worry about the "half a female faculty member" part. Nobody's going to get cut in half. More to the point, it's not unusual for these expected values to come out as fractions.

- **Use the same process to calculate and deposit expected counts for cells B16, C15, and C16.** Here are the formulas and results for each:
  - Put =D4*B17 in Cell B16. The result should be 34.5.
  - Put =D3*C17 in Cell C15. The result should be 40.5.
  - Put =D4*C17 in Cell C16. The result should be 40.5.
  - Notice that each formula picks up the overall percentage for its particular rank category and the overall count for its particular gender category. For example, Cell B15, for female associate professors, refers to the overall percentage for associate professors, while Cell C16, for male professors, refers to the overall percentage for professors. Similarly, Cell B15 refers to the overall count for female professors, while Cell C16 refers to the overall count for male professors.
  - In this example, the expected counts happen to come out the same for females at the associate and professor ranks, and also for males at the associate and professor ranks, but only because the sample happened to have an identical number of associate and full professors overall. Had there been more of one rank type than the other, each expected count would have been unique as a result.

- **Start typing "=chitest(" into an available cell.** Omit the quote marks. We used Cell E1.
  - Tip: Be a little strategic about the cell you pick. When you start typing the =chitest function, Google Sheets will open a pop-up "Help" window. Unhelpfully, the window can cover up cells in the tables that you need to be able to see and click on. The window is about 12 rows tall and about three columns wide, so it can cover up a lot of cells. If it gets in your way, you can close it by clicking the "x" in the help window's upper-right corner.
  - Picking Cell E1, like we did, causes the window to drop down neatly to the right of the tables.

- **Use your mouse to drag across and highlight the observed counts – the ones that came out of the sample.** Those are in cells B9, B10, C9 and C10. Google Sheets will show the range as "B9:C10."

- **Type a comma.** As in any function, the comma signals that you're about to enter the next piece of information.

- **Use your mouse to drag across and highlight the expected counts – the ones you just calculated.** Those are in cells B15, B16, C15 and C16. Google Sheets will show the range as "B15:C16."
- **Press "Enter."** Google Sheets will show you the chi-square test's p-value, which, rounded to the customary three decimal places, is 0.033.

Again, the 0.033 p-value you have calculated represents the probability that our observed counts of females and males at each faculty rank are as different as they are, or more so, from the expected counts we calculated only by the chances of sampling. Since 0.033 is less than 0.050, we can confidently rule out random sampling variation as an explanation for the difference. Ruling out that explanation makes the alternative explanation more plausible: The tenured faculty sample's men were more likely to hold professor rank than its women were because the same pattern exists among the larger population the sample came from: all tenured MTSU faculty. In news-style language, the finding could be summarized in any of the following ways:

- "Fifty-eight percent of male tenured faculty held the rank of professor, compared to only 41 percent of female tenured faculty, a statistically significant difference."
- "Tenured male faculty were statistically more likely than tenured female faculty to have been promoted, according to the data. Fifty-eight percent of the men had been promoted to professor rank, while a significantly smaller 41 percent of the women had been promoted to professor rank."
- "The promotion rate among tenured women, 41 percent, trailed the 58 percent rate among tenured men, a statistically significant disparity."

We said earlier that a finding like this one would suggest that the pay disparity between male and female tenured faculty has something to do with rank. We added that rank differences might even explain all of the pay differences, especially if the pay differences between men and women disappeared when we compared men and women of the same rank. But even that finding would lead to questions about why promotion to professor rank is more common among men than among women, and that institutional discrimination against women might affect women's pay indirectly, by affecting their opportunities for promotion.

You know everything you need to know in order to explore this possible interaction between rank and gender as factors in average pay. You know how to use a two-sample t-test to compare average salaries of men and women (see Figure 6.7). Setting up that analysis involved using a filter applied to the "Gender" column to copy each gender group's salary figures to a different column in a new tab. If you repeat the procedure, but add a filter to the "Job Title" column, you could create the columns depicted in Figure 6.9, then run a two-sample t-test on the male and female salary columns for associate professors, and a second two-sample t-test on the male and female salary columns for

Professor salaries practice space

File Edit View Insert Format Data Tools Add-ons Help   All changes saved in Drive

fx | Male associate

Male associate	Female associate	Male professor	Female professor	t-Test: Two-Sample Assuming Unequal Variances		
67182	68639	79967	75761			
66561	98000	130000	88496		Male associate	Female associate
66199	57934	81642	84140	Mean	71388.02941	68533.36585
78229	102263	74330	64404	Variance	212460843.1	277920448.3
61080	53907	82404	85783	Observations	34	41
86459	68000	92040	86731	Hypothesized Mean Difference	0	
75011	66064	73522	71014	df	72	
99470	63902	123120	82868	t Stat	0.7909082873	
95606	59687	72507	76046	P(T<=t) one-tail	0.215797559	
64401	56019	115085	84370	t Critical one-tail	1.666293636	
72902	61722	86892	71510	P(T<=t) two-tail	0.4315961179	
65000	59669	77678	77164	t Critical two-tail	1.993463539	
63776	64264	88673	82801			
61325	66199	88421	103728		Male professor	Female professor
62757	54443	90571	83977	Mean	89764.82979	86195.82143
59784	52608	87549	95170	Variance	274402135.2	324058961.4
59804	96354	120018	89627	Observations	47	28
57976	63390	91288	83680	Hypothesized Mean Difference	0	
54000	99579	87729	167972	df	53	
114987	62579	112228	69266	t Stat	0.8653123872	
71000	74725	106970	83321	P(T<=t) one-tail	0.1981141766	
62181	58211	74740	79508	t Critical one-tail	1.674116178	
73405	59579	89156	92145	P(T<=t) two-tail	0.3962283532	
67312	56088	89251	82406	t Critical two-tail	2.005745949	

Professor salaries | t-tests by rank | Sheet3 | Pivot Table 3 | Sheet2 | Pivot Table 5 | Pivot Table 4 | Pivot Table 2 | Pivot Table

XLMiner Analysis ToolPak

Sampling

t-Test: Paired Two Sample for Means

t-Test: Two-Sample Assuming Equal Variances

t-Test: Two-Sample Assuming Unequal Variances

Variable 1 Range: C1:C48
Variable 2 Range: D1:D29
Hypothesized Mean Difference: 0
✓ Labels
Alpha: 0.05
Output Range: E15
OK

z-Test: Two-Sample for Means

Help, Examples, Upgrades

Figure 6.9 Setup and results of two separate two-sample t-tests, one comparing average salaries among tenured male and female faculty at the associate professor rank, and one making the same comparison among tenured faculty at the professor rank. Google and the Google logo are registered trademarks of Google Inc., used with permission.

professors. The t-test results show no significant salary differences between tenured men and women of the same faculty rank. The p-value for the directional t-test is 0.216 for associate professors and 0.198 for professors. Both probabilities are less than 0.050. But there's a suspicious pattern in the sample results. Among both associate professor and professors, the sample salaries for males average higher than the sample salaries for females. Also, the gap between the sample salaries for men and women is wider among professors (a difference of more than $3,500) than among associate professors (a difference of just under $3,000). All in all, there's enough of a pattern here to warrant repeating the analysis with a second, larger random sample. It may be that a larger sample could rule out the possibility that the higher average pay for men among both associate professors and professors could be due to random sampling variation. And the results at hand strongly suggest that, for whatever reason, relatively fewer female tenured faculty get promoted than male tenured faculty.

Correlation Between Two Continuous Variables: Regression

What if we want to see whether values for two continuous variables are associated with each other? The MTSU tenured faculty dataset includes only one continuous variable (salary), so we'll look instead at salary data for employees of the Metropolitan Government of Nashville and Davidson County, Tennessee. We created the dataset after downloading records for all 9,358 Metro Nashville employees from the Nashville Open Data Portal mentioned earlier, https://data.nashville.gov. We filtered the data for full-time employees classified as "professionals," which left us with 2,194 individuals. We then used a random sampling procedure to select the 150 workers we included in the "Metro Nashville professional employees.csv" demonstration dataset, which you can download from http://thedatareporter.com/demonstration-files/. Conveniently, Metro Nashville's data includes not only each employee's salary but also the date each employee was hired. A quick formula subtracting each employees hire date from the date we downloaded the file and dividing the resulting number of days by 365 yielded each employee's number of years on the job, expressed up to two decimal places. We also included each employee's job title.

Checking descriptive statistics is a good idea when you're working with regression. Recall that extreme values can distort an average; one or two unusually high or low salaries, for example, can artificially inflate or depress an average. Under the right circumstances, outliers can cause similar trouble in regression. We'll talk more about that later. Descriptive statistics for both the "Annual Salary" column and the "Years on job" column showed averages a bit higher than their medians, an indication that both distributions might include some unusually large values. The "Years on job" column, in particular, showed a maximum value of 44.22 years. That's pretty extreme when you consider that the typical difference from the mean of 13.36 years is only 11.42 years, as indicated by the column's standard deviation. Any time you have questions about how the values in a continuous variable are behaving, you can learn a lot by looking at a particular type of chart called a histogram. You learned in Chapter 2 how to make different kinds of charts in Google Sheets. Making histograms for the "Annual Salary" and "Years on job" columns involves the same process. Highlight the data in the column, click "Insert / Chart," then click "Chart type" on the chart editor's "Data" tab, and scroll down until you can click on "Histogram chart." Figure 6.10 shows the descriptive statistics and histogram charts for both variables after the statistics and charts were copied to a new tab.

A regression analysis can tell us whether there is evidence of a relationship between the "Annual Salary" and "Years on job" variables, and, if so, what direction that relationship exhibits. "Direction," in regression, refers to what happens to the values in one variable as the values in another variable change. Here, we would expect employees with low "Years on job" figures to have low "Annual Salary" figures, and employees with high "Years on job" figures to have high "Annual Salary" figures. After all, the longer an employee works for an organization, the more the employee's salary tends to rise, due to promotions, cost-of-living pay increases, and so on. Such a relationship has a "positive" direction, meaning that as one variable increases, so does the other. But this may not be the case for all employees, and maybe not even for most of them. It could be that Metro Nashville has recently hired a number of new employees at unusually large salaries. If most or all newer employees had higher salaries than all or most longer-term employees, the relationship would exhibit a "negative" direction, meaning that as one variable increased, the other tended to decrease.

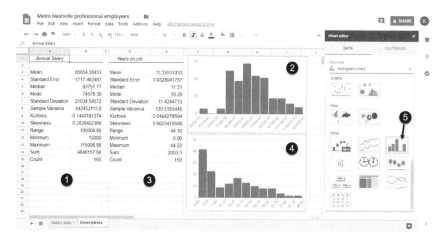

Figure 6.10 Descriptive statistics and histograms. The "Annual Salary" column's descriptive statistics (1) and histogram (2) suggest a few more extreme cases on the right than on the left. The "Years on job" column's descriptives (3) and histogram (4) suggest a little more than 40 extremely low cases and a small number of extremely high cases. A histogram is simply a chart option available in the chart editor (5). The descriptive statistics and histograms shown were generated on the "Salary data" tab and copied to the tab displayed. Google and the Google logo are registered trademarks of Google Inc., used with permission.

The test statistic for a regression equation is referred to as a regression coefficient, or beta. A positive beta indicates a positive relationship, while a negative beta indicates a negative relationship. A zero beta, or an obtained beta that is not significantly distinguishable from a zero beta (a correlation with an associated p-value such that $p > 0.050$), would indicate no evidence of a discernable linear trend in the relationship between "Years on job" and "Annual Salary." In other words, it would mean we don't really see a significant increase or decrease in "Annual Salary" happening as "Years on job" increases.

It is easy to conduct regression analysis in XLMiner. Figure 6.11 shows the steps and results, although we rearranged the output and the plot so that both could show at the same time. Here are details:

- **Go to the salary data tab and activate XLMiner, if it isn't already running.** Click "Add-ons / XLMiner Analysis ToolPak / Start."
- **Click on "Linear Regression" in the XLMiner area.** XLMiner's Linear Regression menu will drop open.
- **Highlight the values in Column A, the "Annual Salary" column.** Remember that you can do so by clicking Cell A1, holding down "Ctrl/Shift" or "Cmd/Shift" on the keyboard, and pressing the down arrow.
- **Click in the "Input Y Range" box.** Doing so will deposit the cell range's address, A1:A151, into the box.

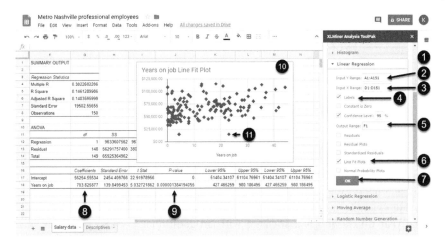

Figure 6.11 Regression analysis setup and results. Click "Linear Regression" in XLMiner (1), highlight the "Annual Salary" data in Column A (not shown) and click on the "Input Y Range" box (2). Highlight the "Years on job" data in Column D (not shown) and click on the "Input X Range" box (3). Check the "Labels" box (4), click an available cell in the spreadsheet as the output location (not shown), then click in the "Output Range" box (5). Check the "Line Fit Plots" box (6), and click "OK" (7). In the output, look for the beta coefficient (8) and its associated p-value (9). Check the line fit plot (10) for outliers and, perhaps, for interestingly unusual cases (11). Google and the Google logo are registered trademarks of Google Inc., used with permission.

- **Highlight the values in Column D, "Years on job," and click the "Input X Range" box.** The range's address, D1:D151, will appear in the box. It doesn't matter much in the end which variable you put in the Y Range box and which one you put in the X Range box. But if one variable can be thought of as at least a possible factor in determining the other, convention calls for putting the possible factor in the X Range box, and the other one in the Y Range box. Here, for instance, it's likelier that "Years on job" is a factor in determining "Annual Salary," or at least more likely than "Annual Salary" to be a factor in determining "Years on job."
- **Check the "Labels" box.** If you forget to do so, and if there are column labels included in the data ranges you defined, XLMiner will complain that your "Input range contains non-numeric data."
- **Click an available cell, like Cell F1, then click on the "Output range" box.** The cell address will appear in the box.
- **Check the box next to "Line Fit Plots."**
- **Click "OK."**

XLMiner will generate the regression output as well as the line fit plot, and put both on the Google Sheet, starting in the cell you specified as the output location. The columns won't automatically expand to accommodate the output, so you'll have to widen them manually by dragging across them with your mouse to highlight them and then double-clicking on the boundary between any two of their column letters.

There are a lot of numbers here. Most are meaningful only to statisticians. Two are particularly important for our purposes, though: the beta coefficient quantifying the association between "Annual Salary" and "Years on job," and the beta coefficient's associated p-value. The beta coefficient will show up in the bottommost table of the output, under the "Coefficients" heading and in the same row as the "Years on job" label. In our example, the beta coefficient comes to 703.83, rounded to two decimal places. It is positive, which means that as "Years on job" increases, "Annual Salary" tends to increase, too. It also tells you how much "Annual Salary" typically increases every time "Years on job" increases by one step. For example, at least among the 150 employees we're looking at, each additional year on the job is associated with an additional $703.83 in annual pay. Some employees get a lot less, of course, and others get a lot more, but that's the overall pattern. The beta coefficient's associated p-value, located three cells to the right, under the "P-value" heading, gives you the probability that randomness, such as random sampling error, could produce a pattern of association as strong as the one the analysis did. The p-value here is 0.000001384194055, which isn't even a blip if you round to the customary three decimal places, 0.000. It's far less than 0.050, so we can confidently rule out randomness as an explanation for the association between "Annual Salary" and "Years on job."

A final component of the output to look at is the line fit plot you requested by checking the "Line Fit Plots" box while setting up the analysis. The plot is simply a picture of the relationship between "Annual Salary," represented by the amounts on the chart's vertical (that is, the "Y") axis, and "Years on job," represented by the numbers on the chart's horizontal (that is, the "X") axis. Each dot represents at least one worker, and the dot's position indicates that worker's position on both the "Annual Salary" axis and the "Years on job" axis. Mouse over the dots in Figure 6.11, and you'll find one that represents a worker who has a salary of $108,242, despite having been on the job only 0.11 years, or barely more than a month. How unusual, right? Go find this person in the data (Hint: Filter "Annual Salary" for "$108,242), and you'll find that the person is an "Assistant Metropolitan Atty 4," that is, a lawyer. That explains the unusually large salary – and perhaps why we should have gone to law school. But perhaps you can see the value, here, of looking at the line fit plot. It will help you find unusual cases, and journalists are always interested in unusual cases. How about the person behind that dot at 23.04 years on the job and a $15,000 annual salary? We figured the person was some kind of low-level clerk or maintenance worker or something, although such workers usually aren't classified as "professional." It turns out that's a "Sr Assistant District Attorney." That person, and two other "Assistant District Attorney" types, are the only professionals in the sample who make $15,000 a year. There's probably a perfectly reasonable explanation. The amounts may be retainer fees, for example. But look at enough unusual cases as a journalist, and you'll eventually find a story. Maybe a really good one.

A less dramatic, but equally important, reason to look at the line fit plot is to check for outliers. An outlier shows up as a dot that is pretty much all by itself on the chart. Imagine, for example, that the chart showed a dot representing someone who had worked only one year but who was making a million bucks. That's several times more than our newly hired "Assistant Metropolitan Atty 4" or, for that matter, anyone else on the chart. Whether the case turns out to be your next Pulitzer or simply a typo in the data (alas, the latter is more likely), the case will definitely wreck your regression analysis. That one case will change the shape of the relationship so dramatically that your beta coefficient will drop to 101.55, and your p-value will inflate to a don't-even-bother 0.859. If you don't check the line fit plot (and if you missed the whopping standard deviation and maximum value in your descriptives), you'll never know that "Annual Salary" and "Years on job" really were strongly related. The opposite can happen, too. Imagine a dot on the chart representing someone with a million a year in pay and a thousand years on the job. Again, typos would be the likely culprits, seeing as Nashville didn't exist in the eleventh century, and anyone who was around back then wouldn't be still working today. But that one outlier would raise your beta coefficient to 942.12 and give you a p-value so small that even Google Sheets would revert to scientific notation to express it: $1.69682348914237E-91$, or 90 zeros to the right of the decimal point before the "169" part even gets started. Finally, a dot showing our sole candidate for employee-of-the-millennium earning just a buck a year would turn the beta coefficient significantly negative: -51.64, and a p-value of 0.017. In short, outliers can mess up a regression analysis the way extreme values can mess up an average. Better check for them.

Examples of ways to write journalistically about regression results include:

- "Salaries tended to range about $704 higher per year on the job, a pattern that proved statistically significant."
- "Salaries correlated positively with years on the job, typically rising by a statistically significant $704 for each year."

Recap

In this chapter we have discussed how statistics calculated using data collected from a random sample of a population can be used to make inferences about that population. This is essentially a matter of probability and confidence.

There is always some chance, no matter how small, that our inferences may be wrong. However, because of the properties of random samples and probability, we can sometimes make inferences with confidence.

Suppose you wrote stories about the analyses we conducted in this chapter and posted them on a website. You might get a comment on the tenured faculty salary story from a tenured faculty member at MTSU saying that he is man who believes he makes less than his female colleagues. You might get a comment on the salary and years on the job story saying that the commenter is a long-time professional employee who makes thousands less than the new hire in the next cubicle. Both of these comments might imply or explicitly argue that your analysis is wrong. But those contentions are anecdotes taken from individual experiences and perceptions, whereas our analyses were conducted using systematically-collected data from random samples of the populations in question, samples that give everyone in the population the same chance of being selected – even the commenters, even if they weren't directly included in the sample. We know there is some small chance that the results of our analysis might not accurately reflect the population, but the results of our analyses are almost certainly more representative of the population than our commenters' anecdotes.

References

Census. 2015. "Income and Poverty in the United States: 2014." Accessed May 8, 2016. www.census.gov/content/dam/Census/library/publications/2015/demo/p60-252.pdf

Census. 2016. "QuickFacts: United States." Accessed May 8, 2016. www.census.gov/quickfacts/table/PST045215/00

Hayes, Andrew F. 2005. Statistical Methods for Communication Science. Mahwah, NJ: Lawrence Erlbaum Associates.

"Qualtrics Sample Size Calculator." Accessed May 8, 2016. www.qualtrics.com/blog/determining-sample-size/

"Survey Monkey Sample Size Calculator." Accessed May 8, 2016. www.surveymonkey.com/mp/sample-size-calculator/

7

Other Functions, Tools and Techniques

In this chapter, we'll list and describe some Excel functions, as well as some general tools and techniques, that can prove especially useful in data journalism but that haven't come up yet or that we feel need further explanation. They're in no particular order, but we'll try to describe each one in a context that shows its potential value. Unless otherwise noted, the functions and tools described here will work equally well in Google Sheets.

DATE, NOW, and DATEDIF

You should know by now how to get Excel to calculate the difference between two values. If Cell A1 contains "10" and Cell B1 contains "3," putting the expression =A1-B1 in Cell C1 would produce the difference: 7. Getting Excel to calculate the difference between two dates, though, isn't so simple. You'll need the DATE and DATEDIF functions to get the job done. The NOW function can come in handy, too.

Suppose you're analyzing a spreadsheet of city parking fines that have gone uncollected for several years. Your spreadsheet includes the year, month and day of each fine's issue date, and you want to calculate how many days old each fine is. Let's say the headings "Year," "Month" and "Day" are in Cells A1, B1 and C1 of your spreadsheet, respectively. The next row contains the data for the first fine's date, which was Sept. 29, 2015. Thus, your spreadsheet has 2015 in A2, 9 in B2, and 29 in C2. The rows below contain hundreds of additional dates for hundreds of additional uncollected fines.

The first task is to convert the date information in Row 2 into a number that Excel can use in calculations. Excel can do this with the DATE function, which takes in the year, month and day of a date and converts them to the number of days between that date and Jan. 1, 1900. No, we're not sure why Microsoft picked Jan. 1, 1900. Yes, the process can go off the rails if you try to convert a date earlier than Jan. 1, 1900. If you come across a parking fine that old, chances are the statute of limitations has run out. Anyway, the function looks like this:

=DATE(year,month,day)

The "year," "month" and "day" arguments can be actual numbers, as in:

=DATE(2015,9,29)

Or they can be addresses of cells that hold the year, month and day information, as in:

=DATE(A2,B2,C2)

Type the latter form of the function into Cell D2 of your spreadsheet, hit "Enter," and Excel will display:

9/29/2015

… or some similar date format, depending on your computer's settings. Underneath, though, Excel will treat the value as 42,276, the number of days since Jan. 1, 1900. Type "Serial date" into Cell D1 as a heading for this calculation's column. Next, you need the current date, which you can tell Excel to fetch for you if you type =NOW() into Cell E2. You might also add "Current time" as a column heading in Cell E1. The NOW function requires no arguments between the parentheses, but don't forget to type the parentheses. The function won't work without them. The NOW function automatically displays the date in a standard, readable format. But, underneath, it's using the same serial approach the DATE function is using. Our final function for this section, the DATEDIF function, can calculate the difference between the two and express it as days, months or years. The function looks like this:

=DATEDIF(start_date,end_date,"unit")

The "start_date" argument is the earlier of the two dates to be compared. The "end_date" argument is the more recent of the two dates. Finally, the "unit" argument controls whether the difference will be shown in days, complete months, or complete years. The "D" argument indicates days. The "M" argument means months. The "Y" argument means years. When you type the function into your spreadsheet, the "unit" argument has to be enclosed in quote marks. The other two functions should not be put in quotes. So, give it a try. Enter "Days old" in Cell F1 as a column heading. Then, in Cell F2 of your spreadsheet, enter:

=DATEDIF(D2,E2,"D")

If you want to, you can add "Months old" and "Years old" headings to cells G1 and H1, respectively, then type these two functions into cells G2 and H2, respectively:

=DATEDIF(D2,E2,"M")
=DATEDIF(D2,E2,"Y")

Copy cells D2 through H2 down the column, and you'll have the age of each uncollected fine, in days, months and years. Of course, if you'd rather choose a fixed second date instead of using the NOW function, just add columns for the fixed date's year, month, day and DATE conversion, then reference the fixed date's DATE conversion cell, instead of the NOW function cell, in the DATEDIF function.

AVERAGE, STDEV, MEDIAN, MIN, MAX

You learned in Chapter 6 how you can use XLMiner to generate a whole series of descriptive statistics for the values in a given column. Descriptive statistics in the output include the average (or "mean," which is a synonym), the standard deviation, the median, the minimum, and the maximum. Sometimes, though, you might want to get these statistics one at a time, or generate them all at once for a range of rows or columns.

Suppose, for example, you had retrieved the unadjusted U.S. monthly unemployment rate data shown in Figure 7.1. Such data is available from the U.S. Department of Labor's Bureau of Labor Statistics at https://data.bls.gov/timeseries/LNU04000000. Also suppose you wanted to quickly generate basic descriptive statistics for each month's rates between 2008 and 2018. In other words, suppose you wanted descriptive statistics for each column. Excel's built-in version of XLMiner, the Data Analysis ToolPak, could generate the table of descriptive statistics for January, shown to the right of the data, in columns O and P. But you would have to regenerate the report for each month. That would take some time. Also, the values in the report's output would not be lined up in the same column as the data they describe.

A better way might be to use the descriptive statistics functions shown in cells B13 through B17, which read:

- =AVERAGE(B2:B12), which calculates the average, or mean.
- =STDEV(B2:B12), which calculates the standard deviation.
- =MEDIAN(B2:B12), which calculates the median, or middle value in the range.
- =MIN(B2:B12), which calculates the minimum, or smallest value in the range.
- =MAX(B2:B12), which calculates the maximum, or largest value in the range.

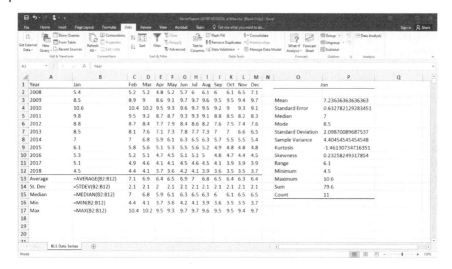

Figure 7.1 Generating descriptive statistics for a series of data columns, using individual descriptive statistic functions. Output from Excel's Data Analysis ToolPak for the January column's figures is shown to the right, in column's O and P. Used with permission from Microsoft.

We've programmed the functions to describe the table's January values, in cells B2 through B12. The values in cells C13 through M17 show the results of copying the functions to the right, a maneuver that will calculate, in a fraction of a second, all five descriptive statistics for the yearly figures in each month's column.

Individual functions are available for several of the lesser used statistics in the descriptives output from XLMiner or Data Analysis ToolPak. Here are examples, programed, like those in Figure 7.1, to summarize the data in Cells B2 through B12:

- =MODE(B2:B12), which returns the mode, or the most frequently occurring value in the range.
- =KURT(B2:B12), which returns the kurtosis of the values in the range. Kurtosis measures how tall and skinny a distribution is. A distribution exactly as tall and skinny as a normal distribution will have a kurtosis value of zero. A distribution that is taller and skinnier than a normal distribution will have a positive kurtosis value, and one that is shorter and fatter than a normal distribution will have a negative kurtosis value.
- =SKEW(B2:B12), which returns the skewness of the values in the range. Skewness measures the degree of symmetry in a distribution. A distribution with the same symmetry as a normal distribution will have a skewness of zero. One that has outlying scores on the left will have a negative skewness value. One that has outlying scores on the right will have a positive skewness value.
- =COUNT(B2:B12), which returns the number of values in the range. The function counts numbers only. It will ignore text and blank cells.

RAND

Any time you need to select a random subset of some records in Excel, the RAND function can help you out. The chapter on inferential statistics described an investigation that involved choosing 150 records at random from a spreadsheet detailing the gender, ranks and salaries of 548 associate and full professors at our university. We wanted to compare rank and salary across gender, but the available data did not include gender information. We wanted to avoid having to find and add gender information for all 548 professors in the database. So, we decided, instead, to do so just for 150 randomly chosen professors, then use inferential statistics to draw conclusions about what we would have found had we done the same for all 548 professors.

We used the RAND function to draw that sample, and you can use it the same way we did any time you need to do something similar. We simply went to a blank column at the right end of the dataset and typed "Random number" as a heading in the column's first cell. Then, in the column's second cell, which was in the same row as the first professor's salary and rank information, we entered:

=RAND()

... then copied the function down the column, putting an =RAND() function in the last cell of each row of salary data. Excel responded by filling each of those cells with a random number between zero and one. Next, we sorted the whole dataset by this newly created "Random number" column. Sorting records by a column of random numbers puts the records in – you guessed it – random order. We copied the first 150 records to a new worksheet, and they became our random sample.

LEFT, MID, and RIGHT

These three functions can help you take apart the contents of a cell. They can be especially helpful when dealing with ID codes made up of parts that have meaning. For example, suppose you're working with a spreadsheet of incident report data for the year 2016 obtained from your local police department. In the spreadsheet's first column is a unique ID for each report. The ID for the first incident report, which is sitting in Cell A2 under the "Report" heading in Cell A1, reads AD041600197. According to the data's documentation, this code has three parts. The first two characters represent the type of crime the report details. An "AD" code, the documentation indicates, is an "Alcohol / Drug Violation." The next two characters represent the month in which the report was filed, with "01" indicating "January," "02" indicating "February," and so on. The next two digits indicate the last two digits of the year. The last five digits indicate the incident's serial position among all incidents of that type for that month. So, the first incident in the spreadsheet details the 197th alcohol / drug violation incident the department investigated in April of 2016. That's all potentially useful information for your analysis, but it's not going to help you much if it stays locked up in that code.

Let's say you insert three blank columns, B, C, and D, to the right of the code and label them "Crime code," "Month" and "Sequence," respectively. First, you can use the LEFT function to pull the first two digits – the crime code – out of the ID and put them cell B2. Just enter this in Cell B2:

=LEFT(A2,2)

The function will show "AD" in Cell B2. The "A2" argument is the cell address for the code. The "2" argument is the number of characters, starting from the left, that you want Excel to extract.

Getting the "Month" out of the middle of the ID is just about as easy. In Cell C2, enter:

=MID(A2,3,2)

The function will show "04" in cell C2. Again, the "A2" argument is the cell address of the ID. The middle argument, "3," is the place number, starting at 1 from the left, of the first character you want Excel to extract. The final argument, "2," is the total number of characters you want Excel to extract. So, the function tells Excel: Go to Cell A2, count from the left until you reach the third character, and, starting with that third character, extract two characters." If you wanted the year, you could use another MID function to get it. Because all of the incident reports are for 2016, though, the year will never vary. A "Year" column that reads "16" for all records wouldn't be all that useful, unless you planned to combine the spreadsheet with identically formatted data from a previous year.

Finally, you can use the RIGHT function to grab the last five digits, which represent the incident's sequence among all of the month's incidents of the same type. In Cell D2, enter:

=RIGHT(A2,5)

The function will show "00197" in Cell D2. The "A2" argument is, as always, the cell address where the ID is. The "5" argument tells Excel to extract the last five characters in the cell. Once you have all of these functions set up, you could copy all three down their columns at the same time, replicating the extraction for each ID number in the dataset.

The "Text to Columns" Wizard

The "Text to Columns" wizard in Excel can help you solve a similar problem. Often, you'll get a spreadsheet in which names have been stored in a single column, with the last name, then a comma, then a first name, like "Smith, John." Or you'll get a single column with a city and state name in the same column, separated by a comma. For instance: "Murfreesboro, TN." For a lot of reasons, you might want to separate the information into one column for the first name and one column for the last name, or one column for the city and one column for the state. However, the LEFT, MID and RIGHT functions described above won't be able to help you. They work only when each piece of information you want to extract from each cell in the dataset starts at the same position and ends at the same position, like when the "Month" code in the example always started at the third position in the ID code and ended at the fourth position. Names of people and cities vary in length.

In such situations, the "Text to Columns" wizard in Excel can help you out. Figure 7.2 demonstrates its use, using, as an example, names of candidates for the U.S. Senate in Tennessee during the 2018 election, as the names appear in the "Cand_Name" field of the Federal Election Commission's downloadable "All Candidates" file, available from www.fec.gov/data/browse-data/?tab=candidates.

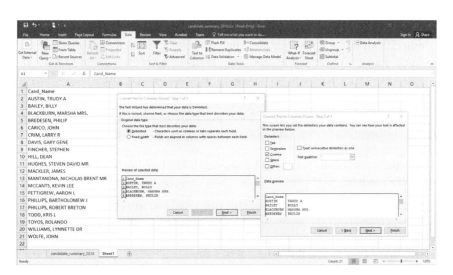

Figure 7.2 The "Convert Text to Columns" Wizard in Excel, which can parse the contents of one column into one or more adjacent columns, guided by a delimiting character, like a comma. Google Sheets offers a similar capability that works differently but produces the same results. Used with permission from Microsoft.

To use the wizard:

- Make sure there is at least one blank column next to the column you want to extract the information from. The extraction process will extract data to as many adjacent columns as there are commas signaling the need for a column break. Note that, if you use commas as delimiters, the wizard can't tell the difference between a delimiting comma and a comma used for some other purpose. A name like "Smith, John" will split neatly into two columns if the comma is the delimiter. But "Smith, John, Jr." will require three columns – and some straightening out of the name after the fact. If the wizard doesn't find enough blank columns to fulfill its task, it will overwrite however many columns it needs. It does ask you first, though, and it gives you the option of canceling the operation if you want.
- Highlight the column you want to split. In Figure 7.2, that would be Column A.
- Click the "Data" tab, then the "Text to Columns" button. The Wizard will open.
- Click "Delimited" to indicate that you want to split the data based on some delimiter in the column. Note that you have the option of choosing "Fixed width." That version of the wizard basically does the same thing the LEFT, MID and RIGHT functions can do, but using a graphic interface. We think the functions are handier, but feel free to try it out and decide for yourself.
- Click "Next." Step 2 of the wizard will show, asking you to specify the delimiter you want Excel to look for. The default is often "Tab." If the box beside "Tab" is checked, uncheck it, then check the box beside "Comma." Note that other delimiters are possible, including the option of specifying a custom one.
- Click "Finish." There is one more step available after Step 2 that will let you specify the type of data in each column. You can use it if you need to, but you probably won't. Clicking "Finish" lets you skip it.

The wizard will close, and Excel will pluck all of the first names and subsequent information from Column A and place them in Column B, leaving the last names in Column A.

Google Sheets offers text-to-columns capability, too, but it works a bit differently. To use it:

- Set the data up the same way, with the delimited text in a column, and enough blank columns to the right of it to accommodate each column of data you plan to extract.
- Use the mouse to select the delimited data.
- Click "Data / Split text to columns …"

Google Sheets will guess which character in the selected text is the delimiter and split the columns based on it. For the data shown in Figure 7.2, which are delimited by a comma, Google Sheets guesses correctly, and no further action is needed. But just in case it guessed incorrectly, Google Sheets will offer a

"Separator:" box toward the bottom of the screen near the selected text. Beside it will be a "Detect automatically" menu that you can click open and change to the delimiter of your choice, including a custom one. Once you designate a different or custom delimiter, Google Sheets will split the data again, this time based on the delimiter you specified.

CONCATENATE

We mentioned the CONCATENATE function briefly in the chapter on mapping, but it deserves a more detailed treatment here. We use the function most often when preparing street addresses for mapping in Google My Maps. Recall that My Maps requires that the street address, city and state for an address be contained in a single column. If these address components reside in separate columns in your dataset, CONCATENATE can put them together for you. Suppose, for instance, cells A1, B1 and C1 of your spreadsheet are labeled "State," "City" and "Street," respectively, and the next row contains "Tennessee," "Murfreesboro," and "1500 Greenland Drive" in cells A2, B2 and C2, respectively. To combine the address components in Cell D2, enter this in the cell:

=CONCATENATE(C2,", ",B2,", ",A2)

The function will display the following in Cell D2, complete with commas and spaces:

1500 Greenland Drive, Murfreesboro, Tennessee

… which, mapped with My Maps, would drop a pin on the campus of Middle Tennessee State University. The tricky part, here, is keeping track of the commas and quotes. The first argument, C2, is, of course, the cell address of the street number, "1500 Greenland Drive." It's followed by a comma, which tells Excel that the first argument is ending and the second one is coming up next. The second argument is a space and a comma, enclosed in quote marks. The quote marks tell the function to treat what's inside them as text and to stick it immediately after the information it pulled from Cell C2. Omit this quote-enclosed comma and space, and you'll get:

1500 Greenland DriveMurfreesboro, Tennessee

… which My Maps might have a difficult time geocoding accurately. Next, another comma signals the end of that argument and the start of the next. The next is Cell B2, which contains the city name, "Murfreesboro." Another comma ends that argument and introduces another "," separator. A final comma introduces the last argument, Cell A2, where the state name, "Tennessee," resides.

You can use CONCATENATE to put together as many cell addresses and separators as you like. A CONCAT function, introduced with Excel 2016, does the same thing the CONCATENATE function does but is also capable of concatenating multi-row ranges of data. We haven't quite figured out a use for that capability yet, though.

IF and IFS

The IF function is another one we've mentioned elsewhere in the book but that deserves a more detailed explanation here. It's easily one of the most useful functions in Excel. In its most basic form, it checks a cell to see whether the cell's contents meet some criteria you've specified. If they do, the function displays one result. If they don't, the function displays a different result.

Imagine you're analyzing finance data for each public school district in your state. The headings "District name," and "Per Pupil Funding" have been entered in cells A1 and B1. The data begin in Row 2, with "Smith County School District" in A2 and "4408" in B2. In the next row, "Smithburg City School District" is in A3, and "6103" is in B3. A nationally comprehensive dataset with these and other variables, by the way, is available from the U.S. Census Bureau (U.S. Census Bureau, 2016a).

You saw during the VLOOKUP demonstration in an earlier chapter that an IF function, given a string of text, can check a cell to see whether the string you've given it matches the text in the cell. Here, we could enter this function into Cell C2:

=IF(A2="Smith County School District","Yes","No")

... and copy it to Cell C3. In Cell C2, the function would display "Yes," because the text string given in the second argument, "Smith County School District," matches the content of the cell specified in the first argument, A2. The third argument tells the function to display "Yes" in the case of a match, and "No" in the case of a mismatch. Accordingly, the function displays a "No" when copied to Cell C3, because that school system name does not match "Smith County School District."

The ability to return a "Yes" in response to an exact match of a text string can be useful. But it might be more useful to be able to return a "Yes" or "No" based on some portion of a string. Notice, for example, that one district is a county school district, and the other is a city school district. City and county school districts can differ substantially, depending on the demographics of their surrounding areas. Faced with a whole column of school district names, some representing county districts and others representing city districts, you might want the ability to automatically classify them as one or the other, based on the content of their names. A regular IF function won't work, because there's no way to get it to match only part of a string in a cell. There is a way, though, that involves combining the IF function with two other functions, the ISNUMBER function and the SEARCH function. Let's assume you've checked to ensure that each county school district has the phrase "County School" in its name, and that every other type of school district does not have the phrase "County School" in its name. If so, you could classify the districts as "County" or "Other" by typing this modified IF function into Cell C2 and copying it to Cell C3 (and all the cells below):

=IF(ISNUMBER(SEARCH("County School",A2)),"County","Other")

The function will display "County" in Cell C2 and "Other" in Cell C3. Explaining how this function works would get pretty tedious. You can learn more about it on the web if you're curious. If you customize the "County School," "A2," "County," and "Other" arguments as needed, the function will work in any situation. You can even use a "*" character as a "wildcard" so the function will recognize subtle variations in the text string. For example, this version of the function:

=IF(ISNUMBER(SEARCH("County Sch*l",A2)),"County","Other")

… will recognize both "County School" and "County Schl" strings, if some districts use "Schl" as an abbreviation for "School." For even more precision, you can "nest" the functions. Here's something to try: Using your mouse, click on the lower boundary of the formula bar and drag it down, to give yourself more than a single line of space in which to type a function. Then, enter this in Cell C2:

=
IF(ISNUMBER(SEARCH("County School",A2)),"County",
IF(ISNUMBER(SEARCH("County Schl",A2)),"County",
"Other"))

It might look complex, but there's a pattern. You can add more "IF(ISNUMBER(SEARCH" statements, one covering each variation you want the search to cover. Just alter each "County School" argument as needed, and be sure to include one ")" character at the end for each such statement. The example has two ")" characters at the end, because it has two "IF(ISNUMBER(SEARCH" statements. You also can use outcome messages other than "County" and "Other."

The IF function can work with numeric data, too. Suppose you learn, through other analyses, that the average per-pupil funding statewide is $5,182. You might want to classify each district's per-pupil spending as "above average" or "average or below." Return the formula bar to its normal size, if you like, by grabbing the lower border and dragging it upward. Then enter this IF function into Cell C2 and copy it to Cell C3:

=IF(B2>5182,"Above average","Average or below")

In Cell C2, the function will display "Average or below," because the amount in Cell B2 is less than $5,182. But in Cell C3, the function will display "Above average," because the amount in Cell B3 is greater than $5,182. In addition to the " > " symbol, you can use " < " or, of course, the " = " symbol to compare values. Combinations of symbols work, too. This version:

=IF(B2>=5182,"Average or above","Below average")

… will classify amounts greater than or equal to $5,182 as "Average or above" and, otherwise, "Below average."

The IFS function, which is new with Excel 2016, can make "nested" IF functions easier. Imagine you learn that districts with a per-pupil funding of more than $5,861 are in the 90th percentile, districts with a per-pupil funding of $4,603 or less are in the 10th percentile, and the rest are in between. You could classify the districts accordingly using this function, entered into Cell C2 and copied to C3:

=IFS(B2>5861,"90th",B2>4603,"Midrange",B2>0,"10th")

In Cell C2, the function will display "10th," and in Cell C3, the function will display "90th." The IFS function will work with strings, too. Like the IF function, though, it is unable to search for and match parts of strings. Microsoft warns against making IF or IFS statements too large and complex, given the potential for errors.

IFERROR

As you may recall from Chapter 5, you can use the VLOOKUP function to match up data stored in one place with data stored in another place. For example, if you have political action committee names and ID numbers listed on one tab in a spreadsheet and have political action committee donation totals to a candidate listed by political action committee ID on another tab, VLOOKUP can pair the donation totals from the second tab with the committee names and IDs on the first tab.

The VLOOKUP function has a potential drawback, though. Every time it fails to find a match, it lets you know by displaying "#N/A" as an error message. The message isn't all that intuitive, though. A message like, "No match found," or even just a blank, would be easier for someone to understand if they were looking at the spreadsheet. But the VLOOKUP function doesn't offer a way to customize the "#N/A" error message.

The IFERROR function was designed to put you in charge of the error message a spreadsheet function displays. You use it by wrapping around whatever function produces the error message you want to control. In Chapter 5, for example, the function =VLOOKUP(A3,'Bredesen aggregated'!D:E,2,FALSE) produced a "#N/A" error every time it couldn't find a donation from a specified political action committee to U.S. Senate candidate Phil Bredesen. Editing the function to read =IFERROR(VLOOKUP(A3,'Bredesen aggregated'!D:E,2, FALSE),"No match") would display a custom "No match" error message instead of the default "#N/A" error message.

COMBIN and PERMUT

Imagine your local city council has consisted of seven members, all men. But an election has replaced one of the men with a woman. One way of quantifying what the election means for gender diversity is to figure out the change in the number of different ways the remaining males on the council could combine to form an all-male majority of four votes. Excel's COMBIN function will help you do it.

Open a spreadsheet and type the headings "Males," "Majority" and "Combinations" in cells A1, B1 and C1, respectively. In the second row, supply the information depicting the situation before the woman's election: A "7" in Cell A2, and a "4" in Cell B2, indicating that there were seven males on the council, and any four could form a majority. In Cell B3, enter:

    =COMBIN(A2,B2)

… which means, "Find the number of unique groups that can be made if you have seven white men (the "A2" argument) and if the group size is four (the "B2" argument). The function will tell you, in Cell C2, there are 35 unique ways to make a four-member group out of seven men.

Now, enter "6" in Cell A3 and a "4" in Cell B3, to model the fact that you now have only six men out of which to form a four-member group. Copy the COMBIN function from Cell C2 to Cell C3, and you'll find that the woman's addition to the seven-member council has cut the possible number of male-only majorities by more than half. There are still 35 unique ways to make up a four-member majority, but only 15 of those ways involve exclusively men. Replace another of the council's men with a woman, and the number of possible all-male majorities drops to just five. One more woman drops the count to just one, and another makes an all-male majority impossible.

Note that the COMBIN function is suitable only for situations in which the order within each group is of no consequence. For example, a four-man majority consisting of councilmen Adams, Jones, Smith and Franklin is functionally the same as a four-man majority consisting of councilmen Franklin, Smith,

Jones and Adams. When within-group order matters, you must use the PERMUT function. Suppose someone on the sports desk wants to know how many different combinations of first, second and third-place finishers are possible in a local 10k race that has 78 entrants. Here, within-group order matters, because even if the top three finishers are Runner A, Runner B and Runner C, an outcome in which Runner A crosses the finish line first, followed by Runner B and then Runner C is not the same as an outcome in which Runner B crosses the finish line first, followed by Runner A and then Runner C.

To answer the question from the sports desk, type "Entrants," "Winners" and "Permutations" in cells A1, B1 and C1, respectively. In Cell A2, type "78," the number of entrants planning to run. In Cell B2, type "3," the number of winner slots available. In Cell C2, type the PERMUT function like this:

    =PERMUT(A2,B2)

… which means "Compute the number of permutations possible if 78 runners (A2) race for three (B2) winner spots, with a placement in each winner spot representing a unique outcome. The answer, Excel tells you, is 456,456.

Google Forms

The Google Drive account you used to work with Google Sheets and Google My Maps has another little gift for you, if you don't know about it already: Google Forms. A Google Form is a web-based questionnaire that stores its results in a Google Sheet. Anyone with a web-connected device, a browser, and the form's URL can complete and submit the form. The possible uses are many. The most obvious application would be using Google Forms to create a survey and administer it via the web. Before your ambitions run amok, remember that conducting a scientifically valid public opinion poll involves a lot more than just distributing a survey and getting some responses, even if you can do so in an innovative, cheap way. Your sample has to be truly random, in that every member of the population you plan to draw inferences about with your results has to have an equal chance of participating in your survey. And writing accurate, thorough questions that don't nudge respondents toward one answer or another takes expertise. But if you want to survey every member of some fairly small, finite group – like all members of your local city council, or each quarter's new members of the local chamber of commerce – you might be able to pull it off with a Google Form and some persistence.

Other uses might be less obvious, but equally valuable. Suppose your town is holding a city-wide election that includes a vote on a key referendum. The city's election commissioner reports precinct-level results as they become available, but by some offline means, like handing out printed results at the

Election Commission headquarters. You have three stringers ready to camp out at the commission headquarters and gather the results. A Google Form, which will work as well on a tablet or smartphone as on a computer, could make things go a lot faster.

To set up a form:

- Log into your Google Drive account and click "New / More / Google Forms." A new window will open showing you the beginnings of a form.
- Click "Untitled form," and replace the text with whatever you want to call your form. For example: "Referendum vote tally."
- Click "Untitled question," and replace the text with whatever you want the text of your first question to be. For example: "Precinct number."
- Click the down arrow to the right of the question text, and you'll see a list of the available question types: Short answer, Paragraph, Multiple choice, Checkboxes, Dropdown, and more. For this demo, let's pick "Dropdown."
- Click "Option 1," and replace the text with the first item you want on the dropdown list. For example: 1, to indicate Precinct No. 1.
- Click "Add option," then type the next option you want on your dropdown list. For example: 2, to indicate Precinct 2. In fact, the latest version of Google Forms can figure out what you are doing and start supplying the numbers automatically.
- Keep this up until you've keyed in all the options you want. We stopped at 20. Obviously, you could enter more.
- If you make a mistake and need to delete an option, click the "X" beside the option.
- Sliding the "Required" button to the right in the bottom-right corner of the window makes the question required. If a question is required, the user has to provide an answer before the form can be submitted. In a data collection scenario like the one we're describing, this option can prevent accidental data omissions.
- When you're done setting up the "Precinct number" question, click the small "+" symbol to the right of the form editing area to close the question's editing window and start editing a new question.
- We added a "Votes for referendum" short-answer box for recording the precinct's number of votes in favor of the referendum and a "Votes against referendum" short-answer box for recording the precinct's number of votes against the referendum. Finally, we added a "Your name" multiple-choice item so we could keep track of which stringer had entered which data. Figure 7.3 illustrates these steps.

Once you've finished setting up all the questions you want to ask:

- Click the "eye" symbol to see what the form looks like from the user's point of view. Google Sheets will open a new tab and show you the form.

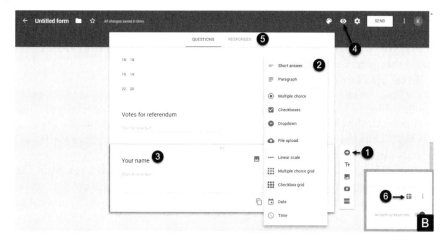

Figure 7.3 Setting up a Google Form. From your Google Drive, click "New / More / Google Forms." Replace the default "Untitled form" text with whatever title you want the form's user to see. Then, you can start editing and adding form questions. Click the "+" symbol to add a question (1), then choose a question type (2) and type the question's text (3). If you've chosen a multiple choice, checkbox, drop-down or similar type of question, you can specify answer choices. Click the preview button (4) to see what the questionnaire will look like to users and to get the URL to distribute to users. Click "Responses" (5) and look for the "Create spreadsheet" icon (6, Inset B) to direct each form submission's results into a Google Sheet. Google and the Google logo are registered trademarks of Google Inc., used with permission.

- Give this page's URL to anyone you want to fill the form out. You also can shorten the URL using any of the free URL shortening services available on the web. You also can create a page in your own web space, one with a simpler URL, and post a link to the form there.
- Go ahead and enter a few test submissions to make sure the form is working. Just don't forget to delete them from the dataset later.
- After you've entered a few test submissions, switch back to the question editing window. At the top of the editing area, you'll see a "Questions" button and a "Responses" button. The "Questions" button is the button for the editing area you've been working in. Click the "Responses" button to see a summary of the test submissions you entered. There's a "Summary" view, which shows you charts and tallies of the responses. There's also an "Individual" view that lets you see any one submission.
- What you really want to do, though, is connect the form to a Google Sheet so the responses will accumulate there. On either the "Summary" or "Individual" view of the "Responses" tab, look for a small, green icon with two white, crossed lines. It's meant to suggest a spreadsheet. Click the icon.
- A "Select response destination" box will appear. Make sure the "Create a new spreadsheet" radio button is checked, then click "Untitled form (Reponses)"

and replace the text with whatever you want to call the Google Sheet the data will collect in. We picked "Precinct tally results."

- Click "Create," and the Google Sheet will open, showing you the test entries you've already submitted.

Note that, by default, Google Forms includes a "Timestamp" column that records the date and time of each submission. The wording of each question becomes the column heading for the question's results. Like any Google Sheet, the sheet is locked by default, so only you can see it unless you decide to share it.

Navigate back to the sheet any time you want to view or download results. Your three stringers can enter data independently and simultaneously. In the Google Sheet, you can click "File / Download as / Microsoft Excel" to download the file for analysis offline. Or you can copy the data to a new tab or new Google Sheet and pursue your analyses there.

Comparing Numbers Over Time

Things change over time. Prices go up. Populations increase. Any time you compare two numbers, one from a time earlier than the other, it's wise to think about whether some adjustment might be needed to make the comparison accurate.

Adjusting for Inflation

Adjusting dollar amounts to account for inflation is one of the most common examples of making two numbers comparable across time. Your grandparents might have paid far less than you do for groceries, clothes and other goods. But their paychecks were smaller, too. Dollar amounts compared across time have to be compared in terms of how much buying power both amounts represent in the same time period.

Suppose, for example, you were writing about how U.S. workers are recovering financially from the "Great Recession." Specifically, you want to examine how much wages have risen since the recession for workers in each of the economy's major segments. You shouldn't just report the difference between average wages then and now, though, because price inflation has occurred between then and now.

Figure 7.4 illustrates one way to report the changing wages accurately, accounting for inflation. Weekly earnings rose for each selected sector during the time period, especially in the "Financial Activities" and "Information" areas. But adjusting for the inflation that occurred during the same time period shows that the increases weren't as impressive as they might initially appear. For example,

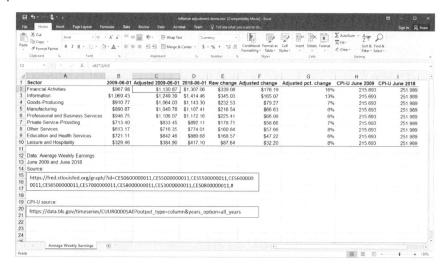

Figure 7.4 Change in average weekly earnings per selected economic sectors between June 2009, the end of the "Great Recession," and June 2018, expressed in raw and inflation-adjusted dollars. The formula in Cell C2, =B2*I2/H2, shows how to convert the June 2009 dollar amount in Cell B2 into its equivalent in June 2018 dollars by multiplying it by the June 2018 Consumer Price Index and dividing by the June 2009 Consumer Price Index. Google and the Google logo are registered trademarks of Google Inc., used with permission.

the $339.08 raw increase in the "Financial Activities" sector is really only a $176.19 increase in buying power, an increase of 16 percent, or 16 cents per dollar. The formula in Cell C2, visible in the spreadsheet's formula bar as =B2*I2/H2, shows how to adjust the 2009 figure by multiplying it by the June 2018 Consumer Price Index, then dividing by the June 2009 Consumer Price Index. The month-by-month Consumer Price Index is available from the U.S. Bureau of Labor Statistics at several locations, but perhaps most conveniently at:

- https://data.bls.gov/timeseries/CUUR0000SA0?output_type=column& years_option=all_years

The "CUUR0000SA0" code is the name of the Bureau of Labor Statistics series that contains the Consumer Price Index for All Urban Consumers, or CPI-U. We used the graph tool at the Federal Reserve Bank of St. Louis to compile the data and download it in Excel format. See: https://fred.stlouisfed.org/graph/.

Adjusting for Population Changes

News media across Tennessee reported in February of 2016 that the state had dramatically surpassed early voting totals from the 2008 primary, at the time the most recent primary in which neither party had an incumbent candidate on the ballot. "Tennessee crushes early voting record for presidential primary," one headline read (Garrison, 2016). The story below the headline, citing Tennessee Secretary of State figures, reported that 385,653 people had cast early-voter or absentee ballots in Tennessee, compared to 329,154 in 2008. The difference came to, the article correctly noted, about a 17 percent increase. The figure had state election officials bracing for a "massive" turnout on election day, and state Democratic and Republican party leaders took jabs at one another in the form of predictions about what the rush to the polls might mean for one another's political fortunes in the state.

Nobody seemed to consider that Tennessee's 18-and-older population had gotten substantially larger since 2008. The best-available U.S. Census Bureau estimates at the time indicated that the number of voting-age residents in the state had grown from 4,736,294 in 2008 (U.S. Census Bureau, 2016b) to around 5,102,688 in 2016, with the latter estimate current as of 2015 (U.S. Census Bureau, 2016c). Obviously, it was possible that at least some, and maybe a lot, of the growth in early voting could be attributed to a simple increase in the number of people available to vote. To figure out how much, enter the headings "2008 18+," "2008 voters," "2016 18+," and "2016 voters" in cells A1, B1, C1 and D1 of a spreadsheet. Next, enter 4,736,294, 385,653, 5,102,688, and 329,154 in cells A2, B2, C2 and D2 of the spreadsheet.

First, figure out the early voting turnout in 2008. You can do it by typing a "Turnout 2008" heading into Cell E1, then entering this expression into Cell E2:

=B2/A2

... which will simply divide the 2008 voters by the 2008 estimate of residents age 18 and older and give the result as 0.069496108, or about a 7 percent turnout. Now, type a "Turnout 2016" heading in Cell F1, then do the same calculation in Cell F2, using the 2016 voter and 18+ figures. Here's the expression:

=D2/C2

... which yields a result of 0.075578401, or about an 8 percent turnout. Yep, that's right. Journalists and election officials and party operatives were flipping out over a 17 percent jump in early voting turnout when all but about 1 percent of it could be explained by population growth.

A lot can change in the time that passes between two events like a salary increase or an early voting tally. Similar problems happen when journalists report about the latest record-grossing box office hit without adjusting their comparisons for inflation, or when they write about a rise in the number of murders in a city compared to last year without using city population estimates for the two time periods to express each murder count as a rate per, say,

100,000 residents. We hope these exercises have shown you how to adjust for inflation and population changes over time and alerted you to the importance of doing so.

Recap

This chapter has offered a cookbook-style introduction to some functions, tools and techniques that, while often more specialized than others we've covered in full chapters, can prove useful in a range of circumstances. We've also elaborated on some that got a mention earlier in the book but we felt needed elaboration here. In each instance, we've tried to provide context that illustrates the item's potential use for journalists.

References

Garrison, Joey. 2016, February 24. "Tennessee Crushes Early Voting Record." *The Tennessean.* Accessed June 12, 2016. www.tennessean.com/story/news/politics/2016/02/24/tennessee-crushes-early-voting-record-08-primary/80853446/.

U.S. Census Bureau. 2016a. "Public Elementary-Secondary Education Finance Data, 2014 Data." Accessed 14 June, 2016. www.census.gov/govs/school/index.html.

U.S. Census Bureau. 2016b. "Population Estimates – Vintage 2008: State Tables." Accessed June 14, 2016. www.census.gov/popest/data/historical/2000s/vintage_2008/state.html.

U.S. Census Bureau. 2016c. "Demographic and Economic Profiles of Tennessee's Electorate." Accessed June 14, 2016. www.census.gov/newsroom/press-releases/2016/cb16-tps24.html.

Index

Page references to Figures are followed by the letter 'f', while those for Tables the letter 't'.

Data Skills for Media Professionals: A Basic Guide, First Edition. Ken Blake and Jason Reineke.
© 2020 John Wiley & Sons, Inc. Published 2020 by John Wiley & Sons, Inc.